☆

THOMAS JEFFERSON

☆

The GREAT AMERICAN THINKERS *Series*

JONATHAN EDWARDS • *Alfred Owen Aldridge*
BENJAMIN FRANKLIN • *Ralph L. Ketcham*
JOHN WOOLMAN • *Edwin H. Cady*
THOMAS JEFFERSON • *Stuart Gerry Brown*
JOHN C. CALHOUN • *Richard N. Current*
GEORGE BANCROFT • *Russel B. Nye*
CHAUNCEY WRIGHT • *Edward H. Madden*
CHARLES PEIRCE • *Thomas S. Knight*
WILLIAM JAMES • *Edward C. Moore*
THORSTEIN VEBLEN • *Douglas F. Dowd*
JOHN DEWEY • *Richard J. Bernstein*

IN PREPARATION

ALEXANDER HAMILTON • *Stuart Gerry Brown*
RALPH WALDO EMERSON • *Warren Staebler*
THEODORE PARKER • *Arthur W. Brown*
JOSIAH ROYCE • *Thomas F. Powell*
THEODORE ROOSEVELT • *William Harbaugh*
ALFRED NORTH WHITEHEAD • *Nathaniel Lawrence*
GEORGE SANTAYANA • *Willard E. Arnett*
DR. W.E.B. DU BOIS • *Henry Lee Moon*
NORMAN THOMAS • *Robert J. Alexander*

THOMAS
JEFFERSON

Stuart Gerry Brown, Ph.D.
Professor of American Studies
University of Hawaii

SERIES EDITORS

Arthur W. Brown, Ph.D.
President, Adelphi University; and

Thomas S. Knight, Ph.D.
Professor and Chairman of the
Department of Philosophy, Adelphi University

WASHINGTON SQUARE PRESS, INC. • NEW YORK • 1966

CONTENTS

PREFACE

Thomas Jefferson is so intrinsically interesting a man, the source of so many ideas and influences in his own country and all over the world, that there is always justification for attempting one more book about him. If this book achieves something of its purposes, it will once again display the vitality of Jefferson in the world of today, where his spirit moves, without wrenching him out of the world of 150 years ago in which he lived. I have, for example, paid little heed to Jefferson's agrarianism. That he hated cities—that is, the crowding of people together in squalor—that he considered the yeoman or independent farmer the most reliable citizen of free society, and that he feared the effects of importing the industrial revolution into the United States are true enough and well enough known. But too often writers have mistaken such prejudices and judgments of a moment for first principles in the Jefferson Canon. They were not. And it is, of course, more to Jefferson than any other American that we owe the initial sharp stimulus to manufactures which set us on the long road we have traveled to today's fabulous world of technology.

Jefferson's mind was, above all, flexible and open. It is in this sense that he was a great liberal, the greatest of the modern era, not because of any specific programs he advocated or opposed. His end was always the life, the liberty, and the happiness of individual human beings. Programs and policies were means to be measured by one yardstick only: how far did they advance mankind toward these ends? Because the agrarian dream foundered on the rocks of Britain's depredations on the seas, Jefferson was willing to alter his views both on manufactures and on navies. But this was because he would not alter his principles.

And I have tried not to separate what Jefferson thought from what he did. He was neither a systematizer nor did he "think with his lips." He was a thoughtfully active man, as close as we are likely to come to Emerson's American scholar. Thus the concluding section of this book is not a formal treatise on Jefferson's philosophy but an essay on his intellectual attitudes and interests, while the sketch of his life tries to show him not as a politician and statesman so much as a man of great intellectual abilities and highly cultivated sensibilities engaged, by conscience and circumstance, in nearly every important political and intellectual development of his time.

Some portions of Part II appeared in the journal *Ethics* (January, 1963), and I am grateful to my friend, editor Charner M. Perry for permission to reprint. Many friends have helped by useful conversations about Jefferson. But I am especially sensible of the debt I owe to Clinton Rossiter, who will disagree with some of what I say about Hamilton in these pages, and to Gregg Sinclair, Ralph L. Ketcham, and William A. Riley, as well as to many students who have sat in my seminars over the years, at Syracuse University and the University of Hawaii, to my great advantage.

As on so many other literary labors, my wife has been a just and trenchant critic and has shared the chores of proofreading with me. This book is for her.

S. G. B.

Honolulu
October, 1963

Part 1

THE LIFE OF THOMAS JEFFERSON

Chapter 1.

YOUNG MANHOOD IN VIRGINIA

If life and myth were one and the same, the intellectual leader of the American Revolution would have been born in humble circumstances of "poor but honest" parents. Thomas Jefferson's parents were honest enough, but they were not poor and their circumstances were humble only by standards of a later and more lavish America. Peter Jefferson, Thomas' father, was one of the early settlers along the upper James River in Virginia, acquired very large holdings of land, married well, and built at least two homes of substantial plantation character. He was largely self-educated, but his intellectual capacity was sufficient to bring him, jointly with Professor Joshua Fry, of the College of William and Mary, the assignment of completing the survey, begun in earlier years by Colonel William Byrd, and marking the boundary between Virginia and North Carolina. Peter Jefferson was the elected lieutenant colonel of the local militia. When he died in 1757, he had become a leading citizen of piedmont Virginia.

Thomas Jefferson's mother was Jane Randolph, a descendant of William Randolph of Turkey Island. More than one biographer has made much of this connection between Jefferson and one of the great aristocratic families of old Virginia. But Jefferson himself, reflecting in his old age upon his ancestry, wrote ironically of the Randolphs: ". . . they trace their pedigree far back in England and Scotland, to which let everyone ascribe the faith and merit he chooses."

Among his two sons and six daughters who survived infancy, Peter Jefferson followed custom and the laws of inheritance in selecting Thomas, his eldest, for such advantages as Virginia offered in the 1740's and 1750's. Born April 13,

[3]

1743, at the plantation known as Shadwell on the Rivanna River, Jefferson was sent to school nearby at the age of five to learn reading and writing. At nine he went to board with a Scottish clergyman named Douglas, who taught Jefferson Latin and Greek "rudiments" and some French. At fourteen, following his father's death, he was sent to the Rev. Mr. Maury, "a correct classical scholar," who prepared him for William and Mary.

These years of Jefferson's boyhood seem to have been happy and healthy in abundant measure. While his brothers and sisters provided him with affectionate companionship, his great friends were his cousin Thomas Mann Randolph, and neighbors John Page and Dabney Carr. With these friends he learned to ride, to hunt, and to fish and acquired the deep feeling for country living which was certainly the continuing passion of his life. At home his mother encouraged his growing fondness for literature and music. He learned to play the violin, an instrument to which he was ever afterward devoted. His father did not live long enough to have taught him all the lore of plantation life, but the boy learned from overseers, neighbors, and books what his father could not teach him. At seventeen, when he took up his residence at the College of William and Mary in Williamsburg, he was over six feet tall, strong and rangy; his sandy hair crowned a well-formed if not handsome face; his carriage was erect, his manners graceful.

Williamsburg in the middle of the eighteenth century, where Jefferson lived during much of his young manhood, is a living legend. The restored town is so attractive that one is tempted to flowing daydreams of the days before the Revolution when Jefferson mingled with the great of Virginia and formed his mind and character. But dreams are not realities, and it is not possible fully to recapture the spirit of the times or of the place. We know enough for certain, nevertheless, to be content.

As Jefferson recollected in later years, the instruction at William and Mary was uniformly inferior. But there were two exceptions, each of which permanently impressed itself upon his young mind. William Small, an Englishman who stayed at Williamsburg only a few years, was a cultivated scholar who introduced Jefferson to contemporary as well as ancient philosophy, encouraged him to philosophical speculation, and helped him to flex the muscles of his critical judgment. George Wythe, only a few years older than Jefferson, was already a commanding intellectual figure in the fields of law and legal philosophy. To these two men Jefferson quickly gravitated. For their part, they were delighted to have a young scholar of such insatiable appetite for learning and unusual intellectual endowment. The fact is that intellectual men were uncommon in eighteenth-century Virginia. Learning was respected but not generally sought. Men like Wythe, Richard Bland, and George Mason were unusual; the Lees, the Washingtons, the Randolphs were the representative men—able, energetic, but scarcely bookish. Thus Jefferson's finding himself a youthful fourth at dinners with Governor Fauquier, Wythe, and Small is not so fortuitous as it might at first appear. In any case, it was with such men and in such times that he was drawn to the new philosophy of the Enlightenment. In an age of high specialization two hundred years later, it is perhaps difficult to appreciate fully the breadth and depth of intellectual life young Jefferson now began to explore, and continued to explore throughout his long life—politics; philosophy; religion; natural science; music; architecture; sculpture and painting; the law; literature and language; and, not least, agriculture and domestic economy. Even this list is not exhaustive; in effect there were no important limits upon the fields of knowledge cultivated by the Enlightenment. And, after Franklin, it is safe to say that Jefferson was more truly the son of that benign dispensation than any other American.

While intellectual cultivation, with a generous admixture of the polite society of the colonial capital, filled Jefferson's life comfortably enough, and the responsibilities of managing his farms—his since the age of fourteen—were sufficient for any gentleman, the young man nevertheless presently decided upon a professional career. After two years he left the curriculum of the college and began to read law under Wythe's direction. This he continued to do intermittently, and served occasionally as a law clerk in Wythe's office until he was admitted to the bar in 1767 at the age of twenty-four.

But much of his time was spent at home. His concern to improve his gardens and lands and to breed better crops grew as he saw how severe were the limits placed by climate, soil, and implements upon the ordinary products of the Virginia soil. He began to make entries in a sort of diary of farm and garden matters in 1766. His first entry, on March 30, reads: ". . . purple hyacinth begins to bloom." This revealing book Jefferson kept until 1824, though with many gaps. It has been published as *Thomas Jefferson's Garden Book*. Another diary, *Thomas Jefferson's Farm Book*, was begun in 1774. Though he owned many thousands of acres in several different parts of Virginia (with more than 150 slaves), the Shadwell plantation in Albemarle County, on which he was born, and Poplar Forest in Bedford County, inherited from his father-in-law, were the chief objects of his attention and the seats of his residence. Long before Shadwell was destroyed by fire in 1770, he had begun to plan for a new and finer home on a hill nearby, to be called Monticello.

But however extraordinary his talents and promise, young Thomas Jefferson was quite ordinary in his failure to escape one of the more interesting pitfalls of youth. Like other young gentlemen of the eighteenth century, he fell passionately in love with his "Belinda." Rebecca Burwell was sixteen when Jefferson, not quite twenty, was smitten by her beauty and grace. For better than two years he dreamed romantically of her, wrote letters to Page and Carr in vain attempts to unburden himself of the freight of emotion he seemed to carry, despaired of winning her, made hesitant approaches to her, and lost out to an older and more self-confident competitor, Jacquelin Ambler. Irony characterized this somewhat awkward first romance, for Rebecca Ambler's daughter became the wife of John Marshall, the future Chief Justice and the chief political enemy of the future President.

This was the first of four affairs of the heart which figured importantly in Jefferson's life. It was innocent, sentimental, and conventional, and except for some felicitous writing in his letters to Carr and Page, it reveals no unusual talents in the young cavalier. The second affair, also unsuccessful, was of a different order. In Jefferson's own words it was "improper," and marks the real man as somewhat different from the matchless hero of American myth. Betsy Walker was his neighbor and the wife of John Walker, a close friend from boyhood who had gone with Jefferson to Maury's school. In 1768, when Walker was absent for several months on a mission to the Indians at Fort Stanwix, Jefferson abused his friend's trust by making tentative advances to his wife. He was twenty-five and robust, and Betsy was singularly attractive. She appears to have turned him away with grace. At any rate nothing came of the affair; the friendship was not impaired, and Betsy did not consider Jefferson's behavior sufficiently aggressive to warrant informing her husband. Not at the time, that is. But many years later, when Jefferson was in Paris as American Minister, she told her husband, or so the latter recorded, a vulgar tale accusing Jefferson of improper advances continuing over many years, even after his own marriage. When Walker and Jefferson found themselves on opposite sides of the bitter political quarrels of a still later era, this story rose to punish Jefferson more than amply for the sins of his youth. The story as told at the turn of the nineteenth century was an evident and fantastic exaggeration, but President Jefferson did not deny that at the age of twenty-five he had behaved badly.

The third in this series of romances drew from Jefferson unmeasured love and devotion to an adoring wife, and gave him the opportunity to become an affectionate and solicitous father and grandfather. Martha Wayles Skelton, the widow of an acquaintance of Jefferson's, was five and a half years younger than her future husband. In 1770 she was graceful, vivacious, and numbered among the belles of Williamsburg. Her father, John Wayles, was a man of wealth and standing. She was a desirable "catch." Jefferson's letters and memoranda suggest that he began his courtship in the fall of the year and had won her hand by the springtime. They were married on January 1, 1772, and drove to Monticello, then only partially constructed, for their honeymoon. They made their home, until the main house was habitable, in the cottage which stands at the end of the walk northwest of the house.

The happiness of the Jeffersons' marriage was diminished over the years by Martha's ill health and by the death in infancy of a son and three daughters. But their first born, Martha, always known in the family as Patsy, was the life-long pride of a doting father, accompanied him to Europe, returned to marry Thomas Mann Randolph, Jr., and became one of the great ladies of her generation in Virginia. Mary, affectionately called Polly, born in 1778, as a little girl also joined her father and sister in Paris. Her marriage to John Eppes in 1797 delighted her father, but both he and his son-in-law were permanently saddened by her untimely death in 1804 at the age of twenty-six. In 1773 Martha and Thomas Jefferson adopted into their home the family of Jefferson's dearest friend, Dabney Carr, when the latter died at the age of twenty-nine. Carr had married Jefferson's beloved sister Mary, and thus he had a double motive for playing the role of father to their six children. While Jefferson was to out-live his friend by more than fifty years, Mrs. Jefferson, like so many others of that day, died young. Her long-declining health finally failed entirely on September 6, 1782, after a little less than eleven years of marriage. But she lived long enough to hear her husband celebrated as the author of the Declaration of Independence and to know that the Revolution he helped to make and to lead had triumphed. Jefferson was never fully consoled for her loss. And his fourth and final romantic adventure was of another order. It lighted with gaiety a moment of his middle years, as we shall see, but offered no challenge to the image of Martha enshrined in his memory.

Chapter 2.

JEFFERSON THE REVOLUTIONIST

Thomas Jefferson "entered upon the public stage," as it was put in the formal language of his day, in 1768 when he was elected to the Virginia colonial legislature, the House of Burgesses. When he took his seat for the session of 1769, he was better prepared for public responsibility than most of the other young men who sat with him. He had not only won the confidence of his neighbors in Albemarle who chose him as their delegate, but he had traveled, three years before, as far north as Philadelphia and New York to observe the ways of life in other colonies and make the acquaintance of public men. One chance encounter at New York, with a young merchant from Massachusetts named Elbridge Gerry, was the beginning of a friendship of more than forty years and a historic political alliance. And at Williamsburg, as we have seen, Jefferson had improved his mind by study and cultivated conversation. His connection with the Randolphs had brought him to the attention of Peyton Randolph, then the esteemed Speaker of the House of Burgesses, and given him access to all the great gentlemen of the day. As a law student in 1765, he had gone to the House of Burgesses to hear Patrick Henry declaim against the Stamp Act. "He appeared to me," recollected Jefferson, "to speak as Homer wrote." His sympathies from the beginning were with Henry and the other younger Burgesses who pressed for common action with the other colonies in defense of their rights.

At his first session Jefferson joined in a resolution protesting to Parliament against the treatment Massachusetts was receiving. Governor Lord Botetourt dissolved the Burgesses, but they promptly adjourned to the Raleigh Tavern's Apollo Room, reassembled, and enacted a resolution against using merchandise imported from England. The members then returned to their homes and stood for re-election on the basis of what they had done. Only those who had refused support to the meeting at the Raleigh were defeated. This episode turned out to be Jefferson's baptism of revolutionary fire, but it was four years before a similar occasion arose.

In the spring of 1773, a new and highly irritating issue provoked the Virginia House of Burgesses, or at least some of the members. A court in Rhode Island had ruled that colonists might be sent to England for trial of charges against them in the colonies, thus depriving the colonial courts of effective jurisdiction. To the young patriots this was intolerable. Jefferson recalled the decisive steps then taken:

> Not thinking our old and leading members up to the point of forwardness and zeal which the times required, Mr. Henry, Richard Henry Lee, Francis L. Lee, Mr. Carr and myself agreed to meet in the evening, in a private room of the Raleigh, to consult on the state of things. There may have been a member or two more whom I do not recollect. We were all sensible that the most urgent of all measures was that of coming to an understanding with all the other colonies, to consider the British claims as a common cause to all, and to produce a unity of action: and, for this purpose, that a committee of correspondence in each colony would be the best instrument of intercommunication: and that their first measure would probably be to propose a meeting of deputies from every colony, at some central place, who should be charged with the direction of the measures which should be taken by all.°

Thus was born the revolutionary organization which, a year later, called together the First Continental Congress and provided the means for developing the sense of national allegiance which was the first necessity in the coming struggle against the British. While, several years before, Samuel Adams

---

° Jefferson's memoirs are contained in his *Autobiography* and *Anas*. The quotations from Jefferson are drawn from the *Papers of Thomas Jefferson*, edited by Julian Boyd, wherever possible, and otherwise from such standard editions as those of Ford or Washington. See bibliographical note (p. 236).

of Massachusetts and others in that colony had set up committees of correspondence, these were for communication among the towns of New England, not between leading groups of the several colonies. These Virginia proposals, introduced into the Burgesses by Carr, at Jefferson's suggestion, were enacted. Peyton Randolph was appointed chairman of the Committee of Correspondence and instructed to notify the other colonies of the action of the Burgesses. The Governor, predictably, dissolved the Burgesses, but, as before, they retired to the Apollo Room and reaffirmed their action. Randolph, in the name of Virginia, sent out the circular letter, which commenced the unification of the colonies.

Events moved even more rapidly at the session of 1774. In May came word that Parliament had passed the so-called Port Bill, ordering the port of Boston to be closed on June 1 in reprisal for the continued noncooperation of Boston merchants. Again led by its young radicals, the Virginia Burgesses took action. Jefferson met again with the two Lees and Henry, and "three or four other members," to plot strategy. According to Jefferson, they "cooked up a resolution," based on records of some old Puritan actions, "for appointing the 1st day of June, on which the port bill was to commence, for a day of fasting, humiliation, and prayer, to implore Heaven to avert from us the evils of civil war, to inspire us with firmness in support of our rights, and to turn the hearts of the King and Parliament to moderation and justice." The resolution was passed unanimously. The Governor, as usual, dissolved the assembly, which, as usual, reconvened at the Raleigh.

This time the rump assembly in the Apollo Room took the fateful step of addressing their sister colonies, through the Committee of Correspondence, with a call "to appoint deputies to meet in Congress at such place, *annually,* as should be convenient, to direct, from time to time, the measures required by the general interest." The response was positive, and the First Continental Congress was called for September at Philadelphia.

Jefferson was not a member of the Virginia delegation to the First Congress, but he nevertheless played a significant part in the events of the following months. After the June "fast day," delegates were elected from the various counties to a convention to be held at Williamsburg in place of the legislature, which was still in dissolution by the action of the Governor. Jefferson was elected a delegate, and immediately interested himself in the instructions of the convention to the delegation to be sent to the Congress at Philadelphia.

At this period Jefferson held more advanced views regarding the legal relations between England and the colonies than any other public person in Virginia except, perhaps, George Wythe, his teacher. He and Wythe considered the matter as in the same case "as that of England and Scotland, after the accession of James, and until the union." That is, Jefferson thought that the King was the executive head both of England and of each of the colonies (because the colonists so willed), but that the British Parliament had no legislative authority over the colonies at all. The consequences of such a position were, of course, that Virginia and the other colonies meeting at Philadelphia would be free to proclaim a legal as well as a moral defiance of British laws, and to petition the King with well-founded expectations of redress. Most of Jefferson's colleagues, on the other hand, "stopped at the half-way house of John Dickinson," conceding that Parliament had limited power to legislate for the colonies. They granted Parliament's power to regulate commerce as an imperial prerogative, and to tax for the purpose of such regulation, though not for revenue. Thus, though Jefferson's views anticipated the commonwealth system of the twentieth century, they were not well tuned to the political realities of the time.

He intended, nevertheless, to press them upon the convention, and for this purpose wrote a substantial memorandum. On his way to Williamsburg he became ill and could not proceed, but he sent copies of his paper to the Speaker and to Henry. The document was laid before the convention and discussed but not adopted. However, it was considered so important a statement that it was ordered to be printed under the title "A Summary View of the Rights of British America." Some months later this paper was published in England and pressed in Parliament by Edmund Burke as a good statement of the constitutional aspects of the American problem. In his old age Jefferson recalled with pride that his authorship of this famous pamphlet—his first serious effort at the formulation of political principles—won him a place on a list of Americans proscribed in a bill of attainder introduced into Parliament. Peyton Randolph told him that John and Samuel Adams, John Hancock, Randolph himself, and Jefferson were among some twenty persons named as dangerous to the security of the British government.

In March, 1775, the Virginia convention added Jefferson to its delegation at the Continental Congress to replace Peyton Randolph, then President of the Congress, who was needed in Virginia. Before going to Philadelphia, however, Jefferson was entrusted with drawing the reply of the Virginia assembly to the new (and final) proposals of Lord North, which were then being submitted to all of the colonial governments. Virginia, in Jefferson's forceful but measured language, expressed its dissatisfaction. On April 19, fighting broke out in Massachusetts, and in May there were skirmishes in Virginia. When the convention voted a call to arms, Patrick Henry led the debate with his famous "Gentlemen cry peace, but there is no peace" speech. Jefferson, as Edmund Randolph recollected, "argued closely, profoundly, and warmly on the same side. The post in the revolutionary debate belonging to him was that at which the theories of republicanism were deposited."

On arriving at Philadelphia in June, Jefferson was almost immediately added to the committee appointed to draft a declaration of causes for the taking up of arms. Feeling was running very high, and the delegates to Congress were deeply divided. One faction, with a lingering hope of conciliation, advocated a moderate approach to the British; the other was convinced that the moment for independence had arrived. The latter group included Jefferson and Richard Henry Lee of Virginia, as well as John Adams of Massachusetts and Benjamin Franklin of Pennsylvania. John Dickinson, then of Pennsylvania (he later moved to New Jersey), widely respected for his learning and his integrity, was a leading conciliator. He and Jefferson worked together in the committee. But Dickinson would not associate himself with the strongly

THE LIFE OF THOMAS JEFFERSON

worded draft prepared by Jefferson and was therefore asked to do it over again. He did so, "preserving of the former only the 1st four paragraphs and half of the preceding one." This declaration was adopted with some considerable misgiving, according to Jefferson. It was, in any case, the last "concili-atory" resolve enacted by the Continental Congress. By the latter part of July all of the colonies had sent in their re-sponses rejecting Lord North's proposals. The Congress acted to present them to the British in a common front. Jefferson again, with Franklin, John Adams, and Lee, formed the com-mittee to draft the appropriate paper. Already noted for his brilliant draftsmanship, Jefferson was asked to do the work, which was then approved by the committee and by the Congress. He incorporated much of the language he had used earlier in the spring when drawing the Virginia paper on the same matter, which accounts for the similarity of these two historic documents.

It was in the work of these committees that the friendship of Jefferson with two of his greatest contemporaries, Adams and Franklin, was formed. His intimacy with the latter con-tinued unbroken until Franklin died in 1790. Jefferson's rela-tions with Adams, unhappily disrupted by the political battles of the 1790's, were restored in after years. Their correspond-ence after 1811, continuing until both men died on the same day, July 4, 1826, forms one of the great works of American literature.

In the following months of 1775, revolutionaries of like mind with Jefferson and his new friends moved to the fore in most of the colonies. They formed a solid majority of those elected to the Second Continental Congress, which met at Philadelphia the following spring.

The events of June and July, 1776, at Philadelphia so altered a small-scale and somewhat confusing war between American colonials and the British army that, in Jefferson's words, it became "a contest which was to change the condi-tion of man over the civilized globe." Americans of the mid-twentieth century have seen this vision spread over the whole world. Because it was these events which determined the course of American history more immediately, and because he played the leading part in them, it will be best to follow Jefferson's own account quite closely.

On Friday, June 7, the Virginia delegation, with R. H. Lee as spokesman, offered a resolution for independence and nationhood. They were carrying out the instructions of the Virginia convention when they moved that

> the Congress should declare that these United colonies are, and of right ought to be, free and independent states, that they are absolved from all allegiance to the British crown, and that all political connection between them and the state of Great Britain is, and ought to be, totally dissolved; that measures should be immediately taken for procuring the assistance of foreign powers, and a Confederation be formed to bind the colonies more closely together.*

The debate took place on Saturday the 8th and Monday the 10th. The principal speakers opposing the resolution were James Wilson of Pennsylvania, Robert R. Livingston of New York, Edward Rutledge of South Carolina, and Dickinson. All expressed themselves as personally favoring the resolution but thought the action would be premature. The middle colonies, especially, had been doubtful about cutting off all ties with England and had not authorized their delegates to take so radical a step. Further, the outcome of the military campaign was in doubt. If it were unsuccessful, it might be expected that Spain and France would wish to join with England rather than oppose her as allies of the faltering American states. But since there were good prospects for the campaign, it would be wiser to wait until its termination in the hope that the European powers would be duly impressed with the opportunity to reduce the power of England by aiding her former colonies. It was argued also that a full-scale plan of government ought to be offered to the states before they were asked to form a union, since they had a right to know how such a union would affect their internal affairs.

---

* H. S. Commager's *Documents of American History* is a useful source book for papers such as these.

Some felt that this latter point was so critical that a precipitate declaration of independence by the Congress might cause some of the states to secede.

Jefferson's side of the argument was represented in the debate by Adams, R. H. Lee, and George Wythe, among others. Jefferson himself does not appear to have taken the floor. Their principal contentions were, in Jefferson's words:

> . . . that no gentleman had argued against the policy or the right of separation from Britain, nor had supposed it possible we should ever renew our connection; that they had only opposed its now being declared:

> That the question was not whether, by a Declaration of Independence, we should make ourselves what we are not; but whether we should declare a fact which already exists:

> That, as to the people or parliament of England, we had already been independent of them, their restraints on our trade deriving efficacy from our acquiescence only, and not from any rights they possessed of imposing them, and that so far, our connection had been federal only, and was now dissolved by the commencement of hostilities:

> That, as to the King, we had been bound to him by allegiance, but that this bond was now dissolved by his assent to the last act of Parliament, by which he declares us out of his protection, and by his levying war on us, a fact which had long ago proved us out of his protection; it being a certain position in law, that allegiance and protection are reciprocal, the one ceasing when the other is withdrawn. . . .

> [That] No delegates . . . can be denied, or ever want, a power of declaring an existent truth. . . .

> That the people wait for us to lead the way:

> That *they* are in favor of the measure, though the instructions given by some of their *representatives* are not:

That the voice of the representatives is not always consonant with the voice of the people, and that this is remarkably the case in these middle colonies. . . .

That it would be vain to wait either weeks or months for perfect unanimity, since it was impossible that all men should ever become of one sentiment on any question:

That the conduct of some colonies, from the beginning of this contest, had given reason to suspect it was their settled policy to keep in the rear of the confederacy, that their particular prospect might be better, even in the worst event:

That, therefore, it was necessary for those colonies who had thrown themselves forward and hazarded all from the beginning, to come forward now also, and put all again to their own hazard. . . .

That though France and Spain may be jealous of our rising power, they must think it will be much more formidable with the addition of Great Britain; and will therefore see it their interest to prevent a coalition; but should they refuse, we shall be but where we are; whereas without trying, we shall never know whether they will aid us or not:

That to wait the event of this campaign will certainly work delay, because, during the summer, France may assist us effectually. . . .

That it would be idle to lose time in settling the terms of alliance, till we had first determined we would enter into alliance. . . .

Documents probably never succeed in conveying an immediate sense of past reality. But these paragraphs do suggest something of the spirit of the moment, something of the tensions and divisions of opinion that marked the birth pangs of the United States for the rackings and rendings they in fact were. At that moment the first great campaign of the war was testing the citizen soldiers of the emerging American states in bloody battles. The citizens behind the lines were feeling the deprivations and sorrows of war. And it was a new kind of war, with no comforting precedents by which to shape emotions. The position of the delegates in the Congress was indeed uncertain, despite the assured attitude of Jefferson and his friends. They had been sent to concert the efforts of the colonies to defend themselves against British troops, and to present to the world the case for American liberties against the oppressions of British laws. But they had not been chosen to make a revolution against the mother country, or to establish a new nation. If one feels a tingle of excitement and anticipation in the words of the radicals, one must at the same time feel a certain sympathy with the moderates.

It was the moderates, at any rate, who prevailed at the moment. The revolutionaries, as Jefferson marshaled the arguments in his memory, finished their plea with the bold assertion that "the only misfortune is, that we did not enter into alliance with France six months sooner, as, besides opening her ports for the vent of our last year's produce, she might have marched an army into Germany, and prevented the petty princes there, from selling their unhappy subjects to subdue us." But this somewhat rash mixture of hope and regret did not move the majority of the delegates. They decided to postpone decision on the crucial issue until the so-called middle colonies might be better prepared for "falling from the parent stem." July 1 was set as the date for returning finally to the question.

But the revolutionaries nevertheless scored importantly. The Congress appointed a committee to draft and have ready for action a declaration of independence. The members selected were Adams, Franklin, Livingston, Roger Sherman of Connecticut, and Jefferson. The committee asked Jefferson to draft the document for their consideration. Between June 11 and June 28 he worked at it intermittently. At hand was the recent Virginia Declaration of Rights, drawn chiefly by George Mason, setting forth principles of government which had been developing in the minds of thoughtful Americans for at least a generation: the natural rights of man in accord with the "laws of nature"; the theory that governments enjoy their power over citizens by contract only and for the sake of securing the rights of the citizens; that by nature all men are "equally free and independent"; that whenever any government is inadequate to the purpose of protecting their equality and rights, the people have an "indefeasible right, to reform, alter, or abolish it, in such manner as shall be judged most conducive to the public weal." These were Jefferson's principles, as well as those of most of his colleagues. We shall have occasion in the concluding section of this book to consider their development in Jefferson's mind as he worked out his political philosophy. Here it is enough to record that Jefferson drew copiously on Mason's document, as upon John Locke's *Second Treatise of Civil Government,* which he had thoroughly absorbed years before. To this then widely known system of political thought Jefferson added a more liberal concept, however, when he enumerated the natural rights of man as including not only life and liberty but the "pursuit of happiness." Mason had used the phrase "pursuing happiness" in a list which also included life, liberty, property, and safety. Thus Jefferson, omitting the specifics, dedicated the new nation to a human objective broader than, but no doubt including, the protection of individual property and safety. To the statement of principles he composed from these elements, he added a detailed account of the "long train of abuses" to which the Americans had been subjected by the mother country.

The committee made only insignificant changes in Jefferson's draft and authorized him to submit it to Congress with their approval, which he did on June 28. On that day it was read and laid on the table pending action on the resolution for independence. The latter—Lee's resolution—was taken up on July 1. In the first tally nine states voted affirmatively; Pennsylvania, Delaware, and New York abstained for lack of authority or lack of agreement within their delegations. This action, in committee of the whole, was reported to the whole Congress the next day, July 2. In the final, historic vote all states except New York approved. New York delegates were for the resolution but still lacked authority from their state convention. Shortly thereafter they received fresh instructions and added the name of New York to make the action unanimous.

Thus July 2, 1776, was the actual date upon which the United States of America was born. The Congress debated for three days the question whether to adopt Jefferson's paper, and amended it in certain important ways. But with its great preamble unchanged it was finally adopted on the 4th, and every member except Dickinson signed it. Thus it is a kind of unspoken tribute to Thomas Jefferson that it is the 4th, not the 2nd of July, that is celebrated by Americans as their independence day. It is clear from the records of those days that the delegates were fully aware that they were not merely declaring the independence of their states and the joining of these states into a new nation; they were announcing also a revolutionary new departure in government. For the first time in modern history men were undertaking to convert a war for independence into an opportunity to build a government on the principles of individual liberty and equality, assuming, above all, that men are capable of full self-government.

But unhappily the men of Congress could not quite agree that "all men are created equal" or that *all* men are capable of self-government. The alteration in Jefferson's text which disturbed him most was the removal of his clause on slavery. This, he recalled, was "in complaisance to South Carolina and Georgia, who had never attempted to restrain the importation of slaves, and who, on the contrary, still wished to continue it." He did not exempt Northerners from responsibility, "for though their people had very few slaves themselves, yet they had been pretty considerable carriers of them to others." The sincerity of Jefferson's wish to bring an end to the slave trade —and to slavery itself—cannot be doubted. A lifetime of effort testifies his devotion to his ideal. But one may, perhaps, fairly question the technique he used in his draft of the Declaration of Independence. The text of the deleted clause reveals both the angry attitude of its author toward the brutal violation of human dignity occasioned by slavery, and the doubtful propriety of trying to make George III a scapegoat to blame for the regrettable institution:

He [George III] has waged cruel war against human nature itself, violating its most sacred rights of life and liberty in the persons of a distant people who never offended him, captivating and carrying them into slavery in another hemisphere, or to incur miserable death in their transportation hither. This piratical warfare, the opprobrium of *infidel* powers, is the warfare of the *Christian* king of Great Britain. Determined to keep open a market where men should be bought and sold, he has prostituted his negative for suppressing every legislative attempt to prohibit or to restrain this execrable commerce. And that this assemblage of horrors might want no fact of distinguished die, he is now exciting those very people to rise in arms among us, and to purchase that liberty of which he has deprived them: thus paying off former crimes committed against the liberties of one people, with crimes which he urges them to commit against the lives of another.

It is remarkable that Jefferson, remembering the debates over the Declaration and characteristically regretting the omission of his demand for an end to the slave trade, should not also have regretted that he had cast it in such a way as to render himself and his colleagues somewhat less than candid in the eyes of posterity. Everything else in the document, including other excised passages, reads true after two centuries, but the English King simply cannot be blamed for the tragic flaw in America's heroic destiny.

Jefferson regretted the excision also of the clause in which he held the British people responsible for the oppressive measures of their Parliament and their King. It was omitted because there were delegates who still held to what Jefferson called the "pusillanimous idea" that the Americans had friends in England who could be helpful and who would be offended by the passage. Whether this contention was well founded remains difficult to determine, but one can, in the perspective of the twentieth century, regret the loss of the passage for other reasons. The persistence of the British government in the face of popular protest shows how little responsive to the people that government was, and underlines the fact that it was the American Revolution, not the British Constitution, which first established popular responsible government.

But what was left when the Congress adopted the Declaration of Independence was enough both to secure the fame of Jefferson and to sting man's lust for liberty in all the years thereafter. A decade later, as Minister to France, Jefferson was to see for himself how insatiable was the yearning for liberty his words expressed.

But at Philadelphia in the summer of 1776, after independence was declared and justified, the Congress had to fight a war and form a government at the same time. Jefferson assisted in formulating the Articles of Confederation, but his part was minor. He took detailed notes on some of the debates, particularly on questions involving slaves and apportionment of voting strength in the new Congress. He seems to have been especially impressed by the arguments offered on these matters by Adams and Franklin, though his own views were probably even more liberal than theirs. However, he does not appear to have taken an active part in the discussions on the floor.

But the great respect Jefferson had earned among his colleagues was evidenced by their asking him to go to Paris on the mission with Franklin to seek an alliance with France. He declined because he was worried about Martha's health. She was in no condition to make so arduous a trip, and he could not think of leaving her and little Martha behind. In fact he was thinking chiefly about going home. He had been chosen delegate to Congress for another term, but he had also been elected to the Virginia legislature, which was about to revise the laws of the state. With this prospect beckoning at Williamsburg, and his concern about his family, his enthusiasm for the congressional responsibilities flagged. In this respect Jefferson was like many of his colleagues. They were fired by the *idea* of the nation, but the more immediate need seemed to them to be the conversion of their own "homelands," the former colonies, into independent and sovereign republics. Jefferson, like Washington and many other Virginians, spoke of Virginia in those days as "my country," and was anxious to get home.

In October, 1776, Jefferson took his seat at Williamsburg for one of the most momentous sessions in the history of free legislatures. His own work in that session was the prime cause of its historic significance. Though he was still to be numbered among the younger members of the Assembly and could not expect to exercise unchallenged leadership as a politician, he could and did press nevertheless for such revolutionary measures as would convert the old aristocracy into a popular republic. Conditions at the moment were propitious for accomplishing radical changes which might otherwise have been left to gradual evolution. Persuasive conversation in the corridors and at the Raleigh, and skillfully drawn bills were Jefferson's revolutionary tools. The measure of his success, given the conservative temper of the older Virginians, was substantial.

It may be useful to list the successes, partial successes, and failures of Jefferson's program before considering them in detail:

1. Abolish entails of land—accomplished.
2. Abolish primogeniture—accomplished.
3. Separate church and state—partially accomplished.
4. Abolish slave trade—accomplished.
5. Reform penal code—accomplished.
6. Establish system of public education—partially accomplished.
7. Complete religious freedom—accomplished by stages.
8. Abolish slavery—failed.

It might be added that by 1779 the separation of church and state, under other leadership, was completed, and that the system of public education was set up piecemeal over many years. Religious freedom was achieved under the leadership of James Madison in 1786 when the legislature enacted Jefferson's bill. His lifelong efforts to abolish slavery were, of course, unavailing.

The measures having to do with the ownership and inheritance of land were among the most far-reaching that could have been advanced to remake the society of old Virginia. The feudal system of entailing property had the effect, as Jefferson put it, of raising up "a distinct set of families, who, being privileged by law in the perpetuation of their wealth, were thus formed into a Patrician order, distinguished by the splendor and luxury of their establishments." It was from these families that the Crown had drawn its councilors, thus binding them in allegiance to the aristocratic ways of life. "To annul this privilege," said Jefferson, "and instead of an aristocracy of wealth, of more harm and danger, than benefit, to society, to make an opening for the aristocracy of virtue and talent, which nature has wisely provided for the direction of the interests of society, and scattered with equal hand through all its conditions, was deemed essential to a well-ordered republic." He might better have said that he, Jefferson, so deemed it, since in fact there were many members of the legislature, led by the redoubtable Edmund Pendleton, who did not agree at all. But the measure was carried, and thus vast tracts of land eventually became available for those "small farmers" who, in Jefferson's vision, ought to form the backbone of a free republic. It remained to abolish the legal right of the first-born male to inherit, so that landowners could make such provision for their children as they wished. This was done, again over the arguments of the conservatives, led by Pendleton. To these laws were added provisions to make the Western lands available to settlers at low prices and to liberalize the property holdings required for the suffrage. Jefferson never favored unqualified universal manhood suffrage. He was persuaded that men who owned land would, because of their stake in the community, be more reliable and responsible citizens than those who did not. But his principle would open the prospect of full citizenship to any man who was willing to take the responsibility of ownership.

These measures laid the basis for an agrarian democracy. But slavery remained to blight the expectation of equality. Jefferson argued that human slavery was unnatural, demeaning both slave and master. The slave trade had already been interrupted by the war, and he now drew a bill to abolish it permanently. In 1778 he succeeded in getting this measure through the legislature. But his arguments against slavery itself fell mostly on deaf ears.

The problem of religious freedom was of a different order. There were several strong and conflicting views on the role of the church and the obligations of citizens to religion. The Church of England had always been established as the state church in Virginia. Now that the rupture with England had cut that church adrift, it looked to the opponents of establishment like the right moment to move for separation. But the Episcopal Church itself and the idea of state support for religion in general had many vigorous supporters. Pendleton, again, as well as men like Robert Carter Nicholas, Washington, R. H. Lee, and even Patrick Henry, believed deeply in the spiritual and social values of the old order. Their strength in the Assembly was such that neither complete separation nor full religious freedom could be achieved in the session of 1776–77. But important steps were taken. Jefferson recalled that he and his party "prevailed so far only, as to repeal the laws which rendered criminal the maintenance of any religious opinions, the forbearance of repairing to church, or the exercise of any mode of worship; and further to exempt dissenters from contributions to the support of the established church; and to suspend, only until the next session, levies on the members of that church for the salaries of their own incumbents."

Despite Jefferson's disappointment, this was in fact a remarkable record of achievement. In pressing for these measures, Jefferson followed to some extent the political leadership of George Mason, and their forces were strengthened by young James Madison, then serving his first term in the Assembly. The complete disestablishment of the Episcopal Church, accomplished in 1779, was, in fact, owing more to the efforts of Mason and Madison than to Jefferson. And it was Jefferson's collaboration with Madison that eventually brought full freedom of conscience to Virginia. In 1779, while the separation bill was going through, Jefferson's famous statute calling for absolute religious freedom was also proposed. At that time the legislature ordered the bill to be printed and circulated, but Madison wisely judged that it was politically impractical to press for passage. In 1786, however, under different circumstances, Madison guided it through in one of the most skillful exhibitions of the legislative art in the annals of democracy.*

Jefferson saw, in the evident need to revise the laws to conform with independence, a great opportunity to liberalize and democratize the legal code of Virginia. It was this objective which had most strongly impelled him to resign his seat in Congress and return to Virginia. On October 24, 1776, the Assembly passed his bill calling for the revision of the whole code and the appointment of a committee to draft the revision and report it back to the legislature. To this committee Jefferson was himself appointed, as he certainly desired, together with Pendleton, Mason, Wythe, and Thomas Ludwell Lee. These men met at Fredericksburg in January, 1777, to outline their massive project. Both Mason and Lee excused themselves from the actual drafting work on the ground that they were not lawyers. To Jefferson fell the revision of the common law and the earlier English statutes. This task kept him occupied to a considerable measure of his time for more than two years. In particular he and his colleagues mitigated the punishments of the criminal law, abolishing the death penalty for any except murder and treason cases, and in many other cases substituting hard labor for whipping. Jefferson regretted that retaliation, that is, the "eye for an eye" principle, was allowed to stand at all.

In addition to his original bill for religious freedom, Jefferson also added to the revisal a set of three bills to establish a system of public education. His developing theory of republican government assumed that the responsible citizens— whose equality was to be recognized under the law, whose worship was to be unhindered by the state, and whose characteristic employment would be independent farming—would require, above all, to be educated to an understanding of the public questions facing them as voters and facing their representatives as officials of government. No part of the whole

---

* Jefferson's views on religion and religious freedom are explored in Part II of this book.

scheme of liberal government for America was dearer to Jefferson's heart. Accordingly he envisioned three levels of public education: (1) the common school "for all children generally, rich and poor"; (2) a higher stage "calculated for the common purposes of life, and such as would be desirable for all who were in easy circumstances"; (3) "an ultimate grade for teaching the sciences generally, and in their highest degree." At the first stage all pupils would be educated at public expense; at the second, those who proved worthy but impecunious would be granted state scholarships; to the third level of training only a small number would be admitted and, again, those who could not afford it would be supported by public funds. The plan also called for a state library to serve as a depository of books and documents at which advanced research could be conducted. This plan, ambitious beyond the imagination of Americans in that day, was never seriously considered by the legislature. A bill for common schools was passed in 1796, but no money was appropriated to carry it into effect. And it was well into the nineteenth century before Virginia caught up with the Massachusetts of Horace Mann in the field of secondary education. Forty years later, in his so-called "retirement," Jefferson himself founded not a state "library," but the University of Virginia.

The whole work of revision, as reported to the Assembly on June 18, 1779, amounted to 126 bills, a substantial reduction in the body of statutes that had grown up since 1607. Though there was action on some of the bills, most of them were not dealt with until 1785, at which time, under the leadership of Madison, the greater part of them was passed.

In sum, Jefferson the revolutionist succeeded to a remarkable degree in the effort to translate his republican ideals into action and to commence the building of institutions to perpetuate them. At Philadelphia, he articulated in unforgettable language the dedication of the new nation to the principles of liberty, equality, and responsible government. At Williamsburg, he guided the lawmakers of his own state toward a more humane and democratic dispensation consonant with the high language of the revolutionary documents penned by Mason and himself.

As if this were not sufficient achievement for a man still well under forty, he found time to work assiduously at improving his farms and building his great house in Albemarle, persuaded his fellow citizens to move the capital of the state to a more central location, and himself designed the permanent capitol building. He was now, in 1779, for the first time to feel the burdens of executive responsibility.

Chapter 3.

WARTIME GOVERNOR OF VIRGINIA

By the spring of 1779, Jefferson's reputation as a public man, his conspicuous leadership in the revolutionary cause, and his personal stature among the elite of Virginia made it a certainty that he would be elected governor. In due course the legislature elected him. On June 1, 1779, he was installed and began a two-year tenure in which he was probably less happy than in any other public post he held during his long life. Certainly it was his least successful effort.

Under the Constitution of 1776, Virginia retained the old colonial pattern of governor-and-council as a kind of multiple executive responsible jointly to the legislature. The governor was the pre-eminent figure, but he could not, in modern terms, be a "strong executive." He was appointed by the legislature, not elected by the people. And his council were likewise appointed by the legislature, not by the governor. On the other hand, the governor was looked upon by the people of the state not only as the civil head of government but also as the commander-in-chief of the military effort. It was an anomalous position for any man to hold, but particularly difficult for Jefferson, whose talents assuredly were not much bent toward warfare.

From the vantage point of the twentieth century, it requires a considerable act of imagination to understand what the Revolutionary War was like and to envision Jefferson as governor of Virginia and commander of the militia under the circumstances that actually prevailed. It was mainly a seasonal war. In late spring the annual "campaign" would begin, and fighting, vigorous or sporadic, would continue until fall. While General Washington's "continental line" was deployed strategically, as were the British regulars opposed to it, the various state militia groups, acting as home guards, were brought into action only in response to such British operations as might take place in their home territory. When a battle was over, militiamen customarily went home. If operations dragged out, many went home anyway. When harvest time came around, farmers thought nothing of leaving battle stations to get home and take care of their crops. Militiamen in units assigned to Washington followed the same practices, so that the main army was never stable. State governments were squeezed between their obligation to supply the continental army with men, money, and matériel and the more immediate pressure upon them to maintain security at home. It is not remarkable that no state governor was a hero of the Revolution.

In his *Autobiography,* Jefferson actually gives more attention to his work for the College of William and Mary, of which he became a Visitor in 1779, than to his administration of the state. This is not quite so incongruous as it may seem, since during much of his period in office there was no fighting in Virginia and his chief administrative concern was trying to meet his obligations to Washington. His correspondence with the General shows that he was indeed doing his best to put the effort of Virginia solidly behind the Commander-in-Chief. But there was abundance of leisure time for other pursuits. It is characteristic of Jefferson that he should have made use of the opportunity to bring about reforms at William and Mary. His juxtaposition of duty and interest is well illustrated in these words:

On the 1st of June, 1779, I was appointed Governor of the Commonwealth, and retired from the legislature. Being elected also, one of the Visitors of William and Mary college, a self-electing body, I effected, during my residence in Williamsburg that year, a change in the organization of that institution, by abolishing the Grammar school, and the two professorships of Divinity and Oriental languages, and substituting a professorship of Law and Police, one of Anatomy, Medicine and Chemistry, and one of Modern languages; and the charter confining us to six professorships, we added the Law of

Nature and Nations, and the Fine Arts to the duties of the Moral professor, and Natural History to those of the professor of Mathematics and Natural Philosophy.

As for his administration as governor, he recommends his reader to look at Girardin's continuation of Burke's *History of Virginia,* since his own doings were not separable from the public history of the state. His only comment is the statement that he "resigned" the office, in 1781, because of his belief that "the public would have more confidence in a military chief, and that the Military commander, being invested with the Civil power also, both might be wielded with more energy, promptitude and effect for the defence of the State."

But Jefferson's governorship of Virginia, despite his own evident willingness to treat it as a nearly inconsequential phase of his career, is nevertheless an important and revealing chapter. It was, for example, during this period that young James Monroe, returning to Virginia after more than three long years of fighting and serving on Washington's staff, began to read law under Governor Jefferson at Richmond, where the state government was moved in 1780. Presently Monroe became a confidential agent of the Governor. Operating in the Carolinas, where Virginia units under Gates and Stevens had been sent to support defenses against the threat of British invasion, Monroe sent reports by courier to his chief at Richmond that showed both that the young scout was observant and gifted with an orderly mind, and that the Governor of Virginia knew how to ask the right questions. Both men were caught uninformed, however, when Camden fell to the redcoats. Jefferson's frustrations are well expressed in a letter of condolence to General Stevens for the unhappy showing of the Virginia militia under his command. "The subsequent desertions of your militia," he wrote, "have taken away the necessity of answering the question how they shall be armed."

Not all desertions were stimulated by homesickness, either. In the summer of 1780, again, Governor Jefferson was forced to report to the President of Congress that there was much disloyalty in Virginia. Disaffection in some southern counties of the state had gone so far that citizens were said to be taking an oath of allegiance to the British Crown and planning insurrection. In October there was a near revolt in Pittsylvania, thwarted by the arrest of several supposed leaders in the dead of night. To some extent these, and numerous other reports Jefferson made to Congress, to Washington, and to the legislature, may have rested on unreliable rumor. One must always keep in mind the slowness of communication and the remoteness geographically of many towns and villages from Richmond or Philadelphia. But there can be no doubt that Jefferson as governor was unable to count on the unity of his people either behind his own leadership or even against the British. His letter of March 10, 1781, to Lafayette shows how Jefferson tried to put the best face on a situation which made for almost certain military disaster:

> Mild laws, a people not used to war and prompt obedience, a want of the provisions of war and means of procuring them render our efforts often ineffectual, oblige us to temporize and when we cannot accomplish an object in one way to attempt it in another.

The friendship between Lafayette and Jefferson, momentous for both the United States and France, began under these inauspicious conditions. But intellectual kinship displayed itself in their first meetings, and the frustrations of the one as a vigorous young military commander and of the other as a civil administrator were soon laid behind them in their common pursuit of human liberty.

As early as September, 1780, Jefferson was talking to his friends about his determination "to retire" from his office "at the close of the present campaign." The thought of a second year at Richmond was excruciatingly painful to him. He was willing to serve the state and the nation, but he was so sensible of his inability to do the job that needed to be done as governor that almost any other service seemed more inviting. To go home to Monticello, if he could honorably do so, was his fondest wish. Friends like John Page and George Mason urged him to reconsider. The legislature, Mason pointed out, was controlled by Henry. A new governor appointed under these auspices was not likely to be dedicated to the cause of liberal government. Whether such arguments prevailed with Jefferson, or his conscience told him that resignation was an unpatriotic course, he did not offer it and served out his term until June, 1781. John Page tried to console him:

> I know . . . the many mortifications you must meet with, but 18 months will soon pass away. Deny yourself your darling pleasures for that space of time, and despise not only now, but forever, the impertinence of the silly world. All who know you know how eminently qualified you are . . . and that circumstances may happen within the compass of the time above alluded to, which may require the exertion of greater abilities than can be found in any other person within this state. [*]

Such "circumstances" did indeed "happen." And sooner than Page could have expected. But there was some question as to whether Governor Jefferson showed the "greater abilities" of Page's flattering letter. For more than two years there had been rumors of imminent British invasions up the James River, but none had taken place. Now, in December, 1780, a British fleet was in fact on its way to invade Virginia's capital. The Governor and legislature, sitting at Richmond, received their first word of the approach of Benedict Arnold's force at eight o'clock on the morning of December 31. Jefferson immediately sent General Thomas Nelson to the invasion area with power to call up the militia wherever needed. Jefferson's diary records the movements of the British fleet daily and hourly as word was brought to Richmond. As the scope of the operation was revealed by fresh intelligence, Jefferson's orders mustering militia and securing military stores at and near Richmond became more comprehensive. On January 4 he sent his family up the river to Tuckahoe, and late in the day went himself to look after them. The next morning he thought it best to move them still farther upriver.

---

[*] The letters to Jefferson are printed in Boyd's edition of *The Papers of Thomas Jefferson*. See bibliographical note (p. 236)

Nearly all the rest of the time between December 31 and the withdrawal of the British on the 6th of January, Jefferson was riding to this point and that, directing salvage operations, endeavoring to rendezvous with General Von Steuben, protecting state papers, and otherwise exhausting himself by taking personal command of the situation.

The legislature adjourned on the 2nd and went quickly home "as the bearers of the orders to their respective counties." But it was impossible to muster sufficient force in time to obstruct Arnold's movements. The British reached Richmond, burned some buildings, tried to persuade Jefferson to bargain for the safety of the city, and failing that, withdrew before they would have to meet the Virginia militia.

The chief damage of the whole episode was to the pride of Virginia's gentlemen. Jefferson recorded in detail the "public losses" in military stores, armaments, and public papers. But the losses were not substantial. No military objectives were achieved by the British, and few if any American lives lost. But Jefferson's reputation suffered permanent injury as scapegoat for Virginia's spiritual wounds. Not long after Jefferson left the governor's chair, in June, 1781, the legislature, on motion by George Nicholas, "a very honest and able man," according to Jefferson, "then, however, young and ardent," called for an inquiry into the conduct of the executive before and during the British invasion. Nicholas sent Jefferson a copy of the questions he proposed to raise at the fall session. Jefferson prepared specific answers, which he, in turn, sent to Nicholas. One of the Albemarle representatives in the Assembly promptly resigned so that Jefferson could be elected in his place and thus be in a position to meet Nicholas on equal terms on the floor of the legislature. By the time of the session, however, Nicholas was satisfied that there had been no misfeasance or nonfeasance in the Governor's handling of his responsibilities and did not press his questions. Jefferson, anxious for vindication, himself read to the assembly the "Objections" and his answers to them. Afterward the legislature unanimously enacted the following resolution:

Resolved, That the sincere thanks of the General Assembly be given to our former Governor, Thomas Jefferson, Esquire, for his impartial, upright, and attentive administration whilst in office. The assembly wish in the strongest manner to declare the high opinion they entertain of Mr. Jefferson's ability, rectitude, and integrity as Chief Magistrate of this Commonwealth, and mean, by thus publicly avowing their opinion, to obviate and to remove all unmerited censure.

In later years, when Jefferson was struggling in the party battles with the Federalists, this resolution was interpreted by his enemies to mean that he *did deserve some censure* and was only being exculpated from censure he did not merit. Some biographers have accepted this interpretation. But in view of the fact that the members of the Assembly were, with few exceptions, witnesses to the events covered by their resolution—Nicholas himself having been absent—and since Jefferson was present on the floor to defend himself, it seems most unlikely that there was any intention to equivocate in the wording of the resolution. It is characteristic of Jefferson's modesty that he made no use of a letter he had received from General Washington—though he no doubt took private consolation from it:

Give me leave before I take leave of your Excellency in your public capacity to express the obligations I am under for the readiness and zeal with which you have always forwarded and supported every measure which I have had occasion to recommend thro' you, and to assure you that I shall esteem myself honored by a continuance of your friendship and correspondence should your country permit you to remain in the private walk of life.

Saddened by the loss of a baby daughter, worried about Martha's health, and unwilling longer to deal with the frustrations of his office, Jefferson had informed the Assembly in the spring of 1781 that he would not serve another term. He went out of office on June 2. It is a grim irony that the episode of his "governorship" which caused him greatest embarrassment over the years took place two days after he had left office. This was the occasion of Tarleton's raid on Charlottesville and Monticello. By June the British forces were greatly reinforced. Indeed, the war was then moving, though no one yet knew it, toward its grand climax at Yorktown. Since the legislature was sitting at Charlottesville, Lord Cornwallis decided to harass the members as much as he could by sending a raiding party into town. A troop under Colonel Tarleton advanced on Monticello on the morning of June 4, while Jefferson and his guests, the speakers of the two houses of the Assembly, were breakfasting. According to political legend, the master of Monticello panicked and fled into the bushes just in time to escape capture by Tarleton. To the image of inefficiency was now added the charge of cowardice. Jefferson was justifiably bitter. The most scathing passage in all his writings came from his pen as he recollected this episode while composing his *Autobiography:*

. . . we breakfasted at leisure [after the first warning] with our guests, and after breakfast they had gone to Charlottesville; when a neighbor rode up full speed to inform me that a troop of horse was then ascending the hill to the house. I instantly sent off my family, and after a short delay for some pressing arrangements, I mounted my horse; and knowing that in the public road I should be liable to fall in with the enemy, I went through the woods, and joined my family at the house of a friend, where we dined. Would it be believed, were it not known, that this flight from a troop of horse, whose whole legion, too, was within supporting distance, has been the subject, with party writers, of volumes of reproach on me, serious or sarcastic? That it has been sung in verse, and said in humble prose, that forgetting the noble example of the hero of La Mancha, and his windmills, I declined a combat singly against a troop, in which victory would have been so glorious? Forgetting, themselves, at the same time, that I was not provided with the enchanted arms of the Knight, nor even with his helmet of Mambrino. These closet heroes, forsooth, would have disdained the shelter of a wood, even singly and unarmed, against a legion of enemies.

One cannot help speculating as to what "pressing arrangements" Jefferson had to make before he was ready to depart—what papers or books he wished to hide from the enemy. He made no record of these hurried moments. But the mere fact that he delayed his departure as long as he did, after sending his family to safety, suggests that concern for his personal safety was scarcely uppermost in his mind.

In a few days the British had withdrawn from the area and the Jefferson family were able to move safely to Poplar Forest to stay for a time before returning to Monticello. Little damage was done by the British at Monticello, but Jefferson's plantation Elk Hill, some miles away, was used for ten days by Cornwallis as his headquarters and left in a shambles of pillage and burning. And all his Albemarle farms were plundered. In his *Farm Book* he noted "losses by the British in 1781," including "9 blooded mares, colts, and ploughhorses, 59 cattle, 30 sheep, 60 hogs, 200 barrels of corn, 500 of the same still growing, 250 bushels of wheat, etc."

The later months of 1781 were filled with the dramatic military maneuvers which ended in Cornwallis' surrender at Yorktown. Washington's regular army and the French under Lafayette, supported by the French fleet, achieved the historic victory. The chaotic Virginia militia fought bravely but played little part. The wartime Governor had no part at all. When the news came to him that the war for independence he had done so much to set in motion and had provided with its revolutionary idealism had at last been won, he was a farmer again, striving to regain his peace of mind.

Chapter 4.

MR. JEFFERSON AND THE AGE OF REASON

Not long after Tarleton's raid, Farmer Jefferson fell from his horse while riding about his lands and was incapacitated for several weeks. Taking advantage of the leisure enforced by his minor but confining injuries, he devoted himself to answering a series of queries about Virginia which had been formulated by the French Secretary of Legation at Philadelphia, the Marquis de Barbé-Marbois. These comprehensive questions, intended to procure for the French government better information about its new ally, were being circulated throughout the states. Jefferson's copy was placed in his hands by his friend (Monroe's uncle) Joseph Jones. He had already had it by him for a year or more, but his hectic life as governor had allowed him little time for reflection and for gathering and sorting the notes about his native state he had been accumulating for many years. Now that he had leisure to deal with the subject, he found it engrossing, and when they were published a few years later under the title *Notes On Virginia*, the queries with their learned and philosophical answers formed a classic of American literature.

Marbois' topics covered everything from geography to government, and from history to economic, religious, and social life. Jones had referred the matter to Jefferson in the belief that he was best qualified among the men of the state to handle it, but he could hardly have anticipated the seriousness and thoroughness with which in his "retirement" the former governor would attack the project. The *Notes on Virginia*, together with the Declaration of Independence, secured Jefferson's international reputation as a prominent figure of the Enlightenment. And his book was a true product of the "enlightened" mind.

Jefferson's approach to geography and natural history was scientific in the modern sense. So far as he could, he reported his own observations, and where possible verified his observations by exact measurements. Thus in his famous dispute with Buffon, the French naturalist who had guessed wrongly at the sizes of American animals, Jefferson was an easy victor. He measured animals himself or got measurements from friends like James Madison. His report on climate and meteorology was based on his own record of temperatures and rainfall. On historical questions and those dealing with earlier Indian culture he made use of the books and articles in his growing library, as well as the testimony of people he had known. Where he had need to guess, he said so frankly. But more often his own knowledge and the information he collected for the purpose were sufficient to warrant a full statement. When he came to such great issues as slavery and the freedom of religion, he spoke his own mind with brilliant clarity, but he did not fail to give an accurate report of conditions he did not approve. The research and writing of the *Notes on Virginia* occupied much of Jefferson's time until well into 1782. The book was published at Paris in 1784 (dated 1782). Thereafter there were many editions in both English and French.

Jefferson's pleasure in his brilliant intellectual achievement was blighted almost as soon as the manuscript was completed. On September 6 Martha Jefferson died. For months she had been in failing health, and her husband had shared with his sister and the servants the daily and nightly round of nursing. Her death brought to a tragic climax the one wretchedly unhappy period of Thomas Jefferson's life. For weeks he was inconsolable. But the realization that he must now serve as more than father to his three girls (the youngest, then only a few months old, was not to survive) brought him gradually back to activity.

And activity was what Jefferson now wished. Retirement at Monticello without Martha had lost its savor. When word came from Philadelphia that he had been appointed to the American mission, as a colleague of Franklin and Adams, to meet with the British in Paris, he accepted. But as it turned out, his preparations to sail for Europe, undertaken with some excitement of anticipation, were premature. British interference prevented his French ship from making its departure at Baltimore. He stayed on in Philadelphia until April, waiting for transportation or for Congress to decide whether they still wished him to join Franklin and Adams. But while he was waiting, word came that the treaty was concluded, and Congress relieved him of his commitment.

At home again, Jefferson was soon asked to take a seat in Congress. He accepted the appointment, largely to have something to fill the emptiness he still felt, and in September set out to find the somewhat disheveled and largely ineffectual body in which the wobbly United States was then embodied. It had been sitting in Princeton, but by the time Jefferson arrived it was again wandering. The session of 1783–84 was finally set for Annapolis, and it was there that Jefferson ended his career as a legislator. Those last months at Annapolis he found somewhat tedious. He would have much preferred to be living in Philadelphia, where there was more interesting intellectual society and good music. But his work was nonetheless creative.

Congress had such limited powers under the Articles of Confederation that the members could do little but debate like lawyers "whose trade it is to question everything, yield nothing and talk by the hour," as Jefferson wrote to Madison. His own conduct, however, was not disputatious. He addressed himself to such important questions as the Congress did have power to deal with, drafted proposals, and without contention explained their purposes and provisions to his colleagues. His chief interests were in the monetary and measurement system which the new nation should adopt and in the future of the western lands which, as he had advocated, were then being turned over to the nation by the states, especially by Virginia.

Currency in the new United States was in chaotic condition. Several states had circulated coins; all had circulated paper notes. British, French, and Spanish coins of all denominations were in common use. The Congress had authority to regulate currency and to coin money, but had had little success in exercising its power, having almost no credit to back up paper, and no metal to coin. But with the end of the war and a national future projecting itself dimly upon the consciousness of the Americans, a new attempt was being made. When Jefferson arrived at Annapolis he found that the most persuasive suggestion yet offered had come from the financier Robert Morris. But the system Morris proposed seemed to Jefferson too complicated for ordinary use, since "the bulk of mankind are schoolboys through life." As an alternative he worked out a decimal system based upon the common Spanish silver dollar. Hundredths of the dollar would be close enough approximations to the widely coined copper pennies of the states, while tenths and halves would be convenient small coins. In gold coinage it would be practical to multiply dollars into larger monetary units without producing pieces too bulky to be carried in the purse. At the same time Jefferson proposed that the decimal principle be applied also to a national system of weights and measures. The latter effort did not succeed with his colleagues. A decade later, when he was Secretary of State, he tried again, but again his views did not prevail. However, he was more successful with his coinage system. He spelled out his views on this subject in a paper he called "Notes on the Establishment of a Money Unit, and of a Coinage for the United States." This paper was studied attentively by congressmen and, in the session of 1785, they adopted Jefferson's system. It was retained, of course, under the Constitution. Jefferson's paper, published at Paris in 1785, was an important contribution to that systematizing of thought and practice which characterized the administrative and economic efforts of the Enlightenment.

At Annapolis Jefferson had been joined in the Virginia delegation by his young friend and disciple James Monroe. The two men took lodgings together and worked together on many of the problems before the Congress. The common interest closest to their hearts was the future of the West. Jefferson, as a son of the piedmont, felt personal kinship with the people whose migrations across the Alleghenies were already extending what he liked to call "the empire of liberty." Monroe, like Jefferson, was not a tidewater planter but a

"Westerner." His amazingly successful political career then just commencing was to be assisted in no small degree by the Western farmers whose cause he earnestly and ably supported. The two Virginians now collaborated on the famous land ordinance of 1784, first talking over in detail the ideas Jefferson incorporated into a committee document called "Report of Government for the Western Territory."

The principal proposal in Jefferson's "Report" was for the formation of ten new states out of the territories that had been ceded to the national government. He suggested naming them Assenisipia, Cherronesus, Illinoia, Metropotamia, Michigania, Pelisipia, Polypotamia, Saratoga, Sylvania, and Washington. Each state should be governed by officials appointed by Congress until it had 20,000 free inhabitants, when it should be allowed local self-government. After that, full statehood should be granted as soon as a new state had as many free inhabitants as the least numerous of the original thirteen. The Congress should guarantee the new states a republican form of government. Suffrage should be universal among free male adults. No hereditary title should be permitted. And after the year 1800 "there shall be neither slavery nor involuntary servitude in any of the said states, otherwise than in punishment of crimes whereof the party shall have been convicted to have been personally guilty."

This far-reaching plan of development and expansion was thought by the Congress to be too specific and was not accepted. But the distillation of its main ideas became the Ordinance of 1784. The latter, in turn, was the basis upon which in 1787 Congress drew the Northwest Ordinance. This last, the one great achievement of the Confederation Congress, became the controlling statute for the westward movement. Jefferson's influence can be seen in almost every line of that famous document, but nowhere more prominently than in the moving language excluding slavery and guaranteeing equal citizenship.

Another Jeffersonian declaration in the 1784 ordinance which was to recur later was that against hereditary titles. At the time Jefferson drafted the language of his "Report," his advice was being sought by Washington regarding the founding of the Society of the Cincinnati. This controversial organization was to admit to membership the commissioned officers of the Revolution and their male descendants in perpetuity. It was intended to bring the elite of the new nation into a body with common experiences, common principles, and, perhaps, common political interests within the republic. Jefferson objected strongly to the whole notion. He so advised Washington. In May the General stopped in Annapolis to talk over the matter with Jefferson before attending a meeting of the Cincinnati in New York. Jefferson's argument was that such a society contradicted the republican principle for which the Revolution had been fought, "the natural equality of man, the denial of every pre-eminence but that annexed to legal office, and particularly the denial of a pre-eminence by birth." Washington was at least partly persuaded by Jefferson's opinions and recommended, unsuccessfully, that the hereditary provision be removed from the society's constitution. But at the Constitutional Convention of 1787 there was full acceptance of the republican principle for which Jefferson was pleading. It was set forth in Article I, Section 9, of the Constitution: "No Title of Nobility shall be granted by the United States: And no Person holding any Office of Profit or trust under them, shall, without the Consent of the Congress, accept of any Present, Emolument, Office, or Title, of any kind whatever, from any King, Prince, or foreign State."

In the spring of 1784 Jefferson was once more asked to undertake a mission to Europe, replacing John Jay and joining Franklin and Adams as commissioners to treat with the various governments that, it was hoped, would enter into trade treaties with the United States. Jefferson accepted with alacrity and pleasurable anticipation. His only regret was that it would be necessary to separate his family. Polly and little Lucy Elizabeth were too young to be subjected to the trials of transatlantic voyaging, so he left them behind in the care of his sister Mary Carr at Monticello. But Patsy, now eleven, would go with her father as an affectionate companion, and have the advantage of schooling in Europe. When Jefferson set out for Boston, Colonel Monroe stood by to bid him farewell. This young man was about to undertake a rigorous trip of his own—to see the Western lands he and Jefferson had been legislating for during the long months preceding. Before the summer was over, he was writing to Jefferson and Madison about the beauties of upper New York State and arranging to buy land there where, in a future never to be realized, he hoped to escape the Virginia plantation system and to farm with free labor as a "republican" gentleman.

At Boston, where he was to sail for France, Jefferson was received with great deference, including the privilege of a seat on the floor of the Great and General Court of the Commonwealth of Massachusetts. His old friend Elbridge Gerry was back at Annapolis, still attending Congress, but Gerry's letters to friends in Boston no doubt helped to produce the cordial atmosphere which surrounded his Virginia colleague in New England.

When he sailed for France on the *Ceres* on July 5, 1784, Thomas Jefferson was already a prominent name throughout the civilized world. But his fame, thus far, was tied to the Revolution. The French, to whom he was now going, knew him as the author of the Declaration of Independence and had been led by Franklin to expect a cultivated gentleman well equipped to speak for the rights of man. They could not yet know much of the breadth of his talents and interests. Indeed, Franklin himself had had little opportunity since their days together at Philadelphia to develop his friendship with the younger man. Jefferson, for his part, looked forward with eager pleasure to renewing his relation with Franklin and to joining the society of philosophers, scientists, and artists whose work he had admired from across the sea. As it turned out, Jefferson's journey into the Age of Reason at Paris was a portentous event both for himself and for the tense, uncertain, but brilliantly civilized nation he was ever afterward to think of as his second home.

The new American Commissioner arrived with his daughter at Paris on August 6, after a comfortable and fairly rapid crossing. Soon afterward he reported to Franklin, the senior member of the commission, at the latter's famous country house at Passy. John Adams soon joined them to plan their course for improving commercial relations between the United States and as many European nations as would treat with them. The three men gave their time and energy and their best ingenuity to their task. But the governments of Europe were hesitant to enter into treaty obligations with a nation so young and facing so uncertain a future. Some agreements were negotiated with the French, and a full-scale commercial treaty was worked out with Prussia. But these were the only fruits of a year's efforts.

In May, 1785, Jefferson received notice of his appointment to succeed Franklin as United States Minister to France. Franklin, now seventy-nine, was finally going home. His career almost ended, his departure from Paris marked the end of a unique relationship—diplomatic, social, intellectual—between the people of one nation and the representative of another. With Voltaire and Dr. Johnson, Franklin belonged to the select intellectual peerage of the Enlightenment. His achievement, indeed, transcended even theirs. His younger friend from Virginia could not expect to match that record. But he was a worthy successor. Franklin introduced Jefferson to all the leading men, accompanied him to the salons of the great ladies at whose parties the best conversation was to be had and the best music to be heard. The statesmen Jefferson was to deal with on a formal footing, but Franklin's auspices and his own advance reputation meant an entrance into French society on terms perhaps no other foreigner could have commanded.

During that first year in Paris Jefferson also renewed his wartime friendship with John Adams and endeared himself to Mrs. Adams, the talented Abigail. Mrs. Adams, for her part, placed herself permanently in Jefferson's debt by her cordial reception and guidance of Patsy. Franklin and Adams disliked each other. Adams, always testy and suspicious and not without a certain arrogance, could not bring himself to approve the gay life that Franklin, even as an old man, liked to lead. He was hostile to the French *philosophes* with their sublime trust in reason, and generally disliked the moral tone of Paris society. Franklin, for his part, had difficulty restraining his contempt for Adams' arrogance and vestigial puritanism. But he appreciated Adams' great intellectual force and rock-solid patriotism. Adams, perforce, recognized Franklin's pre-eminence and grudgingly paid him as much deference as he could. But both men liked Jefferson, who respected Adams, loved Franklin, and cherished his friendship with both.

In May, not long after Jefferson was appointed Minister to France, Adams departed for London to be Minister to the Court of St. James. In July, Franklin went home. For the next four years, Jefferson, with young William Short as his private secretary, conducted United States relations with France, watched over other American affairs on the continent of Europe, and tirelessly reported to John Jay, the Secretary for Foreign Affairs, and Congress not only the political developments at Paris as the distant rumblings of the French Revolution began to be heard, but political intelligence such as he could get from other capitals, quantities of important economic and commercial information, scientific learning and discoveries, and countless incidental matters of interest to his countrymen. In the spring of 1786 he visited England, where his reception was formally correct but understandably cool. In 1787 he toured the south of France and northern Italy. In 1788 he joined Adams at Amsterdam for negotiations with Dutch bankers and thereafter took a trip through the Rhine Valley. These were the outward events of his public career. But what he was doing as a private person is a different and far more interesting story.

The two great events of Jefferson's years abroad were the coming of the French Revolution and the fourth and last of his romantic attachments. It was evidently hard for him to discriminate between them on any useful scale of values, since the one seized upon his political and philosophical attention while the other precipitated a poignant internal dialogue between his head and his heart. In the perspective of a later day, and even in the unfolding of Jefferson's own later life, the French Revolution no doubt commands the higher priority of consequence. But human lives are lived immediately and personally and not with the advantage of the all-seeing eye of the novelist or the historian.

The state of Jefferson's mind and the quality of the expe-

rience he was having in the years when he fell in love with
Maria Cosway, and consulted with Lafayette, Condorcet, and
La Rochefoucauld on the strategy and tactics of the French
Revolution, are well set forth in a letter he wrote to his friend
Charles Bellini, an Italian immigrant to America and a pro-
fessor at William and Mary. It will be useful to quote it in
full:

. . . Behold me at length on the vaunted scene of Europe!
It is not necessary for your information, that I should
enter into details concerning it. But you are, perhaps,
curious to know how this new scene has struck a savage
of the mountains of America. Not advantageously, I assure you. I find the general fate of humanity here most
deplorable. The truth of Voltaire's observation, offers
itself perpetually, that every man here must be either the
hammer or the anvil. It is a true picture of that country
to which they say we shall pass hereafter, and where we
are to see God and his angels in splendor, and crowds
of the damned trampled under their feet. While the great
mass of the people are thus suffering under physical and
moral oppression, I have endeavoured to examine more
nearly the condition of the great, to appreciate the true
value of the circumstances in their situation, which daz-
zle the bulk of spectators, and, especially, to compare it
with that degree of happiness which is enjoyed in America, by every class of people. Intrigues of love occupy the
younger, and those of ambition, the elder part of the
great. Conjugal love having no existence among them,
domestic happiness, of which that is the basis, is utterly
unknown. In lieu of this, are substituted pursuits which
nourish and invigorate all our bad passions, and which
offer only moments of ecstasy, amidst days and months of
restlessness and torment. Much, very much inferior, this,
to the tranquil, permanent felicity with which domestic
society in America blesses most of its inhabitants; leaving
them to follow steadily those pursuits which health and
reason approve, and rendering truly delicious the intervals of those pursuits.

In science, the mass of the people are two centuries behind ours; their literati, half a dozen years before us. Books, really good, acquire just reputation in that time, and so become known to us, and communicate to us all their advances in knowledge. Is not this delay compensated, by our being placed out of the reach of that swarm of nonsensical publications which issue daily from a thousand presses, and perishes almost in issuing? With respect to what are termed polite manners, without sacrificing too much the sincerity of language, I would wish my countrymen to adopt just so much of European politeness, as to be ready to make all those little sacrifices of self, which really render European manners amiable, and relieve society from the disagreeable scenes to which rudeness often subjects it. Here, it seems that a man might pass a life without encountering a single rudeness. In the pleasures of the table, they are far before us, because, with good taste they unite temperance. They do not terminate the most sociable meals by transforming themselves into brutes. I have never yet seen a man drunk in France, even among the lowest of the people. Were I to proceed to tell you how much I enjoy their architecture, sculpture, painting, music, I should want words. It is in these arts they shine. The last of them, particularly, is an enjoyment, the deprivation of which with us, cannot be calculated. I am almost ready to say, it is the only thing which from my heart I envy them, and which, in spite of all the authority of the Decalogue, I do covet. But I am running on in an estimate of things infinitely better known to you than to me, and which will only serve to convince you, that I have brought with me all the prejudices of country, habit, and age.

Despite his critical attitude toward "intrigues of love," Jefferson presently found himself engaged in one. If he was destined to become the victim of those "passions" he feared, it can at the least be said with assurance that the cause of his fall was as worthy as such a cause might be. Maria Cosway, wife of the English artist Richard Cosway, was twenty-seven and one of the most exciting women in Europe when Thomas Jefferson met her in the summer of 1786. Of medium height and graceful carriage, with abundance of golden hair and a strikingly musical voice, Maria seldom failed to charm. If her own interest was sufficiently aroused, she could captivate. Jefferson met her one afternoon when he went with John Trumbull, a young American painter who was his house guest, to examine the structure of the Halle au Blé. Before he quite knew what he was doing he had fabricated an excuse to miss a dinner with the elder Madame de la Rochefoucauld and set off for St. Cloud with Maria and a gay company of young artists and pleasure seekers.

From that moment and for the next several weeks the American revolutionist sought desperately to quell the revolution taking place in his own emotions. Richard Cosway, an eminent miniaturist and a man of Jefferson's own age, seems to have been used to the infatuations of other men for his lovely wife and to have borne them with good grace. At any rate he and Jefferson remained on excellent terms while the latter spent every moment he could in Maria's company. The affair never quite exceeded the bounds of propriety. Maria was greatly flattered by her conquest of the famous American and was certainly affectionately devoted to him. But there is no reason to suppose that she at any time contemplated another sort of relationship. Jefferson for his part seems to have disciplined himself accordingly but to have cherished somewhat deeper feelings than Maria's.

Theirs was a summer idyll. Maria was an accomplished musician, a composer of songs as well as a harpsichordist, and a successful painter. Her interests in art, literature, and philosophy were genuine. For her, Jefferson was a new and exciting kind of companion whose conversation revealed not only his fine taste and cultivation but an experience of the world none of her long-standing friends could match. So much the richer was her attachment to him for the romantic sentiment it evoked in him. In Jefferson she brought a return of that gusto for life he had almost lost with the passing of Martha. In his middle age he found in his friendship with

Maria a kind of second springtime which long outlasted the summer days in Paris.

In October, when Maria departed with her husband for Italy, Jefferson saw her off and then returned to his study to write her one of the most affecting and justly famous letters preserved in American literature. "Seated by my fireside," he wrote, "solitary and sad, the following dialogue took place between my Head and my Heart." Then, in dialogue form, he set forth a classic opposition between feelings and good sense, between dreams and reality, indeed, between Jefferson, in fantasy the perennial spirit of romantic adventure, and Jefferson, in reality the philosopher-statesman. The Head began the conversation: "Well, friend, you seem to be in a pretty trim." *Heart:* "I am indeed the most wretched of all earthly beings . . ." To which *Head* sagely but ungraciously replies: ". . . these are the eternal consequences of your warmth and precipitation. This is one of the scrapes into which you are ever leading us . . ." And so it went, page after page of exquisite sentiment matched by sententiousness merging into genuine sobriety, romantic reverie countered by an understanding which could interpret and sympathize but not, in the end, be quite swept away. If the heart of Jefferson was caught by the charms of the lady and led into impossible dreams, the head could still contemplate a well-constructed bridge over the Seine and meditate on "what a copious resource will be added, of wood and provisions, to warm and feed the poor" of Philadelphia if such a bridge were thrown across the Schuylkill in place of the floating bridge actually in use. Skillfully Jefferson effected a transition from the romantic leanings of the heart to the dangers of sentimentality in more practical affairs, such as the judgment of a people or a program of public action, and the answers of the head moved from self-discipline to the need for a discipline of democracy in order to preserve liberty. Then, momentarily, he would return to the personal note. In the end he had remarkably succeeded in at once relieving his genuine feelings of romantic loss, flattering the lady of his dreams, and maintaining both his self-respect and his special character of philosopher-statesman.

Though Jefferson continued to move in Maria's society for the next three years, until he returned to America, and wrote her frequent affectionate letters during their periods of separation, the intensity of their friendship was not renewed. But the Cosway circle continued to provide opportunities for zestful living which Jefferson indulged with delighted decorum. Among his new friends was another graceful, vivacious, and much sought young lady. Angelica Church was a daughter of General Schuyler and the sister of Mrs. Alexander Hamilton. She had married a wealthy Englishman and become attached to the Cosway circle through her interest in art and cultivated society. Jefferson and she quickly formed bonds of affection which long survived their separation when the American Minister at last went home. Madame de Lafayette was another close companion of this interesting group and brought with her several of the most charming and talented younger ladies of Paris.

The husbands of these vivacious ladies were indulgent, but at least one of them was much preoccupied with serious matters. Lafayette, who had become Jefferson's friend during the American Revolution, was no longer quite the dashing and boyish soldier who had so endeared himself to the Americans and by his generosity and valor won their permanent gratitude. But his maturing mind was more than ever dedicated to liberty, and he was now acting to make his great influence felt in reforming the government of his own country. Lafayette was among the foremost of those French leaders who saw that the irresponsibility of King Louis XVI and Queen Marie Antoinette, unhappily crowning the depressed condition of the French masses, would lead only to a mighty social explosion unless deep-reaching reforms could be quickly effected. With Lafayette were associated other close friends of Jefferson like the brilliant philosopher the Marquis de Condorcet and the epigrammatist the Duc de la Rochefoucauld. These men, leaders of the Patriot party, encouraged such moderate statesmen in the government as Vergennes, Montmorin, and Necker, but were satisfied that the King's advisers could not succeed in bringing about any serious modification of French domestic policy. They sought, rather, the King's permission to hold a national assembly for the writing of a new constitution.

As the Estates-General, convened in 1789 by authority of the King, failed to make substantial progress, and its Third Estate, representing all of France save the nobles and clergy, began to arrogate to itself the powers of a National Assembly, Jefferson found himself in a delicate situation. He was, in the first instance, the official representative of the United States to the King of France. In that role he had a prime obligation to maintain and foster good relations with the French government. His friends, on the other hand, were becoming increasingly hostile to that government and daily less sanguine about the effectiveness of the King's promises to institute constitutional monarchy. Jefferson was thus pressed from both sides.

When, in the spring of 1789, the King at last ordered the nobles and clergy to join the Third Estate in a formal National Assembly, Jefferson was hopeful that constitutionalism could be developed without violence. But he still hesitated to deal openly with the Patriot party. The latter inevitably looked to Jefferson, as a leader of the American Revolution, for advice and counsel. Informally Jefferson accepted this role. At least he could entertain his personal friends at dinner. It would be ungracious to interrupt them if they should happen to talk politics! And his opinion, if called for, as it earnestly was, could always be stated in general terms. His advice, contrary to the evident wishes of some of the leaders, was not to seek the establishment of a republic but to be content for a time with a constitution retaining the monarch as a needed symbol of national unity. There was an amusing irony, but much wisdom, in the recommendation of this once pro-scribed enemy of Britain inviting French attention to the British Constitution as a model of the most enlightened and benign to which they might aspire. On July 11, three days before the dramatic fall of the Bastille, he wrote to Tom Paine in London an optimistic account of the constitutional changes being brought about by the National Assembly and acceded to by the King. The National Assembly, he wrote, "have prostrated the old government, and are now beginning to build one from the foundation." The new constitution would begin with a declaration of the rights of man as the basis upon which the new structure was to be raised. The monarchy would be preserved but its privileges and restrictions set forth as a social contract with the people. The laws would be made by a representative legislature, elected by the people and responsive to their wishes. There would be an independent judiciary.

But the influence of the Queen and ambitious members of the court caused the King to vacillate, and violence could not be avoided. On July 19, Jefferson wrote a long report to John Jay in which he announced the fall of the Bastille to the patriots and the forcible bending of the King's will to that of the revolutionaries. Meanwhile he was consulting with Lafayette on the text of a declaration of rights. The latter wished to adapt Jefferson's Declaration of Independence to the situation then obtaining in France, and to expand its application. Jefferson encouraged his friend, suggesting particularly that instead of the limited term "property" the draft should claim as man's natural rights "the care of his life, the power to dispose of his person and the fruits of his industry, and of all his faculties, the pursuit of happiness and resistance to oppression." In the final text none of Jefferson's actual language was preserved except in those passages which deliberately echo the Declaration of Independence, but Lafayette's clause "the rights of succeeding generations necessitate the revising of all human institutions" well expresses Jefferson's counsel that any form of government the French might establish ought to be subject to change as conditions change.

Jefferson observed many of the exciting events of July, 1789, on the streets of Paris, and made numerous trips back and forth to Versailles to witness the meetings of the Assembly, the goings and comings of the King and other leading public figures. His reports to the United States Congress, addressed to Jay as Secretary for Foreign Affairs, show that he was an alert and sensitive observer. His fears that an excess of zeal by the Patriot party might open a Pandora's Box of chaotic violence were about evenly balanced by his confidence in Lafayette and the other Patriot leaders and his hope that the

King would yield to the counsels of moderation before it was too late. He fully shared the contempt of the French masses for the irreconcilables of the old aristocracy. As he wrote to William Carmichael in August: ". . . seven princes of the house of Bourbon, and seven Ministers fled into foreign countries, is a wonderful event indeed."

By 1789 Jefferson was homesick. Well before the revolutionary events of the summer had commenced, he had applied for a leave of absence to go home. Now that the Revolution had begun, auspiciously as it then seemed, he was anxious to keep the way open for his return, after a year at home, to observe its further progress. When, in August, he received permission to take leave, he was delighted at the prospect.

At home, too, great events had been taking place. Through his copious correspondence with leading men in many states, and especially through his intimate correspondence with Madison and Monroe, Jefferson had learned of Shays' Rebellion and warned that while violence and disobedience were not to be condoned, nevertheless the action of the rebels was symptomatic of the need for the most liberal laws and institutions. "The tree of liberty," he observed, "must be watered from time to time with blood of patriots and tyrants."

His own experience with the Confederation government, added to the continuing reports of the decline of its influence, persuaded Jefferson that a national convention must revise the articles drastically in order to shore up the union. When he received the draft Constitution in the fall of 1787, it was with mixed feelings. In the summer he had written his friend Colonel Carrington that "with all the imperfections of our present government, it is without comparison the best existing, or that ever did exist." In November, when he had examined the draft, he wrote disparagingly to Adams: ". . . the house of federal representatives will not be adequate to the management of affairs, either foreign or federal. Their President seems a bad edition of the Polish King." He thought all the good of the new constitution "might have been couched in three or four new articles" added to the Articles of Confederation. But by the end of December he had had some clarification from Madison and had thought over the matter more carefully. No doubt in part respecting the feelings of his friend, who was the chief author of the document, he wrote to Madison: "I like much the general idea of framing a government, which should go on of itself, peaceably, without needing continual recurrence to the State legislatures." The plan for the separation of powers he approved, especially the provision for the larger House of Representatives. He made strong objections, however, to the absence of a bill of rights and to the omission of a limit on the terms of the President and the senators. His advice to his countrymen, finally, was to adopt the Constitution by the vote of nine states, but that four should withhold approval until a second convention had added a bill of rights and made some other changes. But the agreement, informally made, that a bill of rights would be recommended by the first Congress, after adoption, satisfied him. He still feared, as he wrote Carrington, that the people would be "put to sleep by the unlimited confidence we all repose in the person to whom we all look as our president." After Washington, he was saying in effect, no one could be sure what might happen.

But as Jefferson made arrangements for his return to America in the summer of 1789, Washington had been inaugurated, the new Congress had enacted Madison's Bill of Rights as the first ten amendments to the Constitution, and, in an atmosphere of optimism and cooperation, was working out the necessary measures to establish the executive and judicial departments of the government. Jefferson was interested in these matters, but not deeply concerned. His mind was fixed that he would not again enter into the national government, or any other. After a year of renewal in Paris and perhaps a final tour of parts of Europe, he would return to live out his days at Monticello, farming, reading, writing, and following the bent of his wide-ranging mind. He had no inkling that President Washington had already determined to offer him the first place in the new cabinet as Secretary of State, and no thought of such a possibility seems to have crossed his mind.

But it was to be twenty years before he could truly retire. In those two decades the enlightened philosopher was to serve his country almost continuously in the highest offices, as Secretary of State, as Vice-president, and then for two terms as the third President of the United States. And not least, this man whose leaning was to contemplation was to lead the "republican" faction in the bitter party battles which in the 1790's determined the later course of American history. He was to found the most durable of all political parties, but he was never to return to the "scene of Europe."

Jefferson's mission to France had been for him a matchless experience, an opportunity to study and observe the old world and the old ways, to meet and converse with the most brilliant men of the age, to stretch his own intellectual tendons, and to gain a new and reassuring perspective upon the great experiment in freedom going on in his own country. Henceforward he would measure every proposal for American policy and program against his knowledge of Europe, and greet with seasoned skepticism every suggestion of emulating European systems of government or economy. As he saw it, the culture of the European capitals had been too dearly bought at the expense of the masses of people. Better the new world should borrow what was useful from the old, but mark out new and better and more humane and liberal institutions and customs. For this purpose it was no small part of his own mission in Europe to do what he could to transfer to America the best products of European invention and agriculture. To friends in various states, as well as to Monticello for his own use, he had sent as many things unobtainable at home as he could afford to buy. He had commissioned portraits and busts by European artists. He had bought many books, both for his own library and for his friends. On his travels his eye had always been directed to agricultural achievements that might be useful at home. Olive trees, dry rice for the Carolinas, and merino sheep were among his shipments to America.

Not all of Jefferson's scientific pursuits entirely comported with the dignity of a Minister to the Court of France. To William Drayton he gave a guarded account of his activities in Lombardy in the spring of 1787. ". . . I thought it would be well to furnish you with some of the Piedmont rice, unhusked, but was told it was contrary to the laws to export it in that form. I took such measures as I could, however, to have a quantity brought out, and lest these should fail, I brought, myself, a few pounds." To his old friend Edward Rutledge he revealed his exploit more frankly:

> . . . they informed me . . . that its exportation in the husk was prohibited, so I could only bring off as much as my coat and surtout pockets would hold. I took measures with a muleteer to run a couple of sacks across the Apennines to Genoa, but have not great dependence on its success.

The spectacle of the American diplomat secreting the proscribed rice in his money belt and directing his servant to store it about his person is ludicrous enough, but the formal language he used, in letters like this, to cover his peccadilloes compounds the amusement, if not the felony. The theft of rice was perhaps Jefferson's most extreme act for the advancement of agricultural science in the United States, but, as he wrote to Lafayette, he was "never satisfied with rambling through the fields and farms, examining the culture and the cultivators, with a degree of curiosity which makes some take me to be a fool, and others to be much wiser than I am."

An important example of thus "examining the culture and the cultivators" was his notation in a memorandum made on a trip to Amsterdam in April, 1788, that the plowmen of northern Europe were struggling with ineffective implements. "The awkward figure of their mould-board," he wrote, "leads one to consider what should be its form." The truth was that no one had in fact been led to consider the matter for untold years. But Jefferson's meditations led from a sketch he made at the moment to his invention of a moldboard that was widely adopted, to the improvement of farming in both Europe and the United States. "The plough is to the farmer," he said, "what the wand is to the sorcerer."

Thus did the Virginia *philosophe,* not content simply to admire the surfaces of the Age of Reason, display the ingenuity of the Yankee to probe around and beneath it. Perhaps it may not be too much to suggest that the finest achievement of his five-year mission in Europe was the advancement of his own education, to the enrichment of his own remarkable life and the lasting benefit of his countrymen.

Assuming that he would return in another year, Jefferson made few farewell visits other than those necessitated by his official position. He entertained his close friends—Lafayette, Condorcet, and La Rochefoucauld—at a private dinner to which he invited Gouverneur Morris, the conservative but patriotic American who, as neither then knew, was to succeed him as Minister to France. Then, on September 26, with Patsy, now a cultivated young lady of seventeen, eleven-year-old Polly, who had joined them the previous year, and two servants, Jefferson set out for Cowes, across the channel from Le Havre. There, on October 22, 1789, after a delay of several weeks in which he took his family on some sightseeing trips about the south of England, he sailed for home.

Chapter 5.

PRELUDE TO THE STORM:
JEFFERSON AS SECRETARY OF STATE

The Jeffersons arrived at Norfolk harbor on November 23, 1789. As they disembarked, the vacationing American Minister to France was surprised to find a large welcoming party, including local officials as well as old friends, who greeted him with ceremony as "Mr. Secretary." They explained that President Washington had nominated him to be Secretary of State and that the new Senate of the United States had confirmed the appointment on September 26. A warm letter from President Washington reached him soon afterward, urging him to accept the senior post in the cabinet, where he would have charge of foreign affairs and act as secretary to the government.

There is no doubt that Jefferson was unhappy at the prospect of having to decide between the President's flattering invitation, with its inevitable consequence of heavy responsibilities and perhaps unpleasant political involvement, and his fond wish to have one more year in France and then to retire permanently from public life. From Norfolk to Williamsburg and on to Richmond he made his way by slow stages, seeing many people and refreshing himself on conditions in his beloved Virginia. Everywhere he was assured that the public expected him to join the new government at New York. Two days before Christmas he reached Monticello, where his neighbors and servants turned out to give him an affecting reception. He addressed them briefly, concluding with these characteristic words:

Wherever I may be stationed, by the will of my country it will be my delight to see, in the general tide of happiness, that yours too flows on in just pace and measure. That it may flow thro' all time, gathering strength as it goes, and spreading the happy influence of reason and liberty over the face of the earth, is my fervent prayer to heaven.

During the holidays, Madison, the leader of the new House of Representatives and at that time a close confidant of Washington, rode over from Orange to stay a few days at Monticello. He advised his old friend to accept the position as Secretary of State, since Jefferson was certainly better prepared than anyone else to direct the nation's foreign affairs and since, so Madison judged, the domestic part of the job would be slight enough. A second letter from Washington, arriving at this time, was no doubt decisive in Jefferson's troubled mind. In his response to the first he had advised the President that he would not refuse an insistent request, but that he preferred to return the next year to France. Now Washington emphasized the importance of the central administration at home:

I consider the successful administration of the general Government as an object of almost infinite consequence to the present and future happiness of the citizens of the United States. I consider the office of Secretary for the Department of State as *very* important on many accounts: and I know of no person, who, in my judgment could better execute the duties of it than yourself.

Jefferson now accepted the appointment and, with little enthusiasm, began the task of preparing Monticello for another long period without its master. He was distressed at the condition of his farms after his five years abroad, and now somewhat desperately planned a program to revive and improve them. While some of the seeds and cuttings he had sent from Europe flourished, more had not. But it was some satisfaction to him that other planters in Virginia and the Carolinas fared better with the experiments his shipments stimulated. At this time, too, he made over a portion of Poplar Forest to Patsy, now seventeen, who married Thomas Mann Randolph, Jr. on February 23. The marriage, uniting his beloved daughter to the son of his lifelong friend, was a happy occasion, making it all the more difficult to reconcile himself to the coming separation. But he nevertheless set out for New York on March 1.

On the journey to New York, Jefferson stopped in Philadelphia to visit Franklin. He found his old friend weak and ailing. Each knew that it would be their last meeting. One could wish that there were fuller records of their conversation than those preserved by Jefferson. He noted, in his *Autobiography*, only one transaction in any detail. Franklin, then eighty-four, made no notes at all. Much of the talk, of course, was about the French Revolution, about Franklin's old friends in Paris, and about the politics of Europe in general. Franklin went "over all in succession, with a rapidity and animation almost too much for his strength." Afterward he put into Jefferson's hands a portion of the manuscript of his own autobiography, which he was then still working on, asking Jefferson to read it at his leisure. Twice Jefferson indicated that he would return it; twice Franklin told him to keep it. It seems clear enough that Franklin meant the manuscript as a parting present, but Jefferson somehow missed the point. Shortly after Franklin died, on April 17, Jefferson personally turned the document over to William Temple Franklin, the executor of his grandfather's literary remains. Temple Franklin, Jefferson afterward recalled, after a perfunctory look at the manuscript, casually observed that he already had a copy of it. It was only then that Jefferson realized that Franklin had indeed intended him to keep it. The paper itself never appeared in print during Jefferson's lifetime. He always suspected that it had been deliberately suppressed, since it dealt with an abortive attempt by Franklin to avert the rebellion of 1775, through his friend Lord Howe. The latter told Franklin in confidence that Lord North actually desired the outbreak of a rebellion. Jefferson thought Lord North's behavior so dishonorable as to warrant considerable British pains to suppress Franklin's account of it.

Perhaps the parting with Franklin draws better than any

other event in Jefferson's life at that time the sharp line de-
noting the end of an era. The Enlightenment phase of the
American beginnings was over. The era of bitter and decisive
politics was about to open. Jefferson, more than any other
American, more even than Washington, reflected in his life
and opinions the transition from a time of optimism and anticipation to a time of tenacious and contentious grappling
with the tough problems of building and protecting a nation.

Jefferson's arrival at what has been called the Court of
George Washington was the occasion, however, for a round
of dinners and entertainments which belied the real state of
political affairs. In the cabinet his colleagues were Henry
Knox, Secretary of War, Edmund Randolph, Attorney General, and Alexander Hamilton, Secretary of the Treasury.
Randolph, called to Virginia by his wife's illness, was away
much of the time during the six months before the government was moved to Philadelphia, and played little part in the
decisive actions that were being taken. Knox had little to do,
since the army was demobilized and there was no navy. Thus
Jefferson found, as Madison had led him to expect, that Hamilton, next to the President, was the leading figure of the
government. The Schuylers, parents of Mrs. Hamilton and
of Jefferson's friend Angelica Church, were particularly
cordial. Washington entertained frequently with Jefferson as
honored guest. Both Hamilton and Vice-president John Adams
were solicitous for his welfare.

But there was a disturbing note. In the social conversation
Jefferson heard many remarks that smacked to him of monarchy. Washington was conducting the ceremonial side of
his office much like a king, with levees and other formal occasions and traveling always with a retinue of liveried footmen.
The members of the executive, many members of Congress,
and the social circles around the government were according
Washington a deference that seemed to Jefferson not quite
compatible with republican principles. It is only fair to observe that Jefferson's reactions at the moment, as recorded in
his notes and letters, were less critical than were his recollections in after years. But he nevertheless seems to have felt

uncomfortable. In a private conversation, Jefferson recorded that the President deplored the special attentions he was receiving: "[he] explained to me how he had been led into them by the persons he consulted at New York; and that could he but know what the sense of the public was he would cheerfully conform to it."

Before long Jefferson began to see, so he thought, connections between the social atmosphere and the measures of government being advanced by Hamilton. Many years later, in a letter to Dr. Benjamin Rush, Jefferson recalled the spirit of Hamilton's politics with this anecdote:

> The room [Jefferson's] being hung around with a collection of portraits of remarkable men, among them were those of Bacon, Newton and Locke, Hamilton asked who they were. I told him they were my trinity of the three greatest men the world had ever produced, naming them. He paused for some time: "the greatest man," said he, "that ever lived, was Julius Caesar." Mr. Adams was honest as a politician as well as a man; Hamilton honest as a man, but, as a politician, believing in the necessity of either force or corruption to govern men.

It would be hard to find an encounter that better reveals the depth of difference between the imperious young statesman and the revolutionary philosopher. Bacon, Newton, and Locke were indeed Jefferson's heroes, while Hamilton himself bore no slight resemblance to Caesar.

Hamilton's report on the public credit, with its recommendations for restoring fiscal soundness, had been received and approved before Jefferson arrived. But an additional measure was then pending which Hamilton thought essential to his program for putting the nation on its financial feet. This was a bill to empower the treasury to assume the debts incurred by the states under the Confederation. Hamilton's view was that private creditors, whether banks or individuals, ought to be attached firmly to the federal government as the source of their return on their money. Such an attachment, "the cement of the union" as he called it, had been lacking under the old

Congress, and Hamilton was anxious that the states should no longer have the leverage of their debts to play off against the central authority. But the whole funding plan not only countered the principles of state-righters like Patrick Henry, it offended the sense for justice of such leading federalists as James Madison because it made no discrimination among the various holders of Confederation or state notes. The rumor that the government would fund and pay the debts had led to much speculation by financial men of the cities, who bought up the securities at less than face value, whereas years before many a revolutionary soldier had been forced to sell his holdings to raise money for minimal living expenses. The assumption plan was considered even more unfair, since some of the states, notably Virginia, had paid off all or most of their debts, while others, like Massachusetts, had paid little or nothing. Thus the tax burden would fall unfairly on citizens of the states whose finances were settled, and to the advantage of others. Madison had argued in favor of the funding program if it provided for a premium to original holders and redemption of the securities held by speculators only at face value. This was not done, however, and Madison was now opposed to the assumption plan. The anti-assumption group in Congress was close to having a majority.

In these circumstances Hamilton appealed to Jefferson to intervene and save the measure from defeat. He argued that the future authority of the central government as well as its present fiscal soundness were at stake. Jefferson was no doubt troubled by the pressure thus applied to him. In after years he often observed that he had been forced to act while still largely ignorant of the implications and true purpose of Hamilton's policies. "I was most ignorantly and innocently made to hold the candle," he wrote twenty-five years later. It seems probable that Jefferson did not in fact fully grasp Hamilton's far-reaching plan. But even if he had, he might still have followed the same course, which was to strike a bargain in what is often called the "first great American compromise." On his side in the negotiation was the desire of the South not to have the permanent capital of the United States established in New York or Philadelphia or elsewhere near the financial centers. The issue was being debated in Congress and the matter had reached an impasse. The compromise was found in an agreement by Hamilton to persuade certain Northern Congressmen to vote for locating the national capital on the Potomac near Georgetown, in exchange for an agreement by Jefferson to persuade certain Southern Congressmen to go along with the assumption. The bargain thus struck was carried out. Jefferson noted that Lee and White of Virginia changed their votes, "White with a revulsion of stomach almost convulsive." The long-term consequences of Mr. White's temporary dyspepsia may well have included a more stable federal government than would otherwise have been possible, as well as the capital at Washington. But the immediate consequence of the deal was a rapidly developing distaste on Jefferson's part for Hamilton's brand of federalism and the end of their short-lived collaboration.

The following year, 1791, Hamilton asked Congress to complete his program by establishing a national bank. Jefferson's reaction was immediately hostile. As he saw it, there were two transcendent objections to such an institution. First, a national bank, under private ownership and control with the government as a junior partner only, was an open invitation to the men of finance to exploit the government for their own benefit by controlling credit and squeezing farmers and tradesmen. Second, the Constitution gave no power to Congress to charter a bank or any other corporation; such powers belonged to the states. If Congress could charter a bank, there was really no limit to what it could do. In short, Jefferson thought it would be hard to imagine a measure better calculated to set up in the United States precisely that English system of centralized finance and government the Revolution, as he thought, had been intended to eliminate. He was strongly supported in this view by the group in the House now calling themselves Republican, which was led by Madison, and by the small Republican group in the Senate of which James Monroe was now a member.

President Washington was in doubt about the bank proposal. He saw the advantage that a central bank would bring to the treasury, indeed to the whole fiscal system. But he appreciated the importance of the constitutional question, had no desire to interfere with state rights, and greatly respected the judgment of the opponents of the measure. He asked his cabinet members for written opinions. Jefferson's statement was a finely written paper which laid down the principles of limited government according to a "strict construction" of the Constitution. Hamilton's opinion, also skillfully argued, set forth the principles of implied powers which could expand the enumerated powers of the Congress in terms of the priority of federal over state sovereignty. His view soon became known as "loose construction." In these papers, as well as in the debates in Congress led by Madison against the bank and Winthrop Ames for the bank, theoretical issues were developed which for two decades thereafter underlay the battles between the Republican and Federalist parties.

The debate on the bank question was intense. Theoretical differences were supplemented, if not fostered, by interest and prejudice. The split in the Congress turned out to be irreparable, and two distinct parties formed. In the cabinet Knox sided with Hamilton and Randolph with Jefferson. Washington resolved the issue by deciding, somewhat reluctantly, to give Hamilton his backing. The bank bill carried the House by a close margin undoubtedly owed to the influence of the President. The Senate gave it a larger majority. Madison, who had collaborated with Hamilton on the *Federalist* papers, now broke with him and thereafter led the Congressional opposition to his measures. Though outwardly the relations of both Madison and Jefferson with the President remained warm, there is no doubt that their influence over him now began to decline.

As the party controversies grew more constant and more heated, Washington pleaded with his two chief lieutenants to collaborate instead of working at cross purposes. Parties or factions, he thought, were the cause of social evils and would destroy the American experiment. If he had read Madison's great treatise on parties in *Federalist X*, he did not agree with it. But he could not persuade the leaders to desist. "The seeds of faction" are indeed "sown in the nature of man," as Madison had written. It is freedom which breeds political parties and it is political parties, in turn, which maintain freedom.

And the parties assuredly grew. Hamilton, a determined and brilliant if sometimes unscrupulous fighter, managed to subsidize John Fenno's *Gazette of the United States,* which became a kind of journalistic voice of the treasury. It kept up a barrage of criticism against the Republicans as "Jacobins" who would destroy the new nation, sang the praises of the Federalists, and enthusiastically defended all the measures of Hamilton's party. In Philip Freneau's *National Gazette* the Republicans found an effective counterirritant to denounce Hamilton and the "monarchists." The Secretary of State, who always maintained that he took no part in these political squabbles, nevertheless hired Freneau as a translator in the State Department, gave him contracts for government printing, and never repudiated either his support or his newspaper. In addition to the newspapers, a pamphlet war soon commenced which was to continue almost unabated for ten years. At various times and under various pseudonyms, such men as Madison, Monroe, John Quincy Adams, and Hamilton himself joined the partisan struggles with the strong and often grossly exaggerated language of pamphlet polemics. On one occasion Jefferson, to his consternation, found himself an author of sorts in the pamphlet war. Publisher John Beckley sent him a copy of Thomas Paine's *The Rights of Man,* which he was about to publish. Jefferson wrote Beckley a letter of thanks, speaking of Paine's work in glowing terms and expressing his pleasure that something was at last to be done against the "political heresies" then current. Beckley promptly published Jefferson's letter as a preface to the book, thus bringing forth a bedlam of newspaper catcalls and a buzz of political whispers.

But Jefferson did for a time keep out of these matters as much as he could. If he had been able to guide his official life according to his own pleasure, he would have put party politics at the bottom of his list and attention to the patent office, then under his jurisdiction, at the top, with foreign affairs somewhere in the middle. He did, in fact, devote many fascinated hours to watching demonstrations of gadgets and engines whose inventors applied to him personally for approval of their patent claims. If there is something incongruous, as before long became evident, in a secretary of foreign affairs allocating large portions of his time to such things, it is less incongruous when one remembers that the secretary was Thomas Jefferson. Devoted to science from boyhood, curious and inventive himself, and fresh from years of close observation of the scientific advances of Europe, he was probably better qualified than any of his fellow citizens to judge wisely and accurately of the advances being made at home.

And, as he had done in 1784, he responded with gusto to a request from Congress for a proposal of a national system of weights and measures. Again basing his suggestions on a decimal system, Jefferson, with help from his friend mathematician David Rittenhouse, proposed a complete system of weights, measures, and coinage. But again his plan for weights and measures was rejected because it conflicted so sharply with systems in use elsewhere and commonly known in the United States. His coinage and monetary system, however, was adapted and accepted, with the approval of his rival, Hamilton.

But he could not avoid politics. In 1792 there would be general elections both for President and for Congress. Jefferson hoped for a sweep by the Republican forces so that Congress would bring an end to Hamilton's domination. In that case, he was confident, Washington, whose re-election he thought necessary for the good of the nation, would revert to his earlier Republicanism and conduct a policy less subservient to the monied interests and more friendly to the common man and to the small farmer. The famous "botanizing expedition" which he and Madison had made in May and June of 1791 may have played some part in the increasing activity of the Republicans, both in preparation for the Congressional elections and in backing Governor George Clinton of New York for Vice-president against Adams. But it is only fair to acknowledge that such meetings as may have taken place between the two Virginians and the Republican politicians of New York and New England must have been brief and secondary in their minds. As the travelers made their way up the Hudson to Albany and Lake George, and then across the mountains and down the Connecticut Valley to Long Island Sound and to New York again, Jefferson made voluminous notes on all the flora and fauna he could observe. These leave no doubt that the main purpose of the journey was indeed observation and recreation, not the making of political medicine.

For himself, Jefferson wished to retire at the end of the year 1792. His position, because he was thrown so constantly into association and conflict with Hamilton, was distasteful. He felt that his own influence had been weakened and that only a strongly Republican Congress could shake Hamilton's hold on the President enough to alter the direction of policy. If that could be achieved in the election, there would be no need for him to continue in office and he could honorably indulge his dream of life at Monticello.

But it was not to be. Washington reacted so strongly that, in effect, he rejected Jefferson's resignation. He himself wished, he said, to retire. But he would stay on for the good of the country. Jefferson could do no less. Further, Washington told Jefferson plaintively, he truly feared that the nation would founder on the shoals of party contention unless Jefferson and Hamilton remained at their posts and endeavored to work together. Jefferson took Washington's plea as a kind of order from the commander-in-chief. He agreed to stay another year, to the general surprise of his countrymen, who had been led to assume that his resignation was final, and to the consternation of the Federalists, who had hoped so.

Meanwhile Washington was unanimously re-elected. Adams was chosen for a second term as Vice-president, but by a close vote in a contest with Governor George Clinton of New York, the Republican spokesman. Jefferson, not a candidate for office, nevertheless received four electoral votes. The Republican faction won a clear majority of the seats in the House of Representatives. Jefferson, reporting these results to Thomas Pinckney, the American Minister in London, added a number of observations which reveal his state of mind on the subject of party battles. "An alarm," he wrote, "has been endeavored to be sounded as if the Republican interest was indisposed to the payment of the public debt. Besides the general object of the calumny, it was meant to answer the special one of electioneering. Its falsehood was so notorious that it produced little effect." He referred also to the slogans of the campaign just concluded. "They endeavored with as little success to conjure up the ghost of antifederalism, and have it believed that this and Republicanism were the same, and that both were Jacobinism." In view of this kind of campaign, Jefferson thought, "the result of the election has been promising."

As for Hamilton, his views at this same period can be judged from the fact that he was writing a pamphlet series, signed "An American" and appearing in Fenno's paper, which struck hard and with doubtful integrity at the Secretary of State. Behind the pseudonym he in effect accused Jefferson of treason to the Union and to Washington, of leading a drive to repudiate the public debts, and of hoping to subvert the republic in favor of Jacobin terror. To these attacks Jefferson made no direct answer. In a letter to Edmund Randolph he disclaimed any thought of entering the lists of the pamphlet wars:

I have preserved through life a resolution never to write in a public paper without subscribing my name, and to engage openly an adversary who does not let himself be seen, is staking all against nothing. The indecency too of newspaper squabbling between two public ministers, besides my own sense of it, has drawn something like an injunction from another quarter.

To this extent, he meant, he would be respectful of the President's wishes.

But when he thought the issues important enough, Jefferson could be at least as tough a politician as Hamilton. There were political ways to move against the Secretary of the Treasury, and Jefferson used them. He drafted a set of resolutions which William B. Giles of Virginia, a Republican leader, introduced in the House of Representatives on February 27, 1793. The Giles motions called for heavy censure of

Hamilton's conduct of his office—including charges that he had misappropriated public money, made illegal transfers of funds, borrowed from the Bank of the United States to the benefit of stockholders when there were unused funds in the treasury, and had refused to cooperate with the Congress when asked to supply financial records. In the background lay the unhappy fact that Hamilton's assistant, William Duer of New York, had made use of his advance knowledge of treasury policies to speculate in government paper on his own account and had conveyed information to his friends for the same purpose. This first scandal in the government of the United States had led to the bursting of a wildly speculative bubble and Duer's departure in disgrace. Hamilton himself had not been charged with complicity or of conduct in any way dishonorable. Nor did the Giles resolutions assert that he was personally involved. Through Giles, Jefferson hoped to bring about Hamilton's resignation on the ground of his responsibility for the boom and bust and for the corrupt behavior of his subordinates. Jefferson went so far as to propose a resolution, which Giles perhaps wisely omitted in his speech to the House, categorically calling for Hamilton's removal.

The Giles resolutions served to firm up the party lines, but revealed that the Republicans had won fewer seats than they supposed. The Federalists, led by Ames, mustered a solid majority to defeat the resolutions and vindicate Hamilton. If Jefferson, like his enemy, did not permit himself to appear as the accuser in these proceedings, and so is open to the same criticism he made of Hamilton, it may at any rate be said that his means of attack were aimed to produce open debate and an open roll call between the parties. There is no doubt that the whole episode advanced the formation of parties a long step beyond where they had been during the elections of the year before. And there was no doubt, either, that the Secretary of State, despite the pleas of the President, was the leader of the Republican party no less than Hamilton was the leader of the Federalists.

Despite the Republican defeat Jefferson was soon considering new legal and political means of curbing Hamilton's power. A note surviving from this period indicates how his thoughts were moving and what he was discussing privately with trusted associates like Madison, Giles, and Monroe. He proposed, for consideration, that the treasury be "divided," the national bank "abolished," the excise tax "repealed," and that holders of government securities be barred from election to Congress. These measures would not only have had the effect of drastically diminishing Hamilton's personal power but would have knocked down his whole fiscal structure. Nothing ever came of the idea of "dividing" the treasury, but the attacks on the bank and on the excise tax—both of which benefited the men of wealth at the expense of the small farmer—became basic planks in the Republican platform throughout the 1790's. Though no law was ever passed to make the holding of government securities a disqualification for Congress, or other federal office, Jefferson's strong feeling about it is revealed in his notes of a conversation with Washington on February 7, 1793: ". . . my wish was to see both Houses of Congress cleansed of all persons interested in the bank or public stocks; and that a pure legislature being given us, I should always be ready to acquiesce under their determinations, even if contrary to my own opinions." The issue Jefferson here posed of the "conflict of interest" has never ceased to present the American people and their government with a serious ethical problem.

By the spring of 1793 it was clear that the American Secretary of State would have to be a minister for foreign affairs on a full-time basis. The French Revolution had gone from regicide to Terror. Britain and France were at war. Both sides were hampering American shipping and both sides were menacing American safety and independence. Washington, Jefferson, and Hamilton agreed on the necessity of American neutrality. But the President was unsure how neutrality could be most advantageously proclaimed and maintained. The issues were complex and the pressures great. It is no doubt an oversimplification to say that Hamilton argued for a policy that would be "neutral in favor of the British," while Jefferson preferred neutrality "in favor of the French." But such expressions do reflect the spirit of the time. On the side of treating the British with cordiality were the vital considerations that Great Britain still controlled the Western forts which were to have been turned over to the United States by the Treaty of Paris, and that the British navy effectively controlled the seas where American commerce must move if the new nation were to grow in economic strength. On the other side, weighing at least equally in the balance, were the treaty with France made in 1778, the immense debt of the Americans to the French for assistance in the Revolution, and the French Revolution itself, which, though fallen from republican idealism into demagogic terror, nevertheless still offered hope for the eventual advancement of human liberty. How could the Americans, in their infant weakness, dare offend the rulers of the oceans? How could the revolutionary republican United States, on the other hand, favor a monarchy over a new sister republic? There were, of course, no right answers to such questions. But American policy had to be established.

Washington put the question to his cabinet, actually thirteen questions, on April 17, 1793. There were two leading issues. If there was agreement on a policy of neutrality, how should it be proclaimed? Should the United States officially receive Citizen Genêt, who was coming from France to replace Minister Ternant, and thereby seem to give approval to regicide and extremism?

On the matter of neutrality Washington leaned toward presidential proclamation. In this he was strongly supported by Hamilton and to a lesser extent by other advisers. Jefferson alone among the cabinet group was strongly opposed. In his view there were two serious objections to an executive pronouncement of this sort. First, it would unnecessarily offend the French by seeming to suggest that the Americans no longer valued their alliance with their comrades of revolutionary days. In any case it was perfectly possible to conduct a *de facto* policy of neutrality without announcing it. Second, Jefferson observed that if the President had the power to proclaim neutrality, it was a fair inference that he would also have the power to declare that the United States was not neutral. But this would in effect usurp the power of Congress to declare war. He saw in the proposal another important move by the Federalists to extend the powers of the executive against those of the people as represented in Congress—another instance of "monocratizing." Over these objections Washington finally decided on a proclamation. To the Secretary of State fell the distasteful task of drafting it.

But on the question of receiving Genêt, Jefferson's view prevailed over Hamilton's. The President agreed that the United States could not afford to offend the French government even though it disapproved of its methods of governing, expressed himself as anxious to keep the treaty of 1778 in being and to improve rather than harm relations with France. The decision was to bring Jefferson a heavy burden of political misery before the year was out, but as a matter of principle he never regretted having advised it.

Citizen Edmond Charles Genêt, certainly the most colorful if not the most popular emissary ever to serve his country in the United States, arrived at Charleston on April 8, 1793, where he was received with acclaim as the envoy of revolutionary France. That is, he was greeted enthusiastically by plain citizens and by Republican politicians. Federalists and substantial men of affairs were cold both to him and to the nation he represented. Genêt made the first in the series of mistakes that wrecked his mission before he reached Philadelphia. At every point on the route he stopped to make speeches and addresses against Great Britain and against Americans who were not actively sympathetic to the French cause. Acting more like a political agitator than a diplomat, he quickly alienated many Republicans and caused Jefferson to look upon his arrival at Philadelphia with misgivings.

But Genêt, it turned out, was not merely conducting a political campaign. Following his then secret instructions, he immediately arranged to hire and arm four merchant vessels at Charleston to privateer on the Atlantic. These ships, manned by Americans Genêt recruited, dashed out and successfully attacked British merchant ships. These they brought into Charleston as prizes of war. News of these developments embarrassed Jefferson and infuriated Hamilton and the Federalists. In the cabinet the question was raised whether the vessels should not be ordered out of the country. Hamilton and Knox were for drastic action against Genêt's little navy. Jefferson was acutely conscious of the undiplomatic conduct of the French Minister whom he was trying to befriend and assist, but argued that the Treaty of 1778, by forbidding enemies of France to fit out privateers in American ports, implied that the French could do so. At the same time he held that the prizes could be legally retained by the French. But Attorney General Edmund Randolph found a middle ground, which Washington accepted, in a proposal that the privateers be ordered out but that the prizes not be returned to Great Britain.

Genêt reacted to this adverse decision by going to the newspapers and stirring up a storm of criticism of the Administration, especially the President and the Secretary of the Treasury. He continued, in his public behavior, to treat the American government with outrageous contempt, blithely ignoring the repeated warnings of Jefferson that he was doing his cause irreparable harm. In July matters came to their inevitable head. Hamilton, through his close friend George Hammond, the British Minister, learned that a French privateer had captured a British vessel, the "Little Sarah," and brought it as a prize into Philadelphia, where Genêt was outfitting her to serve as a French privateer. Jefferson, who had long rightly suspected that his conduct of foreign affairs was being undercut by the Secretary of the Treasury and that his intentions were customarily disclosed by Hamilton to Hammond, was skeptical but sufficiently alarmed to follow up the complaint. It turned out to be true. The President was out of communication at Mount Vernon and the vessel was about to sail. Under the circumstances it fell to Jefferson to make a grave decision. He ordered the sailing to be stopped, and wrote a formal opinion for the President holding, somewhat inconsistently with his earlier view, that the Treaty of 1778 did not justify Genêt's conduct and that United States neutrality required an end to the fitting out of privateers by any belligerent.

Shortly thereafter, on Jefferson's recommendation, and with most of the country howling for the French Minister's scalp, the President asked for the recall of Genêt. It was a bitter experience for Jefferson, the lover of liberty and ardent supporter of the French Revolution. As late as May 19 he had expressed to Madison the conviction that both the neutrality proclamation and the policy against French privateering reflected in the Administration a "fear lest any affection" for France creep into the policies of the United States. In his view the people, "our constituents," were unhappy with the government and, through the newly forming "democratic societies," were finding ways to express their displeasure. But Genêt's behavior, coupled with news of continuing terror in France, was too much. Jefferson could no longer argue for the support of France either in the councils of the government or as a political leader.

At this stage of his career Jefferson's political fortunes were probably at the lowest ebb they ever reached. He had misjudged the French Revolution and supported it to such an extent that he could not extricate himself from the web of anti-French propaganda the Federalists were weaving around him. He had to repudiate the French Minister and the French Terror, yet he could not swing in the other direction, toward closer relations with Britain. His distrust of Britain was as great as ever. The Federalists, it seemed to him, were not only monarchists who wished to subvert the American republic, they were an "English party" who were prepared to betray the whole worldwide cause of liberty for commercial advantage.

Deeply concerned for the future of his country and unable any longer to reconcile his desire to influence American policy by serving Washington with the political position in which he found himself, Jefferson with determination resigned his office. In a frank letter to Madison, June 9, he pictured himself as

. . . worn down with labors from morning to night, and day to day; knowing them as fruitless to others as they are vexatious to myself, committed singly in desperate and eternal contest against a host who are systematically undermining the public liberty and prosperity, even the rare hours of relaxation sacrificed to the society of persons in the same intentions, of whose hatred I am con-

scious even in those moments of conviviality when the
heart wishes most to open itself to the effusions of friendship and confidence . . .

That a coolness had developed between the President and
the Secretary of State is certain. Though his sympathies were
often with Jefferson, Washington's judgment led him to concur
on most questions with Hamilton. After the Genêt affair,
Washington's irritation with the French turned to deep vexa-
tion, and it seems likely that he regretted Jefferson's identifica-
tion in the public mind with the French cause and felt that
Jefferson had indeed been too much swayed by sentiment.
Nevertheless he made an earnest effort, as he had done the
year before, to persuade his Secretary of State to stay on.
He called on Jefferson at the latter's house in the country on
August 6. Jefferson made notes on a long conversation in
which, at least as recollected many years later, he spoke to
Washington with great emphasis about the anti-Republicans
in the Administration, and his own resolve to have no more
to do with them. But he did agree to stay until the end of the
year. Washington, now resigned to losing Jefferson, wrote him
a cordial letter of appreciation for his services.

Jefferson had stayed on in Philadelphia tending to duty
until a plague of yellow fever in late summer made it imperative for him to leave the city. At first he merely moved to
the outskirts, where the President called on him. His friend
Dr. Rush was working heroically to overcome the dread
disease, but medical knowledge still scarcely went beyond
bloodletting and there were no effective medicines. The best
available antidote against the spread was cleanliness, and Dr.
Rush crusaded for a clean city. Jefferson fully cooperated
with Rush, but by mid-September he thought it best to go
home until the Congress should reconvene.

At Monticello the Secretary of State could for a month
largely ignore the squabbles of politics and was little troubled
by affairs of state. His lands were not in good condition, and
as his son-in-law had written to him earlier, there had been
too little rain and the corn crop was too parched to be abundant. He had waited anxiously all summer for word that a

new threshing machine, being sent to him from England by Minister Thomas Pinckney, had arrived. But it did not reach Monticello in time for that year's harvest. In his garden he experimented with tobacco suckers for compost, spreading them generously on flower beds and on the asparagus patch, then covering them with earth.

The month at home whetted Jefferson's appetite for the tranquil life he imagined to lie ahead of him after the first of the year. But before he could settle down permanently, as he intended, to the life of a farmer and philosopher, he had to return once more to public duty. Leaving his daughter Maria, who had been his constant companion during the years at New York and Philadelphia, he set out for the temporary capital at Germantown, on the outskirts of Philadelphia, where the plague did not reach. Politics immediately came to the forefront again. When he discovered that Freneau was suspending the *National Gazette* for lack of money, Jefferson proceeded to help him raise a fund to revive it. And the pamphlet war was as brisk and bitter as ever.

But the most interesting thing that happened before he could leave the government for good, at least to Jefferson's mind, was the arrival of a model of Eli Whitney's cotton gin, for which a patent was pending. Jefferson, fascinated by the new machine, quickly saw its long-run implications for the cotton economy. One of his last official acts was to assign his friend Whitney his historic patent.

Washington made one more effort to persuade Jefferson to stay on, no doubt still believing that it was better to continue to try to contain the two political parties than to accept a fixed association with either. Madison and Monroe, with whom Jefferson lodged after the government returned to Philadelphia in November, also pressed upon their friend the importance of his role to the Republican party. But this time Jefferson was not to be diverted from his resolve to retire. His reasons were not only fatigue and frustration and satiety with politics. They were deeper. In June, when he tendered his resignation, he had written with feeling to Madison:

I have now been in the public service four and twenty years; one half of which has been spent in total occupation with their affairs and absence from my own. I have served my tour then. No positive engagement, by word or deed, binds me to their further service. No commitment of their interests in any enterprise by me requires that I should see them through it. I am pledged by no act which gives any tribunal a call upon me before I withdraw. Even my enemies do not pretend this. I stand clear then of public right on all points—my friends I have not committed. No circumstances have attended my passage from office to office, which could lead them, and others through them, into deception as to the time I might remain, and particularly they and all have known with what reluctance I engaged and have continued in the present one, and of my uniform determination to return from it at an early day. If the public then has no claim on me, and my friends nothing to justify, the decision will rest on my own feelings alone. There has been a time when these were very different from what they are now; when perhaps the esteem of the world was of higher value in my eye than everything in it. But age, experience and reflection preserving to that only its due value, have set a higher on tranquility. The motion of my blood no longer keeps time with the tumult of the world. It leads me to seek for happiness in the lap and love of my family, in the society of my neighbors and my books, in the wholesome occupations of my farm and my affairs, in an interest or affection in every bud that opens, in every breath that blows around me, in an entire freedom of rest, of motion of thought, owing account to myself alone of my hours and actions.

At the end of December he had his books and furniture sent aboard ship for Richmond. On January 4 he took leave of the President and of his friends and set off for Monticello. He was approaching fifty-one. Into his span of years he had compressed more action and more service, more learning and more meditation, more travel and more turmoil than most men experience in a long life. He was ready for retirement. The author of the Declaration of Independence had given a quarter of a century to the pursuit of other people's happiness; he would now seek his own.

Chapter 6.

AN EMBATTLED VICE-PRESIDENT

Jefferson reached Monticello on January 16, 1794, intending never again to reside elsewhere and never again to pursue any occupation save that of farmer. No one who knew him then, either observing him, as did his family and neighbors, or receiving news of him in letters, could doubt that he was in earnest.

While in the previous year there had been time for only one entry in his cherished *Garden Book,* he could now record numerous details of planting and landscaping. On March 1, for example, he noted the sowing of "Charlton peas, lettuce and radishes." And on May 19, he could enter the pleasant fact that his "peas of Mar. 1. come to table." In his *Farm Book* Jefferson set down an account of his landholdings as of 1794. In Albemarle County were 5,581 ⅔ acres, while in Bedford, Campbell, and Rockbridge counties he owned 5,258 ½ additional acres. These farms and forests, plus some lots on the James River and in Richmond, came to about 11,000 acres. Jefferson was not one of the very great landowners of his time in Virginia, but his farms and shops were large and active enough to require more than 175 laborers, mostly slaves, as well as overseers.

Now that he was residing at home he gave the farms his personal supervision. As he himself many times observed, this was a full-time job. He was up early, breakfasted heartily, and then rode off for the day's affairs. In midafternoon he would return for dinner. Afterward he would sometimes nap, frequently receive visitors, tend to his correspondence— though with much less diligence than in previous years—and after supper, which was served about eight o'clock, he would retire early.

When Tench Coxe wrote to Jefferson about the growing Terror in France, the former Secretary of State replied characteristically that the villains of the piece were the "kings, nobles, and priests" who had for so long been "deluging with human blood." But he went on to observe, "I have so completely withdrawn myself from these spectacles of usurpation and misrule, that I do not take a single newspaper, nor read one a month; and I feel myself infinitely happier for it." He wrote in a similar vein to both President Washington and Vice-president Adams, April 25:

> The difference of my present and past situation is such as to leave me nothing to regret, but that my retirement has been postponed four years too long. The principles on which I calculated the value of life, are entirely in favor of my present course. I return to farming with an ardor which I scarcely knew in my youth, and which has got the better entirely of my love of study. Instead of writing ten or twelve letters a day, which I have been in the habit of doing as a thing in course, I put off answering my letters now, farmer-like, till a rainy day, and then find them sometimes postponed by other occupations.

But the President and his new Secretary of State, Edmund Randolph, were reluctant to leave Jefferson to his bucolic contentment. By summer they were speculating on the possibility that he could be persuaded to go again to Europe, this time to Spain. At another period in his life Jefferson would certainly have been tempted. Spanish control of the lower Mississippi was a severe hardship to farmers who had moved out from Virginia and the Carolinas across the Alleghenies and the Smokies into Kentucky and Tennessee, as well as to the "whiskey farmers" of western Pennsylvania. The latter were then openly rebelling against the stiff excise taxes of 1791, as both Jefferson and Madison had feared they would. Their uprising posed a difficult problem for the "republican interest," who sympathized with them yet could not condone armed defiance of the national government. A treaty with Spain opening up the Mississippi to American navigation through a free port at New Orleans would thus be a great service. Commissioners of the United States, dispatched the year before by Jefferson himself, had been in Madrid for many months trying to reach an agreement but meeting only with frustration. Now, in the summer of 1794, the Spanish Minister at Philadelphia had suggested to Secretary Randolph that an envoy of "character, conduct, and splendor" might be able to negotiate successfully in Madrid.

With Jefferson's great reputation in mind, the President instructed Randolph to ask him to undertake the mission. Randolph put it in these terms:

> Notwithstanding you have fenced out from the purlieus of Monticello every thing which assumes a political shape, you must permit me to bring before you a subject once extremely near to your heart, often the employment of your pen, and always a deep interest to the United States. The delays and evasions which you know to have been practised towards our Commissioners at Madrid have at length terminated in absolute stagnation. The people of Kentucky, either condemning or ignorant of the consequences, are restrained from hostility by a pack thread. They demand a conclusion of the negotiation, or a categorical answer from Spain.

Randolph admitted that the President felt "some hesitation" in asking Jefferson to go to Spain, but believing that it would be a short mission he nevertheless tendered the invitation. Randolph, speaking for himself, pointed out that the danger of Kentucky's going to war with Spain was real, that "the lopping off of Kentucky from the union is dreadful to contemplate," and that he feared nothing could stop "the mischief but . . . a vigorous effort of our government thro' the medium of one possessing their confidence." This was, of course, a reminder to the farmer of Monticello that he had political strength in Kentucky which he might wish to shore up against a different but not impossible future.

Jefferson, however, seems not to have been tempted. And it is apparent that Washington had not seriously supposed that he would be, for Randolph's letter enclosed another addressed to Patrick Henry with the request that Jefferson forward it if he should decide not to accept himself.

But Jefferson's blood was nevertheless stirring. The Whiskey Rebellion had presented the hated "monocrats" with a rich opportunity to talk about the dangers of too much liberty for the masses and to make a show of the power of the central government. To the disgust of the Republicans, Hamilton had persuaded Washington to allow him to go as commander of a military force to put down the insurrection. By the time his troops reached the scene of action, however, the rebellion had ended, under persuasion from Pennsylvania Republican leaders like Albert Gallatin. But the show of force was nevertheless completed by a number of arrests. It was followed, under Hamilton's prompting, by a direct attack in the President's annual message to Congress on the so-called Democratic societies.

These clubs, formed initially to show sympathy for the French Revolution and continuing as Republican caucuses, Washington now denounced as "self-created societies," bent only on stirring up public disorder and disaffection for the government. Jefferson was angered. His letter of December 28 to Madison reveals that he was doing a good deal of talking about the matter with friends and neighbors, and perhaps even reading a newspaper or two!

> The denunciation of the Democratic societies is one of the extraordinary acts of boldness of which we have seen so many from the faction of monocrats. It is wonderful indeed, that the President should have permitted himself to be the organ of such an attack on the freedom of discussion, the freedom of writing, printing, and publishing. It must be a matter of rare curiosity to get at the modifications of these rights proposed by them, and to see what line their ingenuity would draw between democratical societies, whose avowed object is the nourishment of the republican principles of our Constitution, and the society of the Cincinnati, *a self-created* one, carving out for itself hereditary distinctions, lowering

over our Constitution eternally, meeting together in all parts of the Union, periodically, with closed doors, accumulating a capital in their separate treasury, corresponding secretly and regularly, and of which society the very persons denouncing the democrats are themselves the fathers, founders, and high officers.

He went on to observe that he had "never heard, or heard of, a single expression or opinion which did not condemn" the President's statement as "an inexcusable aggression." The retired farmer was evidently now aroused sufficiently to be taking some political soundings.

After the storm over the Democratic clubs had quieted down, Jefferson again sought to avoid public affairs. More congenial to his mind was an approach to him in 1705 by the exiled Genevan scholar François d'Ivernois on the subject of moving a college of letters and philosophy from Geneva to Virginia. The project interested Jefferson for a time but was judged to be unrealistic. In the same year he redesigned his moldboard for submission to the American Philosophical Society. He began the remodeling of the upper story of the house at Monticello. His diary for 1795 in the *Farm Book* is one of the fullest he ever wrote. It is hard to believe that he meant to be taken literally, but the description of his life in a letter to Henry Knox, June 1, 1795, is certainly a fair indication of his feelings:

I am become the most ardent farmer in the state. I live on my horse from morning to night almost. Intervals are filled up with attentions to a nailery I carry on. I rarely look into a book, and more rarely take up a pen. I have proscribed newspapers, not taking a single one, nor scarcely ever looking into one. My next reformation will be to allow neither pen, ink, nor paper to be kept on the farm. When I have accomplished this I shall be in a fair way of indemnifying myself for the drudgery in which I have passed my life. If you are half as much delighted with the farm as I am, you bless your stars at your riddance from public cares.

About a year after he wrote this letter, Jefferson was pleased to be elected President of the American Philosophical Society, succeeding his friend Rittenhouse, who had died. This post of intellectual distinction he held for twenty years. In the summer of 1796, also, he was delighted to have a visit from his old and warm friend of Paris days, the Duc de la Rochefoucauld. The French intellectual leader, who had been among the original revolutionaries of 1789, made an extended tour of the United States between 1795 and 1797, and in his *Travels Through the United States* he wrote in detail about his stay at Monticello as one of the more engrossing events of his long journey. His account of Jefferson's farming methods is highly critical, particularly because the Monticello farms were not, so he thought, adequately fertilized. But he admired Jefferson's plow, his threshing machine, and his drilling machine. His observations on Jefferson himself vividly picture the "retired farmer" as seen through contemporary eyes:

In private life, Mr. Jefferson displays a mild, easy and obliging temper, though he is somewhat cold and reserved. His conversation is of the most agreeable kind, and he possesses a stock of information not inferior to that of any other man. In Europe he would hold a distinguished rank among men of letters, and as such he has already appeared there; at present he is employed with activity and perseverance in the management of his farms and buildings; and he orders, directs and pursues in the minutest detail every branch of business relative to them. I found him in the midst of the harvest, from which the scorching heat of the sun does not prevent his attendance. His negroes are nourished, clothed, and treated as well as white servants could be. As he cannot expect any assistance from the two small neighboring towns, every article is made on his farm; his negroes are cabinetmakers, carpenters, masons, bricklayers, smiths, etc. The children he employs in a nail factory, which yields already a considerable profit. The young and old negresses spin for the clothing of the rest. He animates them by rewards and distinctions; in fine, his superior mind directs the management of his domestic concerns with the same abilities, activity, and regularity which he evinced in the conduct of public affairs, and which he is calculated to display in every situation of life. In the superintendence of his household he is assisted by his two daughters, Mrs. Randolph and Miss Maria, who are handsome, modest, and amiable women . . .

Maria "Polly" Jefferson augmented the Monticello company and delighted her father by her marriage in October, 1797, to John Wayles Eppes, a cousin on her mother's side. The picture of domestic contentment would have been complete if Jefferson's farms had been productive enough to keep him out of debt. But they were not. His tastes always tempted him to overestimate his income. His books, his scientific equipment, his imports of all kinds from Europe, his earlier purchases in Paris, involved great expenditures of cash, which he was forced frequently to borrow. For security he gave mortgages on his lands, but their productivity was never sufficient to earn the necessary profit. Thus his was a long, losing battle with the balance sheet.

In the world outside Monticello political events were moving with such inclusive turbulence that Jefferson was slowly but inescapably drawn in. John Jay's treaty with England had been published and was being considered by both the executive and the Congress at Philadelphia. Jefferson, like a great majority of his fellow citizens, was dismayed by provisions in the treaty which were not only offensive to France but demeaning to the United States. The Republicans, having failed in an all-out effort to prevent its ratification in 1795, were now striving to prevent its going into effect by denying to the executive the necessary funds. Madison, in the House of Representatives, was leading the fight. Jefferson gave Madison, as well as Gallatin, William Giles, and other Republicans, his strongest assurances that he hoped the treaty would be voided. He felt, as he had felt so many times before, that President Washington was being made the tool of the pro-British "monocrats."

Perhaps his feelings were, at least at some moments, even

stronger. On April 24, 1796, he wrote a fateful private letter to his old friend and former neighbor, the Italian physician and horticulturist Philip Mazzei—a letter which appeared in the press a year later and thereafter haunted his political career. But the fact that it was a private letter, sent to a friend in Italy, may suggest that it was a truer revelation of Jefferson's thoughts and feelings than what he was saying aloud or writing to his friends at Philadelphia. To Mazzei he wrote of the "Anglican monarchical aristocratical party," pitted against the "main body of our citizens" who "remain true to their republican principles." He then classified the American people, in 1796, according to their political leanings:

> . . . the whole landed interest is republican, and so is a great mass of talents. Against us are . . . all the officers of the government, all who want to be officers, all timid men who prefer the calm of despotism to the boisterous sea of liberty, British merchants and Americans trading on British capital, speculators and holders in the banks and public funds, a contrivance invented for the purposes of corruption, and for assimilating us in all things to the rotten as well as the sound parts of the British model.

The next sentence, when Mazzei proved so indiscreet as to give the letter to the press, was immediately and no doubt correctly interpreted by Washington and others as referring to the President:

> It would give you a fever were I to name to you the apostates who have gone over to these heresies, men who were Samsons in the field and Solomons in the council, but who have had their heads shorn by the harlot England.

Washington, whose coolness toward Jefferson had been slowly growing at least since 1791, could not forgive this attack and finally broke off relations with his long-time colleague.

Jefferson, always conscious, as a skilled politician, of the value of Washington's good opinion, wished never to cross the older man if he could help it. He had sincerely believed, in addition, that Washington's personal views were republican and democratic. But he could not reconcile such views with Washington's conduct of the presidency. He was thus forced to conclude that the great man was being somehow duped by Hamilton and the Federalist influence. Jefferson's own convictions were so deep-running and so well defined that he seems to have been quite unable to entertain the notion that Washington's support of the funding system, the excise, the bank of the United States, and even the Jay Treaty was given in each case because of his considered judgment as to what was the best course for the nation.

The truth is that Washington and Jefferson were wholly different men, not only in character and temperament, but in their estimate of human society and the problems of politics. They could work together in harmony and comradeship in the common cause against the British in a war for independence. But to Jefferson that war was also a revolution; to Washington revolution was anathema. The Father of his Country was, indeed, a great conservative; the author of the Declaration of Independence was a great liberal. What is remarkable is not that they should have fallen out in 1797, but that they should have collaborated as long as they did.

When the appropriation for the Jay Treaty was carried in the House by a very close vote, Jefferson attributed the result exclusively to the influence of Washington. He also calculated that the Washington influence would carry over into the coming elections for President, Vice-president, and Congress. By midsummer it was clear to him that he could not avoid a contest with John Adams for President. But he could and did let others conduct the campaign. His lack of enthusiasm may have been partly owing to his doubts about Republican chances. If, as has often been asserted, there was some mixture of motives in his aloofness toward the election and his repeated protests that he did not desire the presidency, the fact is that his personal letters reveal no hidden ambition. His attitude was consistent from the beginning of the year. To every overture he replied that he had no desire to hold any office, that he was happy in his retirement, and that he honored John

Adams. He never said that he would not accept office, but he did not in fact take any action to obtain it. He hoped earnestly for a Republican victory in the congressional elections, as he had done in 1792, believing, perhaps, that a Republican Congress would keep Adams as President out of the clutches of the more extreme Federalists. He knew that Adams shared his distrust of Hamilton, and he seems in a general way to have had more confidence in his old colleague from Braintree than did other Republicans. Hamilton, as both men knew, was in fact exploring the possibility of sidetracking Adams in favor of Thomas Pinckney.

The campaign of 1796 was largely directed from New York City. Hamilton, now a New York lawyer, gave orders to his followers, received visitors, and conducted a large political correspondence in the Federalist cause. Also in New York were stirring the beginnings of a national Republican organization through the efforts, often conflicting, of Governor George Clinton and Aaron Burr, leader of the Tammany Society. By the time the voting began the two embryonic parties had secured a fair measure of agreement around the country that the tickets would be for the Federalists, Adams and Pinckney, and for the Republicans, Jefferson and Burr. The *Aurora,* a Republican organ edited by Franklin's grandson, put it this way:

> . . . it requires no talent at divination to decide who will be the candidates for the chair. Thomas Jefferson and John Adams will be the men, and whether we shall have at the head of our executive a steadfast friend to the Rights of the People, or an advocate of hereditary power and distinctions, the people of the United States are soon to decide.

Thus in the fall months Jefferson was forced to face the prospect that he might again have to leave Monticello for national service. However, he does not appear ever to have supposed that he would win the presidency. News moved very slowly and often inaccurately. Jefferson was remote, at Monticello, from its centers, though Madison spent much of

the summer and fall at Philadelphia and kept his friend as
well informed as possible on the progress of the election. The
electors were in many cases chosen by state legislatures, so
that state elections had also to be watched closely to see what
the national trend might be. Madison on several occasions
was encouraged to believe that the Republican ticket might
win the election. But by November he was discouraged. There
seems to be no doubt that the name of Burr was detrimental
to Jefferson's chances. Burr was not well known in the South,
nor well thought of in New England and the middle states.
That brilliant and strikingly attractive young politician was
already so patently ambitious as to raise suspicions in the
minds not only of Federalists but of Republican leaders as
well.

On December 28, before he knew for certain the outcome
of the election, Jefferson wrote what was in effect a letter of
congratulation to Adams. It is worth quoting at length because it sums up the feelings of the aloof and unenthusiastic
Republican candidate:

... I knew it impossible that you should lose a vote north
of the Delaware, and even if that of Pennsylvania should
be against you in the mass, yet that you would get
enough south of that to place your succession out of
danger. I have never one single moment expected a different issue; and though I know I shall not be believed,
yet it is not the less true that I have never wished it. My
neighbors as my compurgators could aver that fact, because they see my occupations and my attachment to
them. Indeed it is possible that you may be cheated of
your succession by a trick worthy the subtlety of your
arch-friend of New York who has been able to make of
your real friends tools to defeat their and your just
wishes. Most probably he will be disappointed as to you;
and my inclinations place me out of his reach. I leave
to others the sublime delights of riding in the storm,
better pleased with sound sleep and a warm berth below, with the society of neighbors, friends and fellow-
laborers of the earth, than of spies and sycophants. No

one then will congratulate you with purer disinterestedness than myself.

The trick Jefferson refers to here was to have a few Federalist
electors vote for Pinckney and Burr, thus giving Pinckney a
slightly larger total than Adams'. Since under the system then
prevailing the President would be the recipient of the most
electoral votes and the Vice-president would be the runner-
up, Pinckney could become President and Adams would continue as Vice-president, contrary to popular wishes. There
was, of course, the further assumption in Hamilton's plan
that the Federalist electors would substantially outnumber
the Republican. Both his calculations proved in error, while
Jefferson's forecast was correct. Adams was elected by three
votes over Jefferson, 71 to 68, with Pinckney and Burr trailing
out of contention. Jefferson, as he had foretold, did not get all
of the Southern votes, else the result would have been reversed.

Given the frame of mind with which he approached the
election, Jefferson could not have been entirely displeased
by its outcome. On New Year's day, 1797, he wrote to Madison that the office of Vice-president which he was now to assume was "the only office in the world about which I am unable to decide in my own mind whether I had rather have it
or not have it." At the same time he suggested to Madison
what he thought the Republican line ought to be at the outset
of the Adams administration:

If Mr. Adams can be induced to administer the government on its true principles, and to relinquish his bias
to an English constitution, it is to be considered whether
it would not be on the whole for the public good to come
to a good understanding with him as to his future elections. He is perhaps the only sure barrier against Hamilton getting in.

His personal attitude toward serving under Adams he put in
these affecting words:

I can particularly have no feelings which would revolt at a secondary position to Mr. Adams. I am his junior in life, was his junior in Congress, his junior in the diplomatic line, his junior lately in the civil government.

On February 20 Jefferson set out for Philadelphia for John Adams' inauguration and his own installation. He might have stayed at home, but made the journey because he felt that his appearance would be "a mark of respect to the public." He reached Philadelphia on March 2, and immediately called on the President-elect. The call was returned the next day and the two men held an important conversation, which Jefferson recorded in detail. The President, much concerned about deteriorating relations with France, proposed to send Elbridge Gerry and James Madison, as well as General Charles C. Pinckney, to Paris to try to improve the situation. He wished Jefferson to approach Madison and use his influence to persuade him to undertake the mission. Adams asserted that his first choice would be Jefferson, but that he feared such an appointment would be taken as an attempt to get rid of his chief political rival. Jefferson, for his part, made it clear that he would not consider another journey abroad. But he seems to have been pleased by Adams' manner and satisfied with his attitude on the French question.

The following day, March 4, Jefferson was sworn in as Vice-president and made a brief address to the Senate. Imploring his colleagues to believe that he would not prefer one party over the other, he emphasized his understanding of his new office as servant of the Senate and impartial administrator of the rules. In his concluding paragraph he asserted his confidence in and devotion to the President, "whose talents and integrity have been known and revered by me through a long course of years; have been the foundation of a cordial and uninterrupted friendship between us." The sincerity of this feeling cannot be doubted, and for several months nothing overt happened to break the "uninterrupted friendship." Jefferson, in fact, returned to Monticello almost immediately and did not take up his duties in Philadelphia until May. As late as May 13 he could write to Elbridge Gerry about knowing the "worth" of Adams "as intimately and esteeming it as much as anyone." He referred to his own new position with satisfaction: "The second office of the government is honorable and easy, the first is but a splendid misery."

But the second office of the government was not then what it is now. The mode of election could easily place an opposition party leader directly below the President. And that, of course, was the way it turned out in 1796. Though Jefferson hoped that he would be able to support rather than oppose Adams, his hopes were soon proved to be without foundation. The break was, indeed, presaged during the first week of their term. Jefferson noted that he followed up the President's request and approached Madison about the mission to France, which was declined. On March 6 he dined with Adams at General Washington's, where he had an opportunity to report his failure with Madison. President Adams "immediately said, that, on consultation, some objections to the nomination had been raised which he had not contemplated; and was going on with excuses which evidently embarrassed him, when . . . our roads separated and we took leave." Thereafter, Jefferson records, he was never consulted "as to any measures of the government." It is significant that in his memoranda over the next few years Jefferson repeatedly sets down anecdotes, often unsubstantiated rumors, which show Adams as distrustful of democracy and Hamilton as an avowed monarchist. He does not again suggest that the former was being politically victimized by the latter, though such was certainly the case.

Adams' cabinet was infiltrated by Hamiltonians like Oliver Wolcot, who continually bent the government toward Britain and away from *rapprochement* with France, pointed the finger of suspicion at Republican critics, warned the President against Republican newspapers as seditious, and whispered suspicions of such French aliens as Samuel DuPont and Volney, both friends of Jefferson. Monroe was recalled from Paris by Secretary of State Timothy Pickering in disgrace for being too pro-French, though the purpose of his mission had been to offset the Jay mission to London by reassurances that the American-French alliance was as strong as ever. By summer, 1797, the crisis in American-French relations erupted into an undeclared naval war.

How far political relations among Americans had deteriorated in a few months, and how desperate Jefferson considered the posture of the United States before the world, can be seen in the following letter to his old friend Edward Rutledge, written from Philadelphia on June 24:

We had, in 1793, the most respectable character in the universe. What the neutral nations think of us now, I know not; but we are low indeed with the belligerents. Their kicks and cuffs prove their contempt. If we weather the present storm, I hope we shall avail ourselves of the calm of peace, to place our foreign connections under a new and different arrangement . . . As to everything except commerce, we ought to divorce ourselves from them all. But this system would require time, temper, wisdom, and occasional sacrifice of interest; and how far all of these will be ours, our children may see, but we shall not. The passions are too high at present to be cooled in our day. You and I have formerly seen warm debates and high political passions. But gentlemen of different politics would then speak to each other, and separate the business of the Senate from that of society. It is not so now. Men who have been intimate all their lives, cross the streets to avoid meeting, and turn their heads another way, lest they should be obliged to touch their hats. . . .

Presently Jefferson himself became one of those of "high political passion."

Under pretext of national security, in July, 1798, the Federalist majority in Congress by a narrow margin passed the Alien and Sedition Laws. These laws, providing severe punishment for publishing "malicious or defamatory" matter regarding the Congress or the President and authorizing the President to deport any aliens whose presence in the country he considered undesirable, were aimed directly at the Republican opposition and their French friends. To Jefferson they were simply intolerable. Like all other patriots he was shocked and angered by the revelations of French attempts to bribe the American commissioners in the XYZ affair. But he was not prepared to go to war because Talleyrand was underhanded, and he could see no justification whatever for such repressive laws against American citizens or alien friends. President Adams himself seems to have had some doubts about their wisdom, as, at first, did Hamilton. But Adams signed the measures into law, and countenanced a series of arrests of Republican propagandists, who were promptly charged under the Sedition Law. One victim was a Congressman, Matthew Lyon of Vermont. Party feeling now reached a bitterness without parallel in all later American history. Talk of splitting the Union was not uncommon; talk of disobedience to the offensive laws was common indeed.

Jefferson, no longer able to maintain even a semblance of impartiality, now personally took the lead in organizing the Republican opposition. Since his political activity during the next year has been the subject of almost continuous controversy ever since, it will be well to examine it closely.*

The Federalists had begun their direct attack on the writings of the Republicans in the courts, by means of a federal grand jury presentment against Samuel Cabell of Albemarle County, Virginia, on May 22, 1797. Cabell was representative from Jefferson's own district and his strong supporter, so that an attack upon him was readily construed as a way to get at the Vice-president. The presentment accused Cabell of calumny against the government in a circular he had sent out to his constituents. Jefferson reacted by drawing a "petition" to the Virginia legislature, arguing that the grand jury had no authority to charge a man for his political opinions and was itself guilty of "perversion" of a legal institution into a political one. This document was circulated and signed by citizens of Albemarle and other counties and then taken up in the Assembly, where it was approved as a formal expression of the opinion of the legislature. Though a document of this sort coming out of a state legislature could not legally affect a

---

* I am much indebted in these pages on the events of 1798–1800 to an article by Adrienne Koch and Harry Ammon, "The Virginia and Kentucky Resolutions: An Episode in Jefferson's and Madison's Defense of Civil Liberties," *William and Mary Quarterly*, third series, V (April, 1948), 146 ff.

federal court, it may have had some influence. Cabell was never prosecuted.

But the following year, when Congress began to consider the bills against sedition and against aliens, Jefferson immediately saw that the Federalists were laying the ground for the destruction of the Republican party before the approaching election of 1800. Mere petitions would not suffice for retaliation. To Madison, who had just retired from Congress, Jefferson wrote on June 7:

> They have brought into the lower house a sedition bill, which among other enormities, undertakes to make printing certain matters criminal, tho' one of the amendments to the Constitution has so expressly taken religion, printing presses etc. out of their coercion. Indeed this bill and the alien bill both are so palpably in the teeth of the Constitution as to show they mean to pay no respect to it.

It is important to observe in these words Jefferson's basic contentions—(1) that the laws in question are violations of the Constitution and (2) that the Federalists know it—for it is only upon these two contentions that Jefferson's line of retaliation can be properly understood. Now, as always, the author of the Declaration of Independence was concerned to secure the liberties of individuals. His consistent first premise was liberty, not union. The Federalists were now seeking to suppress liberty in the name of securing the Union, and Jefferson would not be intimidated. When the laws were enacted a month later, he went immediately into action. At Monticello he met with Wilson Cary Nicholas, a devoted political friend, to whom he entrusted for delivery to John Breckinridge of Kentucky a set of resolutions to be brought before the legislature of that state. At the same time he was working out with Madison a plan to offer similar resolutions in the Virginia Assembly. These documents were drawn and put into circulation with great care to conceal their authorship, since if Vice-president Jefferson, in particular, were known to be endeavoring to influence state legislatures against the national government, a new issue would be raised and even more serious difficulties might well face the Republicans in the election of 1800.

Jefferson's draft as delivered to Breckinridge was based upon the proposition that the Constitution was a compact among the states of the Union and that the states, therefore, had a natural right both to declare their view that a law of the Congress was unconstitutional and to disobey such a law. He proceeded then to maintain that the Sedition Law violated the First Amendment by restraining freedom of speech and of the press. The Alien Law, he asserted, violated Article I, Section 9, which forbade Congress to interfere before 1808 with the "migration or importation of such persons as the states shall think proper to admit." In the latter case Jefferson has always been accused of deliberately misinterpreting a passage he knew was meant to refer to slaves. But Jefferson's ground was better than has been generally realized. He knew from Edmund Randolph, author of the original draft of the article at the 1787 convention, that it had been intended in the first instance to refer to aliens.*

As the Jefferson resolutions were actually introduced and adopted in the Kentucky legislature, the now famous clause "where powers are assumed which have not been delegated, a nullification of the act is the rightful remedy" was omitted. In the Virginia resolutions, drawn by Madison, no such language appeared at all. Thus the effect of the resolutions was not to urge disobedience but to put the state legislatures of Virginia and Kentucky on record as holding the Alien and Sedition Laws to be unconstitutional and inviting their sister states to concur with them in this judgment. They were therefore propaganda documents intended to influence public opinion and to attract followers in the coming campaign. As such they failed to elicit any formal concurrence from other state legislatures, but they were enormously successful with the citizens generally.

Jefferson was quite prepared, in his own mind, to take the stronger position contained in his Kentucky draft. But he had

---

* See *Omitted Chapters of History, Disclosed in the Life and Papers of Edmund Randolph*, ed. M. D. Conway (1888), p. 78.

no belief that disruption of the Union would be necessary. That he thought the tactic of protest would succeed is indicated in his letter to Madison of November 17, 1798, enclosing the copy of the Kentucky draft:

> I think we should distinctly affirm [in Virginia] all the important principles they contain, so as to hold to that ground in future, and leave the matter in such a train as that we may not be committed absolutely to push the matter to extremities, and yet may be free to push as far as events will render prudent.

Madison replied wisely and persuasively, agreeing in general but calling Jefferson's attention to the crucial point that it had been the states *in convention,* that is, the people of the states, who had ratified the Constitution, not the state legislatures. This distinction was never again obscured in the political writings of either of the great Republicans. And for this reason, if there were no other, it would have been improper for extreme Southern state-righters of later times to invoke their names. But there is another reason. Jefferson and his friends were defending the civil liberties upon which free government depends. They were employing the tactic of state legislative resolutions as a part of their broad strategy to defend republican government. They were standing for the rights of man. Later state-righters, invoking Jeffersonian doctrines improperly, were upholding the enslavement of man, not his liberty, or defending the segregation of men of one color from those of another, not insisting upon their equality. Jefferson died before the great schism over nullification and secession developed, but happily Madison was able, in the 1830's, to denounce these unconstitutional devices with the authority of the original Republicans and of the founding fathers themselves.

After the Kentucky and Virginia resolutions were put into circulation, the party warfare grew even more intense. The Federalists, not content with arrests and prosecutions under the Sedition Law, began to charge that the Republicans were planning violent insurrection. John Nicholas, brother of W.

C. Nicholas and a Republican, was convinced by this utterly unfounded charge and turned Federalist. The Republicans, for their part, continued to print their papers and broadsides accusing the Federalists of plotting the conversion of the government into a monarchy with the suppression of all liberties. There were street fights and pub brawls. Federalist youngsters wore black cockades like the British while young Republicans wore the tricolor.

In 1799 Jefferson, not at all dismayed that none of the other states had joined with Kentucky and Virginia, proposed to his Kentucky friends, as well as to Madison, that the theme of the resolutions be repeated by the legislatures. And again he and Madison drew resolutions, with some advice from John Taylor of Caroline, W. C. Nicholas, and Breckinridge. The new resolutions were in due course adopted at Lexington and Richmond. Their tone, however, was a bit more moderate than those of the previous year, perhaps reflecting growing Republican confidence.

In November, 1799, Jefferson followed up the Kentucky and Virginia resolutions with a broad statement of strategy for the coming election. To Madison he wrote:

> Our objects, according to my ideas, should be these: 1. peace even with Great Britain, 2. a sincere cultivation of the Union, 3. the disbanding of the army on principles of economy and safety, 4. protestations against violations of the true principles of our constitution, merely to save them, and prevent precedent and acquiescence from being pleaded against them; but nothing to be said or done which shall look or lead to force, and give any pretext for keeping up the army. If we find the monarchical party really split into pure Monocrats & Anglo-monocrats, we should leave to them alone to manage all those points of difference which they may choose to take between themselves, only arbitrating between them by our votes, but doing nothing which may hoop them together.

It was on this platform that the Republicans the next year

asked votes for Thomas Jefferson for President of the United States. And the "monarchical party" was indeed split.

Feelings remained inflamed. The quality of the Federalist press may be seen from such a passage as this, which appeared in the *Connecticut Courant*, appraising the prospects for the nation if the Republicans should win the election:

There is scarcely a possibility that we shall escape a *Civil War* . . . Murder, robbery, rape, adultery, and incest will be openly taught and practiced, the air will be rent with the cries of distress, the soil will be soaked with blood, and the nation black with crimes.

Republican writers, for their part, kept up a running fire of criticism and invective against the Federalists, often sinking to the language of the gutter.

The prime target of the Federalists was Jefferson personally. Few American leaders have ever been subjected to such unconscionable abuse as filled the Federalist newspapers and broadsides in 1799 and 1800. He was charged with treason, with intent to overthrow the government and make himself dictator, with plotting to free the slaves and to destroy all property rights, with being the agent of Napoleon, and with being personally dishonest and immoral. He was whispered to have fathered countless mulattoes and to have taken a fictitious Negress to Paris as his mistress, and he was publicly denounced and caricatured as a lecher and an adulterer. His financial transactions were said to include robbing widows who were his clients and misappropriating funds entrusted to him by his friends. Above all, he was accused of being an atheist. Perhaps among all American Presidents only Lincoln and Franklin Roosevelt were so vilified and slandered, but neither so openly. Jefferson ignored the attacks as much as possible and did not often refer to them. But his feelings may be judged from this passage from a letter to his young friend Peregrine Fitzhugh:

I have been for sometime used as the property of the newspapers, a fair mark for every man's dirt. Some, too, have indulged themselves in this exercise who would not have done it, had they known me otherwise than through these impure and injurious channels. It is hard treatment, and for a singular kind of offence, that of having obtained by the labors of a life the indulgent opinions of a part of one's fellow-citizens. However, these moral evils must be submitted to, like the physical scourges of tempest, fire, etc.

Under the circumstances what was most remarkable was that the torrent of words was so ineffective. Jefferson's hold on the popular mind was so great, his reputation so finally unreachable, and his contribution to human freedom so well understood that his chances of election grew almost in proportion to the increase in the flow of anti-Jefferson propaganda. By April, 1800, Jefferson was beginning to be optimistic. To Philip Nicholas, another brother of W. C. Nicholas, he wrote that "the people in the middle states are almost rallied to Virginia already; & the eastern states are recommencing the vibration which had been checked by XYZ."

The problem for the Republicans now was to arrange their presidential ticket and organize to win the election. Monroe, rewarded by the citizens of Virginia for his "disgrace" in France by election as governor of the state, corresponded extensively with Republican leaders, as did Madison, Albert Gallatin of Pennsylvania, Republican leader in the House of Representatives, and Aaron Burr, George Clinton, and the Livingstons of New York. The basis of the effort was to be the already established alliance between New York and Virginia. In New York, as in 1796, Clinton and Burr could only agree on their hatred of the Federalists and their support of Jefferson—at least Clinton was sincere in his support of the Vice-president. Burr, never entirely trustworthy, worked hard and was rewarded, against the better judgment of Monroe and others, with the nomination for Vice-president. Jefferson himself played no part in settling the ticket or in organizing the campaign. His views were well known to his followers and to the country at large; he was prepared to accept the presidency if elected; but he would not directly enter the lists against Adams, whom he still honored for his great earlier services to the nation.

During the greater part of the fateful year, 1800, Jefferson was at home. He was inevitably far more preoccupied with political affairs than he had been in previous years, or than he wished to be. But he nevertheless found time to think about and plan for a university for the state of Virginia, a project he had first advanced when he was working at the revision of the laws of the state almost twenty-five years before. Joseph Priestley, the eminent British scientist and philosopher, and like Jefferson an outstanding figure of the Enlightenment, was then living in the United States, and Jefferson hoped to persuade him to take the leadership of the projected university, or at least to advise on matters of curriculum and selection of faculty. In his letters to Priestley Jefferson outlined his own ideas of a modern curriculum of sciences, humanities, and arts for Priestley's consideration. At the same time his interest in the philosophy of law was revived by a correspondence with Edmund Randolph on the question whether the common law was the law of the United States or only of the states. Jefferson considered the attempt to make the inherited British common law applicable in the federal courts an even more serious violation of the Constitution than the Alien and Sedition Laws.

While the campaign raged and Jefferson was denounced as a would-be Napoleon or as an agent of France, it is interesting to see what he was himself thinking about French events. His sympathy with the French people had never wavered since the days of the American Revolution. His hopes for them had been raised to the heights by the events of 1789. But over the years thereafter both his own experience with Genêt and the steady stream of bad news from France had disappointed and disillusioned him. What marked him off, however, from many of his fellow citizens, and of course from the Federalists, was that he never saw in French misfortunes or failures reasons for attachment to Britain or for losing faith in republican government. Now, in 1800, came news that Napoleon had brought an end to the French republic and declared himself First Consul. To his neighbor, Dr. Bache,

Jefferson set forth these conclusions from reflection on French events:

> Our citizens . . . should see in it [Napoleon's *coup*] a necessity to rally firmly and in close bands round their Constitution. Never to suffer an iota of it to be infringed. *To inculcate on minorities the duty of acquiescence in the will of the majority;* and on majorities a respect for the rights of the minority. To beware of a military force, even of citizens; and to beware of too much confidence in any man. . . .

These sentiments, closely related as they were to the Republican platform he had laid down earlier, contrast so sharply with the caricature of Jefferson as a man and the distortion of his ideas by propaganda that in retrospect one cannot fail to see an element of humor in the situation. But the times were not characterized by the comic spirit. Jefferson's most famous words of the campaign, written to his friend Benjamin Rush, were in deadly earnest:

> The returning good sense of our country threatens abortion of [the Federalists'] hopes [of establishing religion] and they believe that any portion of power confided to me, will be exerted in opposition to their schemes. And they believe rightly: for I have sworn upon the altar of God, eternal hostility against every form of tyranny over the mind of man. But this is all they have to fear from me: and enough too in their opinion.

In November, when the electoral votes of the states began to come in, Jefferson was at the new capital, the city of Washington, to preside over the lame-duck Senate. He seems to have been fairly confident of the outcome until he saw how complicated the election had become, as the result both of political intrigue and the faulty provisions of the Constitution for the choice of President and Vice-president. While there was agreement among Federalists to drop one or two of their votes from General Charles C. Pinckney, thus assuring Adams of the larger total, and an arrangement among Republicans to drop a vote or two from Burr to secure a majority for Jefferson, these plans were upset.

By the middle of December there was great doubt about the outcome. Everyone knew that the popular vote had heavily favored Jefferson. But the Federalists saw in a possible tie between Jefferson and Burr the remote chance that they could dictate the final choice, to be made by the Federalist-controlled House of Representatives, which had been elected in 1798 and would still hold over. In the House they might perhaps declare an interregnum, voiding the election of Jefferson and appointing a temporary chief executive to hold office until another election could be held. By this means some hoped to force Jefferson permanently into retirement. Others preferred to make a deal with Burr, exacting his pledge to co-operate with the Federalists, in exchange for bringing about his election. Hamilton, who had tried to replace Adams with Pinckney, would have neither alternative and used his waning influence on behalf of Jefferson. Burr had wrested control of New York from Hamilton, thus thwarting his personal ambition, and the former Secretary of the Treasury now thought Jefferson, his ancient enemy, the lesser of two evils. In his diary arch-conservative Gouverneur Morris noted that "it seems to be the general opinion that Colonel Burr will be chosen President by the House of Representatives. Many of them think it highly dangerous that Mr. Jefferson should, in the present crisis, be placed in that office. They consider him as a theoretic man, who would bring the National Government back to something like the old Confederation."

Under these circumstances Jefferson wrote to Burr a letter calculated to smoke out the New Yorker if he were in fact intriguing on his own behalf. Jefferson referred to the "badly managed" effort of the Republicans to give Jefferson a vote or two more than Burr and to the prospect of a tie, which would open the way for a Federalist plot to seize the government. He then went on to offer Burr, in effect, an opportunity to withdraw from the contest in order to accept a place in a Jefferson cabinet. The proposal was composed with great political skill:

While I must congratulate you, my dear Sir, on the issue of this contest, because it is more honorable, and doubtless more grateful to you than any station within the competence of the chief magistrate, yet for myself, and for the substantial service of the public, I feel most sensibly the loss we sustain of your aid in our new administration. It leaves a chasm in my arrangements, which cannot be adequately filled up.

Jefferson here made it plain to Burr that he had no thought of giving up the presidency because of the accidental situation then obtaining. He did not approach Burr as an equal, in spite of the prospective tie. But he flattered him sufficiently and appealed to his pride as a colleague so effectively that in a week Burr replied with a forthright disclaimer:

I do not apprehend any embarrassment even in case the votes should come out alike for us—my personal friends are perfectly informed of my wishes on the subject and can never think of diverting a single vote from you—on the contrary, they will be found among your most zealous adherents. As to myself, I will cheerfully abandon the office of V. P. if it shall be thought that I can be more useful in any active station. In short, my whole time and attention shall be unceasingly employed to render your administration grateful and honorable to our country and to yourself.

This was written on December 23. But the decision was still a long way off. In the interval Jefferson became convinced that Burr was in fact trying to intrigue for the presidency. His suspicion of Burr gradually turned, over the ensuing years, to animosity. He never, of course, actually offered him a cabinet post.

Congress convened on February 11, 1801. But long before that, it was known that the electoral votes would show a tie, 73-73, between Jefferson and Burr. Federalist intrigue, after the result was made official, included overtures to Burr, desperate talk of a coup, and even offers of a deal to Jefferson.

"Many attempts," said Jefferson, "have been made to obtain terms and promises from me. I have declared to them unequivocally, that I would not receive the government on capitulation, that I would not go into it with my hands tied." Gouverneur Morris told him flatly that the election would be "instantly . . . fixed" if he would simply agree to keep the Federalists in office, maintain the navy and the debt. He replied as flatly that he would "certainly make no terms." He would never, he said, "go into the office of President by capitulation."

In the end he did have to make a deal of sorts. Great power had come by accident into the hands of James Bayard, the lone Representative of Delaware. The Constitution specified that if a tie developed in the Electoral College, the House should choose the President on a ballot by states. States with large delegations in the House had therefore to resolve their differences among themselves if they were to be effective in the actual tally. But Bayard was his own man. It was he who, after thirty-five ballots, determined, for a price, to end the deadlock by throwing his support to Jefferson. He told General Samuel Smith of Maryland, chief of the Jefferson organization, that he would bring about Jefferson's election if the latter would agree to retain Federalists in posts below cabinet rank and leave the funding system undisturbed. Smith took up the matter with Jefferson and soon reported back that Jefferson entirely agreed. On February 17, Bayard acted. Jefferson was elected on the thirty-sixth ballot. But there had certainly been a misunderstanding between Bayard and Jefferson, as General Smith afterward admitted. Jefferson categorically denied that he had given any promises to keep the Federalists in office. He said that he had understood that he was being asked to protect one officeholder, a relative of Bayard's, and this he agreed to do. As for the funding system, he had never had any thought of *altering* or *rescinding* it. His fiscal policy, soon to be entrusted to Albert Gallatin, was quite simply to *end* the funding system by paying off the debt.

Under these heavy clouds of suspicion, intrigue, and bitter contention, Thomas Jefferson at last became the third President of the United States. To a man as sensitive as he, it was a period of almost unrelieved misery. But the "theoretic and visionary" philosopher was also a tough-sinewed man. His fears for his country were deep; his resolve to put it once more on its true course, firm. At fifty-eight he had learned the lessons of "practical" politics, as his election showed, but he had not ceased to believe in the efficacy of ideas or in the capabilities of his countrymen. And he had one warm consolation for the storm that raged about him and for the separation from his home and family he had now once more to face: the people of the nation, to the extent that they could vote and voice their opinions, were overwhelmingly for him and with him. And so he was well prepared to be not only the founder of the Democratic party but the first Democratic President of the United States.

Chapter 7.

PRESIDENT JEFFERSON:
FIRST ADMINISTRATION

At noon on March 4, 1801, Thomas Jefferson, accompanied by a throng of well-wishers, walked from Conrad's boarding-house to the Capitol to be inaugurated President of the United States. In the muddy streets outside the unfinished building stood a large crowd, come from near and far to witness the great change-over. To some Jefferson's election was a second revolution sorely needed to complete that of 1776 and led appropriately by the revered author of the Declaration of Independence; to others it was a grim moment for meditating the dangers to which radical democracy would no doubt subject the nation under the leadership of the "theoretic philosopher." President John Adams, embittered by his defeat and his pride wounded by the opposition of his long-time friend, had already left not only the White House but the city of Washington.

In the Senate chamber, with Aaron Burr presiding, Jefferson read his inaugural address in a voice so low that only persons seated quite near could hear him distinctly. Chief Justice John Marshall, who was for eight years to be his arch political enemy, sat beside him and administered the oath of office. Marshall heard well enough and was pleasantly surprised at the conciliatory tone of the address. His reaction was typical. The fame of the address has ever afterward rested mainly on Jefferson's theme of national unity:

Let us, then, fellow-citizens, unite with one heart and one mind. Let us restore to social intercourse that harmony and affection without which liberty and even life itself are but dreary things. And let us reflect that having banished from our land that religious intolerance under which mankind so long bled and suffered, we have yet gained little if we countenance a political intolerance as despotic, as wicked, and capable of as bitter and bloody persecutions. . . . But every difference of opinion is not a difference of principle. We have called by different names brethren of the same principle. We are all republicans—we are all federalists.

It is not necessary to question Jefferson's sincerity in order to observe that these words are thoroughly political. Faced with the immediate responsibility of governing the nation for four years, the new President meant to make as many friends as he could.

But conciliation was not the most effectively articulated theme of his first inaugural, it was only the most popular. The very next words provided the key to Jefferson's mind and life, and to the democratic spirit with which he approached his task:

If there be any among us who would wish to dissolve this Union or to change its republican form, let them stand undisturbed as monuments of the safety with which error of opinion may be tolerated where reason is left free to combat it. I know, indeed, that some honest men fear that a republican government cannot be strong; that this government is not strong enough. But would the honest patriot, in the full tide of successful experiment, abandon a government which has so far kept us free and firm, on the theoretic and visionary fear that this government, the world's best hope, may by possibility want energy to preserve itself? I trust not. I believe this, on the contrary, the strongest government on earth. I believe it is the only one where every man, at the call of the laws, would fly to the standard of the law, and would meet invasions of the public order as his own personal concern. Sometimes, it is said that man cannot be trusted with the government of himself. Can he, then, be trusted with the government of others? Or have we found angels in the form of kings to govern him? Let history answer the question.

This was rhetoric of a high order, as might have been expected from so gifted a literary man. The barbs may have pricked only gently, but their direction was unerring. The epithets "visionary" and "theoretic" were at last applied where Jefferson thought they belonged, to the doubters of democratic faith. And the smooth assertion of the popular will to defend the nation was another way of underlining his republican distrust of such standing armies as had set out after the whiskey rebels. The people's militia would be the backbone of the national defense henceforward. The dangling question about kings might well have set the extreme Federalists on their guard; for Jefferson was himself about to make the history that would answer the question.

That Jefferson's mind had indeed reverted to the days of the Revolution and to the republican faith that stirred in the land in those days is attested not only by such passages in his inaugural address but by three remarkable private letters he wrote during his first days in office. Each was to a man, a good deal older than himself, who had been his comrade in the Revolution. The first was a reply to a letter of congratulation from John Dickinson, once the voice of caution in the Continental Congress, but now a patriarch and a Republican. To him Jefferson wrote, in his favorite figure:

> The storm through which we have passed, has been tremendous indeed. The tough sides of our Argosy have been thoroughly tried. Her strength has stood the waves into which she was steered, with a view to sink her. We shall put her on her republican tack, and she will now show by the beauty of her motion the skill of her builders.

The second was to Tom Paine, hated and feared by the Federalists and despised even by Washington and Adams. He was, in fact, guilty of scurrilous attacks on both men. Nevertheless, Paine had been the author not only of *The Rights of Man* but of *Common Sense* and *The Crisis*, which, together with the Declaration of Independence, had fired the revolutionary spirit in 1776; Jefferson now quickly heeded his call for help in returning to the United States, a call which the previous Presidents had ignored:

> I am in hopes you will find us returned generally to sentiments worthy of former times. In these it will be your glory to have steadily laboured and with as much effect as any man living.

He ordered the U. S. warship "Maryland" to take Paine on board and bring him home.

The third letter was the most remarkable, under the circumstances. It was to Samuel Adams of Massachusetts, then seventy-nine years old and one of the few of the original revolutionaries still living. This cousin of President Adams had been a firebrand in his youth, an effective propagandist against the British and a leader in the Massachusetts committees of correspondence. He had sat in the revolutionary Congress with Jefferson. Though he had grown conservative in his later years, especially in his support of the state church in Massachusetts, Adams was nevertheless a target of Federalist vilification. Jefferson, to whom state aid to religion was both benighted and vicious, now completely overlooked his old friend's views, revealing in his letter his preoccupation with the Revolutionary era and with the meaning of the Revolution:

> I addressed a letter to you, my very dear and ancient friend, on the 4th of March: not indeed to you by name, but through the medium of some of my fellow-citizens, whom occasion called on me to address. In meditating the matter of that address, I often asked myself, is this exactly in the spirit of the patriarch, Samuel Adams? Is it as he would express it? Will he approve of it? I have felt a great deal for our country in the times we have seen. But individually for no one so much as yourself. When I have been told that you were avoided, insulted, frowned on, I could but ejaculate, "Father, forgive them, for they know not what they do." I confess I felt an in-

dignation for you, which for myself I have been able, under every trial, to keep entirely passive.

He went on to say much the same thing he had said to Dickinson about the change in the political situation. He declared his intention to discharge a few "officers who have perverted their functions to the oppression of their fellow-citizens," but asserted his willingness otherwise to let public opinion direct public affairs. Then he concluded:

How much I lament that time has deprived me of your aid! It would have been a day of glory which should have called you to the first office of the administration. But give us your counsel, my friend, and give us your blessing; and be assured that there exists not in the heart of man a more faithful esteem than mine to you, and that I shall ever bear you the most affectionate veneration and respect.

If it is permissible to doubt that Jefferson was giving much thought to Sam Adams while composing his inaugural address, and if the picture of Adams as Secretary of State is quite beyond anything either Jefferson or anyone else could seriously entertain, the letter is nevertheless sincere enough in its sentiment. President Jefferson did approach the presidency in the spirit of vindication. These letters express that spirit. To steal a figure from one of his successors of a much later era, he might have said that the moneychangers had fled from their seats in the temple; Jefferson would restore them to the revolutionary truths.

But if the Federalist leaders had fled their seats, their followers occupied all the other seats of the government. How to replace them with deserving Republicans without violating his inaugural pledge of national unity was the first problem Jefferson as President had to face. No one questioned the propriety of selecting only his own supporters for the cabinet. Madison, as everyone had expected, became Secretary of State, and Gallatin, again as a foregone conclusion, took over the Treasury. Monroe was Governor of Virginia and not immediately available. Levi Lincoln of Massachusetts was appointed Attorney General; Henry Dearborn of Maine, Secretary of War; and Robert Smith of Maryland, after several refusals from better-qualified men, became Secretary of the Navy. Gideon Granger of Connecticut was appointed Postmaster General, though that officer was not yet a member of the cabinet. But when it came to the lesser offices, Jefferson's difficulties quickly multiplied.

When Burr recommended his friend Matthew Davis for a post in New York City, Jefferson seems to have taken the occasion to let Burr know that he did not have and would not again have the President's support. Davis followed Jefferson to Monticello in the spring, hoping to persuade him to make the appointment, but Jefferson showed him only hospitality. Thereafter, though he made one last appeal to Jefferson in 1806, there was no real doubt that Burr's political career was ruined. By giving the patronage in New York to George Clinton and the Livingstons, the President hoped to keep that state in the Republican column, as he succeeded in doing, while Burr, like Hamilton on the Federalist side, was consigned to leading a splinter group without important political strength.

Jefferson refused to recognize John Adams' "midnight" appointments, which had filled every vacancy, mostly judicial, that existed in February and the first three days of March. One of the commissions denied under this policy was that of John Quincy Adams, son of the ex-President and in his boyhood well-loved by Jefferson. There was no intentional slight, but the Adamses took it as such and the rupture between them and Jefferson was complete. Six years later the younger Adams, as Senator from Massachusetts, was to swallow his pride and "cross the aisle" of the Senate to support President Jefferson's embargo, in flat opposition to the will of his principal Federalist constituents, but with his father's grudging approval. And eleven years later the friendship between the elder Adams and Jefferson was to be renewed by correspondence, to the permanent enrichment of American civilization.

Meanwhile Jefferson handled the patronage problem with

considerable political skill. Though he satisfied neither the unreconstructible Federalists nor the more vindictive Republicans, he appointed enough Republicans to office during the first year of his administration to convince his followers that he was true to his party, and retained enough Federalists of competence to persuade the people as a whole that he meant to bind up the political wounds of the 1790's. Though he was the first President to make of the patronage a calculated weapon of party politics, filling vacancies as rapidly as was seemly with members of his own party to the advantage both of the party and of his own political position, Jefferson was not the real founder of the "spoils system." That distinction was reserved for another good Jeffersonian a generation later —Andrew Jackson.

But it was Jefferson who introduced "republican" customs and dress into the White House. As a people's President he thought it proper to dress in plain clothes and to eliminate every remaining trace of court manners and ritual. The levees were abolished. At state dinners "pell mell" replaced protocol, to the special disgust of newly arrived British Minister Merry. This was a system by which a gentleman, at the announcement of dinner, escorted whatever lady he was standing with to a seat at a table where there were no place cards and no ceremonial seating. As for his dress, Jefferson was often criticized for wearing carpet slippers when receiving guests. Some unfriendly gossips even reported that he was not careful about his linen. He had, of course, a fine wardrobe, and in his earlier years had displayed a taste for elegance. But times were now different and he intended to lose no opportunity to underline the republican simplicity of both the new Administration and its chief.

The new President was fortunate in many of the circumstances under which he took office. His pledge to get rid of the troublesome excise tax, for example, was feasible. Gallatin at the Treasury soon produced a budget, sharply reducing expenditures for the navy and paring the fat in other places, which could be financed by import duties and by the sale of the public lands. The President so reported to Congress, and the excise taxes were repealed. The Alien and Sedition Laws

THE LIFE OF THOMAS JEFFERSON

expired, after their three-year trial, soon after Jefferson's inauguration; and the President took advantage of the altered political climate to ask for and receive a relaxation in the immigration laws. In his first annual message he asked in moving language:

> And shall we refuse to the unhappy fugitives from distress that hospitality which the savages of the wilderness extended to our fathers arriving in this land? Shall oppressed humanity find no asylum on this globe?

As President, Jefferson could effectively support his belief in freedom of conscience by a powerful statement of presidential policy. The occasion he chose was not without political significance. He received in 1802, among numerous other greetings, a New Year letter of congratulation from the Danbury Baptist Association. Connecticut was the last nearly impregnable stronghold of Federalism. The Congregational Church was still established there, and the New England Congregational clergy in general were bitterly and chronically opposed to him. A strong statement on the separation of church and state might serve both to underline the well-known Jeffersonian view and to assist the dissenters of New England to break from their Federalist leaders, lay and clerical:

> Believing with you [he wrote] that religion is a matter which lies solely between man and his God, that he owes account to none other for his faith or his worship, that the legislative powers of government reach actions only, and not opinions, I contemplate with sovereign reverence that act of the whole American people which declared that their legislature should "make no law respecting an establishment of religion, or prohibiting the free exercise thereof," thus building a wall of separation between Church and State. Adhering to this expression of the supreme will of the nation in behalf of the rights of conscience, I shall see with sincere satisfaction the progress of those sentiments which tend to restore to

man all his natural rights, convinced he has no natural
right in opposition to his social duties.

As an exercise in political writing this paragraph has few
equals. Not only did it address effectively a political situation then prevailing in Connecticut, but it laid down the
classic position on church and state which has been American
doctrine ever since. So firmly established has the Jeffersonian
statement become, in fact, that the Supreme Court has cited
it as though it were an official act of the government. Discern-
ing students may see in the statement another instance of
Jefferson's consistent elevation of libertarian principle over all
other considerations. It is the priority assigned to civil liberty
that links the letter to the Danbury Baptists with the Kentucky
Resolutions, while the diametrically opposed interpretations
of the origin of the Constitution seem to divorce the two
statements. The political theorist, or indeed anyone who requires logical consistency, must balk at the notion that for one
purpose the Constitution is a compact among the states but
for another it is the "act of the whole American people." Yet
if Jefferson was at all aware of his inconsistency it must not
have mattered to him. Fidelity to his democratic values was
what did matter.

In foreign affairs Jefferson at first felt less pressure than had
his predecessor. The undeclared naval war with France had
come to an uncertain end as Napoleon went in search of more
formidable opponents. But both the British and the French
harassed American merchant vessels and posed for the new
President a continuing dilemma. If he were to give naval
protection to American ships, he would be inviting new involvements in sea warfare and perhaps full-scale war with
one or the other of the great powers. Such a policy would, in
any case, require much larger expenditures for the navy. But
it was precisely the budget of the navy which could most
easily be reduced in order to bring expenditures of the government into line with income from duties and land sales, so that
the hated excises could be forgotten. Jefferson was on record
in emphatic terms against "foreign entanglements," both
because he hated war and because he believed that American

prosperity would need a long period of peace. But to cut down the navy and submit to depredations upon American commerce was to surrender the libertarian doctrine of the freedom of the seas to which he also strongly adhered, and to demean the young nation in the eyes of the world. There was no "right" policy under such circumstances. And Jefferson followed a makeshift middle course by keeping the Mediterranean battle squadron at sea to protect American shipping in that area, while withdrawing some other ships from service and reducing construction.

During Jefferson's first term the Barbary pirates of Tripoli and Morocco were more troublesome than the British or the French. The President was anxious to establish good relations with the rulers of these states and willing to pay substantial fees for passage through the seas they were "patrolling." This was blackmail, of course; but if it was cheap enough, it was Jefferson's view that it would be better than war. When agreed payments brought only demands for more, Jefferson angrily ordered the fleet to take whatever measures were necessary to police the waters for American ships. Morocco was soon persuaded to respect her treaty with the United States, but Tripolitan guns fired upon the warship "Philadelphia," disabled her, and forced her to surrender. Jefferson was infuriated by this affront to American dignity and, unsatisfied with the efforts of United States diplomats in Europe to secure release of the ship and some three hundred prisoners, he orderd an attack on Tripoli. In the summer of 1804 the U.S.S. "Constitution," famed as "Old Ironsides," led a task force into Tripoli harbor and bombarded the city for many weeks. Other ships were added to the engagement until ultimately the Pasha of Tripoli asked for mercy. Thereafter American ships were safe from Barbary pirates.

The victory over the pirates was a considerable achievement and the news was well received by the Congress and the public. But the epochal event of Jefferson's first term was the Louisiana Purchase from France. The acquisition of the vast territory of the South and West doubled the "empire of liberty" and guaranteed, as Napoleon assuredly did not at the time appreciate, that the United States would become a great power. The events preceding Napoleon's offer to sell the territory belong to the dark recesses of Franco-Spanish relations in the eighteenth century. It would be both tedious and unnecessary to recount them here. It is enough to say that by the Treaty of San Ildefonso, Napoleon had, in 1800, acquired New Orleans and the Spanish territories of the Mississippi. By a dubious oral agreement the Floridas were said also to have been placed at French disposal. Thus the United States had a new opportunity to try to secure freedom of navigation for her irate citizens of Kentucky and Tennessee. The situation was exacerbated, however, in 1801 and 1802, by the anti-American behavior of the Spanish authorities, who still had not turned over New Orleans to the French. As in 1794, there was talk of direct hostilities.

Under these circumstances Jefferson and Secretary of State Madison decided to make an effort to purchase the port of New Orleans from France, together with as much of the territory east of the Mississippi as they could get. Supporting the President against a treacherous attack from eccentric John Randolph of Roanoke, Congress in the spring of 1803 appropriated two million dollars to be spent at the sole discretion of the President in dealing with the Louisiana question. Thus armed, Jefferson sent Monroe to Paris to negotiate with Napoleon.

Meanwhile, for months, United States Minister Robert R. Livingston in Paris had been talking to Talleyrand, now Napoleon's minister, on every suitable occasion. These conversations had been fruitless, since Napoleon then had in mind a major military operation in the Caribbean, to suppress insurrection in San Domingo and consolidate his North American territories. But suddenly and without prior hint that he might change his mind, Napoleon reversed himself. To Minister of State Barbé-Marbois, Jefferson's old friend, the emperor announced his new policy on April 10. "They ask of me only one town in Louisiana," he said, "but I already consider the colony as entirely lost; and it appears to me that in the hands of this growing Power it will be more useful to the policy, and even the commerce of France than if I should attempt to keep it." Marbois, of course, informed Livingston of Napoleon's new attitude.

The next days were tense indeed for Robert Livingston. He had neither authority nor money to purchase the whole of so vast a territory; yet he wished, understandably, to have the credit for making the transaction. Monroe, he knew, was about to arrive with authority superior to his own. He tried to temporize with Talleyrand, but only succeeded in annoying Napoleon, who was under pressures from his brothers to change his mind again and now threatened to do so. Monroe arrived at Paris on April 13 and immediately took charge of the negotiation. He was careful to consult with Livingston, but no doubt because of his long and intimate relationship with the President and Secretary of State, he was far more self-confident than the New Yorker. In short order he decided to bargain for the whole territory. But for several days he was confined to his quarters by illness and Livingston conducted the actual negotiations. The agreement was finally made at a figure of 60 million francs, about $16,000,000. The cession included all of the French territory both east and west of the Mississippi, and Florida, if French title to that area was ever cleared. Monroe and Livingston afterward insisted that Florida was included without qualification, but the Spanish-French protocols and treaties do not bear them out. At any rate, the United States did not acquire Florida until the administration of Monroe himself after the Napoleonic Wars.

The American envoys had committed the United States to a sum eight times greater than Monroe's secret fund, as they reported to Jefferson and Madison somewhat apologetically. They had also committed the Congress to fashioning states out of the new territory and conferring citizenship upon the European inhabitants. Jefferson was convinced that the treaty was unconstitutional on all counts. But his concern about strict adherence to the Constitution was evidently less intense than his delight at the acquisition. After consultation with the members of his cabinet, with congressional Republican leaders, and with trusted old friends, he sent the treaty to the Senate, called the Congress into special early session, and reported to them in his third annual message. He said nothing about constitutionality. After a brief review of the difficulties with Spain and the continued unhappiness of the Westerners, he reminded the Congress of their grant to him of two million dollars to seek the purchase of New Orleans. This, he said, "was considered as conveying the sanction of Congress to the acquisition proposed." This bit of bravado, flaunting both the Congress and the Constitution, succeeded. Indeed, the record shows that the members of Congress were much less concerned about the constitutional question than was the President. With their assurance that they approved his action, the President dropped the matter with a sigh that must have been audible, at least figuratively, to many a Federalist who remembered how tenaciously Jefferson had held to a strict construction on matters dear to them. But the national bank, the indiscriminate redemption of government paper, and the Alien and Sedition Laws were not popular measures. The purchase of Louisiana was the most popular event since Yorktown. The Federalists could and did cry out in protest, but their voices were scarcely heard outside the clubs and countinghouses of Boston, New York, and Philadelphia. Jefferson commented somewhat wryly in a letter to General Horatio Gates:

I find our opposition is very willing to pluck feathers from Monroe, although not fond of sticking them into Livingston's coat. The truth is, both have a just portion of merit; and were it necessary or proper, it would be shown that each has rendered peculiar services, and of important value. These grumblers, too, are very uneasy lest the administration should share some little credit for the acquisition the whole of which they ascribe to the accident of war.

More important than the constitutional question was the meaning of the Louisiana acquisition for the future of the nation. Jefferson, in his message, dealt with both the economic and the political consequences:

While the property and sovereignty of the Mississippi

[121]

and its waters secure an independent outlet for the produce of the western states, and an uncontrolled navigation through their whole course, free from collision with
other powers and the dangers to our peace from that
source, the fertility of the country, its climate and extent,
promise in due season important aids to our treasury, an
ample provision for our posterity, and a wide-spread
field for the blessings of freedom and equal laws.

From Congress he asked legislative action to bring the government of the United States to the new lands:

With the wisdom of Congress it will rest to take those
ulterior measures which may be necessary for the immediate occupation and temporary government of the country; for its incorporation into our Union; for rendering the
change of government a blessing to our newly-adopted
brethren; for securing to them the rights of conscience
and of property. . . .

It was characteristic that "conscience" preceded "property"
in Jefferson's list of rights.

Since this message affords a fair example of Jefferson's
treatment of the Congress, it may be useful here to consider
his handling of the presidency from this point of view. Jefferson is rightly listed among the so-called strong Presidents of
American history. In the same category fall Jackson, Lincoln,
and both Roosevelts, and perhaps also Polk, Wilson, Truman,
and Kennedy. Though these men have differed in the degree
of their success, and in party, program, and policy, they
shared the belief that the President of the United States is
the "steward," to use Theodore Roosevelt's term, of the
people's welfare. All but one believed that the President, as
the only elected spokesman for the whole nation, should give
leadership to Congress, not take it. The single exception was
Jefferson, and he is only partially an exception.

As the message on Louisiana shows, it was not his practice
to ask the Congress for specific legislation. His attitude was
deferential. He appeared, at least, to suggest his recognition

of a coequal status of the Congress in the distribution of national power. Other strong Presidents seldom showed such deference and characteristically spelled out in pretty clear language what they wished the Congress to do. If Congress was balky, they would, on important matters, "go to the people" to generate pressure on Congress. Jefferson's theory of the presidency was different in this important respect. His strict construction of the Constitution led him to see the President as confined, formally, to the powers set forth in the document. While he violated the Constitution in the case of the Louisiana Purchase, he did so knowingly and unwillingly. He would have preferred a constitutional amendment to make his authority clear. That he did not press the point is evidence not of his political theory but of his mode of political behavior.

The key to understanding Jefferson as President is to be found precisely in his politics, not in his theory of government. The Constitution said nothing about political parties or who should lead them. But in a system of government where parties had become the informal but actual vehicles of power, the party leader could wield powers nowhere set forth in Constitution or statute. And Jefferson was the undisputed leader of the Republican party. That party held a big majority in the House of Representatives and, after 1802, a normally decisive margin in the Senate. Thus Jefferson's formal deference to Congress in his messages and in other dealings conceals at least as much of the reality of his administration as it reveals. He could in good faith say to the Congress that it was up to them to deal with this, that, or the other problem, but as party leader he made his views privately known to the leadership on every measure he thought important. In fact, he often drafted legislation himself to be introduced by his congressional followers. By such means the Congress enacted his program, and his only. In the case of Louisiana he wished to move cautiously. In private he asked congressional leaders to provide appointive government in the territory, including New Orleans, until the French and Spanish were adjusted to American civil institutions. Congress obliged, and it was not until 1805 that New Orleans was granted a measure of self-government. The wisdom of Jefferson's views on Louisiana was amply demonstrated during his second term by the Burr conspiracy, as we shall see.

It was Jefferson's leadership of the party that annoyed such stalwarts as John Randolph of Roanoke and Nathaniel Macon to a point where they could no longer endure their political chains and went into opposition. One of the amusing ironies of the Jeffersonian era, in fact, was that Randolph's followers, known as the "tertium quids," always insisted that they opposed Jefferson because he was not sufficiently "Jeffersonian." But their opposition was never effective for more than brief moments. It was only after he had himself retired to Monticello that there would be revealed in his unhappy successor, Madison, the weakness of a President who followed Jefferson's theory without his gift for political leadership.

With the addition of the great trans-Mississippi territories another important element of Jefferson's program came into full perspective. This was the expedition of Lewis and Clark up the Missouri River, across the mountains, and down the valley of the Columbia to the Pacific. On January 18, 1803, the President sent a confidential message to the Congress recommending an exploration of the waters of the Missouri with a view to improving trade with the Indians and otherwise increasing public knowledge of the vast Western lands. As a boy Jefferson had known the forests on the western slopes of the Alleghenies, and his sense of the importance of the West for the American future had grown with the years. His Ordinance of 1784, his Spanish policy as Secretary of State, and now his Louisiana policy were consistent expressions of his dream of an "empire of liberty." There was also his insatiable scientific curiosity. Such an expedition as he now proposed to the Congress would answer to both purposes:

The river Missouri, and the Indians inhabiting it, are not as well known as is rendered desirable by their connection with the Mississippi, and consequently with us. It is, however, understood, that the country on that river is inhabited by numerous tribes, who furnish great supplies of fur and peltry to the trade of another nation, carried on in a high latitude, through an infinite number of portages and lakes, shut up by ice through a long season. The commerce on that line could bear no competition with that of the Missouri, traversing a moderate climate, offering, according to the best accounts, a continued navigation from its source, and possibly with a single portage, from the western ocean, and finding to the Atlantic a choice of channels through the Illinois or Wabash, the lakes and Hudson, through the Ohio and Susquehanna, or Potomac or James rivers, and through the Tennessee and Savannah rivers.

The need for exploration and mapping is underlined for later Americans by the lack of a realistic grasp of the sheer extent of the West revealed in these words. Yet it is likely that Jefferson was at least as well informed on the geography of the Missouri and the Northwest as any American of his day. The unbelievably modest scale upon which this greatest of American exploring expeditions was launched is indicated by the remarkable sentence which followed:

An intelligent officer, with ten or twelve chosen men, fit for the enterprise, and willing to undertake it, taken from our posts, where they may be spared without inconvenience, might explore the whole line, even to the western ocean; have conferences with the natives on the subject of commercial intercourse; get admission among them for our traders, as others are admitted; agree on convenient deposits for an interchange of articles; and return with the information acquired, in the course of two summers.

For this heroic undertaking the President asked an appropriation of $2,500 "for the purpose of extending the external commerce of the United States."

Congress authorized the expedition and appropriated the money. The message was secret and the plans for the enterprise were developed with as little public attention as possible, since it was doubtful, to say the least, that the two great

European powers would have consented to the proposed attack upon their trade with the Indians or condoned the cavalier manner in which Jefferson assumed that one day the whole area would be American. Secretary Madison persuaded the French and the British to grant permission for the explorers to cross their territories, on Jefferson's pretext that it was a "literary" excursion.

To head the expedition Jefferson chose his own private secretary, Captain Meriwether Lewis, a Virginia native and neighbor of the President's in Albemarle. Lewis had had some prior experience of the West in his army service, knew something about geography and mapping, and was gifted with a fine intelligence and a clear prose style. As his deputy Jefferson appointed William Clark, also of Albemarle and a brother of the famous Indian fighter George Rogers Clark. To these young men Jefferson gave detailed instructions on the scientific aspects of their expedition. He charged them to observe all forms of plant and animal life, to take note of climate and rainfall, to be on the lookout for fossils and other evidences of life in earlier times, and to take careful note of the customs, language, and other characteristics of the Indians they met along the way. The skill, tenacity, and courage with which they lived up to the last syllable of their instructions is recorded in Lewis' great journal, which, as edited a few years later by Nicholas Biddle, became a masterpiece of American literature.

The "two summers" of Jefferson's message became more than two and a half years, from May, 1804, when Lewis and Clark set forth from St. Louis, just then turned over to the United States by the French, to January 10, 1807, when Lewis reported to the President in person. Lewis and Clark traveled nine thousand miles from St. Louis up the Missouri, across the mountains, down the Columbia to the Pacific, and back again. Their story cannot be told here. But perhaps it is permissible to guess that Jefferson, who took immense pride in their achievement, would have been stirred by the lines of the poet Archibald MacLeish, which brilliantly distilled for a later generation the meaning of that achievement:

To Thos. Jefferson Esq. his obd't serv't
M. Lewis: captain detached:
                              Sir:
Having in mind your repeated commands in this matter,
And the worst half of it done and the streams mapped,

And we here on the back of this beach beholding the
Other ocean—two years gone and the cold

Breaking with rain for the third spring since St. Louis,
The crows at the fishbones on the frozen dunes,

The first cranes going over from south north,
And the river down by a mark of the pole since the
    morning,

And time near to return, and a ship (Spanish)
Lying in for the salmon: and fearing chance or the

Drought or the Sioux should deprive you of these dis-
    coveries—
Therefore we send by sea in this writing.

                                        Above the
Platte there were long plains and a clay country:
Rim of the sky far off, grass under it,

Dung for the cook fires by the sulphur licks.
After that there were low hills and the sycamores,

And we poled up by the Great Bend in the skiffs:
The honey bees left us after the Osage River:

The wind was west in the evenings and no dew and the
Morning Star larger and whiter than usual—

The winter rattling in the brittle haws.
The second year there was sage and the quail calling.

All that valley is good land by the river:
Three thousand miles and the clay cliffs and

Rue and beargrass by the water banks
And many birds and the brant going over and tracks of

Bear, elk, wolves, marten: the buffalo
Numberless so that the cloud of their dust covers them:

The antelope fording the fall creeks, and the mountains and
Grazing lands and the meadow lands and the ground

Sweet and open and well-drained.
                                        We advise you to
Settle troops at the forks and to issue licenses:

Many men will have living on these lands.
There is wealth in the earth for them all and the wood
    standing.

And wild birds on the water where they sleep.
There is stone in the hills for the towns of a great
    people . . .*

Though the Lewis and Clark adventure was justly celebrated, it is worth adding that Jefferson also sent Zebulon M.
Pike to the headwaters of the Mississippi and later to the
Southwest, where he studied and mapped the great mountains
of the Rockies, one of which bears his name.

Despite the achievements of Jefferson's first years in office,
the personal attacks on him, which had diminished somewhat
just after his election, were before long renewed. In particular he suffered at the hands of a supposed political supporter, James Callender. This scamp had been a hack writer
in the Republican cause and had been jailed in Richmond for
violation of the Sedition Act. Jefferson, soon after his inauguration, ordered him released and the remainder of his sentence
remitted. But there had also been a fine, which Callender
thought Jefferson ought to pay as a reward for services to the
Republican cause. Jefferson did so privately, only to let himself
fall into the clutches of a blackmailer.

For Callender, informed apparently by Colonel Henry Lee
of Jefferson's unfortunate adventure with Mrs. Walker many
years before, and of Betsy Walker's later wild exaggeration of
it, presently demanded more money on pain of revealing the

* Archibald MacLeish, "Frescoes for Mr. Rockefeller's City," *Collected
Poems, 1917–1952,* (New York: Houghton Mifflin Company, 1952).

Walker story. Jefferson refused, and Callender gave the story to the Federalists, who gave it to the papers. The scandal raged until Walker himself approached Jefferson to join him in an effort to quiet it down. He proposed that Jefferson write a public letter clearing Mrs. Walker of the presumed adultery. Jefferson was willing enough to write the letter, but despite the insistence of Lee, he refused to do so for publication. He did eventually reply to the increasingly nasty and fantastic stories by means of a letter to the Richmond *Enquirer* by his secretary, William Burwell. The end of the miserable story came only in 1809, when Walker was dying. Through Monroe an approach was made to Jefferson asking him to visit the Walkers and forgive them. He would not see them, but he sent them a present of figs as a token of his willingness to forgive.

Other stories were continually whispered, blackening the President's character, and the Federalist press, still flourishing though the numbers of the Federalist party constantly dwindled, never let up in its charges of sedition, treason, dictatorship, and corruption. Jefferson's patience was severely strained, and he sometimes thought that it might be good for the country if some Federalist editors were tried for libel in the state courts. He has often been charged with inconsistency for taking this view. While it is certain that he was much more disturbed by Federalist than by Republican journalistic excesses, it does not follow that his recommendation of libel actions in the state courts was in opposition to free speech and press. The Sedition Law, which Jefferson so forcibly opposed, had been intended to shut off criticism of the government as a matter of principle. But suits for libel could be instituted only after publication had taken place, and the accused could offer the truth of the allegations as defense against the charges. The purpose, as Jefferson intended, was not to stifle criticism but to put an end to slander. If there was nevertheless a certain inconsistency in his behavior, it is at least understandable in view of the remorseless and virulent attacks to which he was subjected. To demand government action against newspapers cannot quite be squared with his famous aphorism that if he had to choose between "newspapers without government and government without newspapers," he would choose newspapers!

In one case President Jefferson did more than urge prosecution in the state courts. When Justice Samuel Chase of the Supreme Court made a direct attack from his bench in Baltimore, not only on the government but on democracy and civil liberty, Jefferson thought he should be impeached. In the light of the behavior expected of a modern Justice of the Supreme Court it is hard not to see in Chase's words an unpardonable breach of political decency as well as an insufferable attack on Jefferson's principles of free speech and opinion:

> The modern doctrines by our late reformers that all men in a state of society are entitled to enjoy equal liberty and equal rights, have brought this mighty mischief upon us; and I fear that it will rapidly progress until peace and order, freedom and property, shall be destroyed.

So said the Justice. Acting characteristically as party leader rather than in his official capacity, Jefferson suggested to Joseph Nicholson of the House Republican leadership that proceedings should be started against Chase. The Republican majority promptly voted the impeachment on a straight party vote. In the trial before the Senate, John Randolph, in one of his last services to Jefferson, conducted the prosecution. Though he was found guilty by a majority on several counts, Chase was acquitted, since the Republicans did not control two-thirds of the Senate, the number necessary for conviction. Thus Jefferson lost the battle. However, since there is no subsequent record of similar behavior by a federal judge, it may perhaps be said that he won the war.

The public events great and small of his first term in the White House did not, in spite of their demands upon his time and energy, entirely prevent Jefferson from giving attention to his long-time interests in science and in learning. In previous years he had followed closely the efforts of his friend Dr. Rush to control plagues of yellow fever and malaria, and he now received with interest news of experiments in smallpox inoculation being carried on by Dr. Benjamin Waterhouse of Boston. At Jefferson's request Waterhouse sent him some live pustulant matter from his smallpox patients to be used in immunization. The President forwarded it to Virginia, where experiments were conducted at Monticello and elsewhere in Albemarle, with results which certainly advanced the limits of knowledge in this vital medical field.

In 1802 Jefferson persuaded Congress to appropriate a sum of money for the purchase of books for the use of its members in the preparation of legislation. It was his hope that from such a beginning there might grow up a national library. Twenty-five years before, he had prepared a bill to establish a state library in Virginia, and he had never lost sight of that long-delayed project. But a Library of Congress was an even more tempting opportunity, and it was at hand. In such a matter both Congress and the executive branch automatically deferred to the scholar President, who undertook personal responsibility for the purchases. Some books were ordered from American booksellers, but the main work of acquisition was assigned by Jefferson to his old friend and former secretary William Short, who still served in the American legation at Paris. Thus President Jefferson, the devoted believer in the separation of powers, happily superintended the earliest stages of building the Library of Congress. A year or so later he was corresponding again about books, this time with Littleton Tazewell, who was trying to advance the plans for a University of Virginia. Jefferson indicated his intention to bequeath his library to the university. It had cost, by 1804, more than $15,000, but since, as he thought, much of it could no longer be duplicated, it was really priceless.

Nor did he neglect his farms or the improvement of his house, as he had been forced to do so often in earlier years. He made it a practice to spend a few weeks at Monticello each spring, superintending the planting of his fields and gardens and laying out with his overseer and builder the program for the year. In the summer he was usually at home for a much longer period, often not returning to Washington until just before the convening of Congress in November. He occasionally visited Poplar Forest, but his account book and his farm and garden books show that most of the time was spent at Monticello.

The only inhibition upon Jefferson's complete happiness in his beautiful house was his growing debts. No measures of economy seemed to be effective. With Carrs and Randolphs and Eppeses to lavish his care upon, with his own expensive tastes, and with indifferent crop yields and a falling tobacco market, there was seldom a year when income even approximated expenditures. Jefferson knew, of course, that his affairs were worsening all the time, but he either could not or would not take the kinds of drastic action which might have saved him from the bankruptcy which caught up with him in his old age.

The year 1804, which brought his first term to a close, was filled with sadness for Jefferson personally and with public tragedy. On April 12, his daughter Maria died after a long period of uncertain health and spirits. Thus Jefferson finally lost all but one of his children. "Others may lose of their abundance," he wrote to John Page, "but I, of my want have lost even the half of all I had." Quite unexpectedly he received a letter of condolence from Abigail Adams. Her letter touched him and stimulated him, in his grief, to make a somewhat clumsy effort to restore his relations with her and her husband. But the political wounds were still too raw, and he only succeeded in drawing Mrs. Adams into a momentary controversy from which both were glad to escape.

In July, Vice-president Burr shot and killed Alexander Hamilton in a duel. Burr, knowing that he was to be dropped by Jefferson from the national ticket and bent on making one more desperate bid for power, had made an alliance between his own followers and a Federalist faction in New York that had broken away from Hamilton's leadership. With this backing he offered himself as a candidate for governor of the state. Governor Clinton, Jefferson's choice for Vice-president, gave his support to Morgan Lewis. During the fierce campaign, some of the more extreme Federalists deserted Burr because he would not commit himself unequivocally to splitting the Union by the secession of the New England states and New York. Hamilton and his followers attacked him vigorously and continuously. Hamilton, beyond doubt, wrote and spoke of Burr in language too abusive even for a tough political campaign. Losing to Morgan Lewis, Burr attributed his defeat to Hamilton's machinations and libels. But instead of bringing a libel suit against him as he might have done, he challenged him to a duel. At Weehawken, New Jersey, on July 11, Burr mortally wounded his opponent. Party bitterness was put aside for the moment while the shocked nation mourned the death of one of its most brilliant founders. Burr's career was ruined. When he returned to Washington Jefferson made it clear that he could not expect to continue his career as a Republican leader, though as a kind of recognition for his earlier work for the party the President appointed two of Burr's relatives to federal posts.

As the election of 1804 approached, the only question was how large Jefferson's majority would be. He would still have preferred to retire, but this time his gestures in that direction were halfhearted. He knew well enough that popular expectation would have to be satisfied. The victory over the Barbary pirates, the Louisiana Purchase, and the repeal of the excise taxes had made his Administration the first really successful one the young country had known. Federalist rearguard action had been feverish but ineffective. The last Federalist hope had, in fact, evaporated when Burr went down in New York. General Pinckney of XYZ fame, and a perennial Federalist candidate, allowed himself to be put forward as the Federalist nominee against Jefferson. But he knew it was no more than a gesture.

When the voting began, it soon became apparent that the popularity of the Administration's measures and the immense prestige of the President would give the Republican ticket a sweeping victory. Not only was the South "solid" for the "Democratic-Republican" candidate—as it was to be most of the time for 150 years thereafter—not only were the big states of Pennsylvania and New York faithful to the coalition of 1800, but even Massachusetts toppled into the Jefferson column. In the end only Connecticut, by a very small margin, and Delaware gave their votes to Pinckney. The tally was Jefferson and Clinton 162, Pinckney and Rufus King 14.

Only James Monroe in 1820 and Franklin D. Roosevelt in 1936 afterward scored such overwhelming victories.

Jefferson was happy with the outcome, and said little about the burdens he must continue to carry for the coming four years. He thought that the country was in good shape. Relations with Britain he considered—rashly, as events proved—to be cordial; with France excellent; with Spain chronically poor but not dangerous. The budget was balanced, the debt greatly reduced, the people prosperous. Jefferson's only regret was that the Federalists had, despite their rapidly shrinking numbers, remained stubbornly unpersuaded of the benefits of Republican rule or of his own leadership. If they had been more friendly, he wrote to William Short, he would have allowed them to hold some offices in the government, but as it was, he said, to him had "fallen the drudgery of putting them out of condition to do mischief." His successor, he hoped, would "have smoother seas." But it was to be twelve more years before the Federalists' power to annoy Republicans, and even to threaten the security of the nation, would finally disappear; and Jefferson's own seas were to be far from smooth for the sailing of his second term.

Chapter 8.

PRESIDENT JEFFERSON:
SECOND ADMINISTRATION

When Thomas Jefferson for the second time spoke to his fellow citizens in an inaugural address, it was in a spirit of quiet pride in the accomplishments of the intervening years. If he had known for certain, what he partly felt, that the world situation was about to deteriorate so abruptly that his second term would be one endless and frustrating struggle, he would have been glad indeed to forget the adulation of his followers and once and for all put aside the burdens of state for the placid delights of Monticello. But on March 4, 1805, the intransigence of England and France seemed more remote than it was, and the wretched expedition of Aaron Burr, with its wake of political chaos and corruption, could not have been anticipated.

As he noted in later years, it had been the purpose of his first inaugural to declare the principles upon which he would govern the country; it was the intention of the second inaugural to review the record in the light of those principles. And the record was good. On the international side, an accommodation with Napoleon had brought Louisiana under the American flag, as well as a dubious claim to the Floridas, and relations with Britain were at least no worse than they had been. On the domestic side Jefferson's fiscal policy had been successful beyond the most optimistic Republican expectations. How successful it was can be seen in the famous rhetorical question the President put to his fellow citizens—a question which from the vantage point of the twentieth century sounds as though it emanated from a different world, as indeed it did. "It may be the pleasure and pride of an American," said Jefferson, "to ask, what farmer, what mechanic, what laborer, ever sees a tax gatherer of the United States?" It was a safe question, for the internal taxes had been repealed, as import duties and land sales produced an overflowing treasury.

The government's problem, as Jefferson saw it on March 4, 1805, was not how to meet expenses in the future but what to do with the federal surplus when, as would happen very soon, the national debt was wholly retired. Because of his insistence upon a strict construction of the Constitution, his creative policy for meeting this desirable situation has been somehow detached from Jefferson by the American mind and identified exclusively with the views of Henry Clay a generation later. But what Jefferson proposed was an ambitious program of internal improvements, applying surplus revenue "to rivers, canals, roads, arts, manufactures, education, and other great objects." He envisioned an amendment to the Constitution which would permit the Congress to distribute the federal surplus to the states after earmarking by Congress for such purposes. A year later, in fact, he asked Secretary of the Treasury Gallatin to work up a plan for internal improvements in accordance with which the states would be expected to expend their shares of the federal grants. Gallatin's plan, fully approved by Jefferson in his sixth annual message, was more detailed than anything later proposed by Clay in his "American System."

But nothing came of the Jefferson program, partly because after the Chesapeake affair of June, 1807, it was necessary to increase federal expenditures for defense, thus putting off the day when surpluses would be available for internal development, and partly also because not only Jefferson but all his successors down to the Mexican War differed with Congress as to the government's power to execute such a program without a Constitutional amendment. A different sort of "internal improvement," it should be added, Jefferson did succeed in obtaining. To him, fittingly, fell the honor of asking Congress to exercise the authority granted in the Constitution to end the slave trade in 1808. Jefferson did so in his message of 1806, and Congress acted promptly in 1808.

In his second inaugural Jefferson gave a good deal of attention to Indian affairs. His administration had made a number of treaties and agreements with the Indians which had resulted in vast additions to United States territory. Jefferson's policy was to educate the Indians in modern agriculture and domestic arts as rapidly as possible, so that they would not be likely to resent the loss of their hunting grounds. But the Indians often proved resistant to the new ways and frequently took the war path in desperate efforts to reclaim their ancient lands. Jefferson saw an important analogy between the problems thus posed for the government and the continuing intractableness of the Federalists. He made no direct reference now to his political opponents, but no one missed the point of what he was saying:

These persons [some Indians] inculcate a sanctimonious reverence for the customs of their ancestors; that whatsoever they did, must be done through all time; that reason is a false guide, and to advance under its counsel, in their physical, moral, or political condition, is perilous innovation; that their duty is to remain as their Creator made them, ignorance being safety, and knowledge full of danger; in short, my friends, among them is seen the action and counter-action of good sense and bigotry; they, too, have their anti-philosophers, who find an interest in keeping things in their present state, who dread reformation, and exert all their faculties to maintain the ascendance of habit over the duty of improving our reason, and obeying its mandates.

A final major topic upon which Jefferson touched as he took office for his second term was the irresponsibility of newspapers. Though the Federalist party had so diminished in numbers as to be ineffective politically, anti-Republican newspapers still flourished and still cried their message of hate, particularly against the President personally. He had hoped that prosecution of some of these papers for libel in the state courts would change the minds of the hostile editors. But there had been no serious move by Republican prosecutors to employ this method of redress, and Jefferson would not condone repressive measures by the federal government. In his address he suggested his disappointment that the states had not been more vigorous, but chiefly he emphasized his ancient faith in truth and reason to counter falsehood:

> . . . since truth and reason have maintained their ground against false opinions in league with false facts, the press, confined to truth, needs no other legal restraint; the public judgment will correct false reasonings and opinions, on a full hearing of all parties; and no other definite line can be drawn between the inestimable liberty of the press and its demoralizing licentiousness. If there be still improprieties which this rule would not restrain, its supplement must be sought in the censorship of public opinion.

Then, with an appropriate recognition of the likelihood that he would make mistakes in the coming term, and with good Jeffersonian expressions of need for popular indulgence, Mr. Jefferson again took the oath of office at the hands of John Marshall and entered upon the last phase of his long and still unparalleled public career.

The history of Jefferson's second administration is best understood as a chapter in the Napoleonic wars. Jefferson's policy was to keep his own country out of war. From the beginnings of government under the Constitution he had argued and urged that the United States stay clear of foreign entanglements. At the same time he had advocated friendly commercial relations with all nations. This policy had always been difficult if not impossible to achieve; now, in 1805 and the years immediately following, the President more than ever determined to maintain it in the face of steadily worsening international conditions.

The United States had three foreign powers with which to contend, each presenting a different set of problems. Nearest at hand was Spain, still occupying the Floridas, still obstructing American commerce at Mobile, and still not showing any willingness to settle the boundaries of Louisiana. Jefferson's policy was to force Spain out of North America altogether by any means short of overt war. He had sent

Monroe to Madrid in the hope of reaching an amicable agreement to be ratified in a treaty. But Monroe had no better success with the Spanish government at Madrid than had Charles Pinckney, who had preceded him there. The Spanish, indeed, perhaps encouraged by Napoleon, adopted an attitude so close to belligerence that Monroe was left with no course but to ask for his passports.

Upon receipt of the news from Madrid, Jefferson resolved to ask Congress for power to deal with Spain by whatever military means might be necessary. His annual message in December, 1805, dealing with Spain in such strong language as to border on a call for a declaration of war, was enthusiastically received. In the Southwest particularly, Spain was more of a nuisance than ever, and other sections of the country seemed to take pride in the President's determination not to be intimidated by the unwelcome Southern neighbors. But Jefferson had no desire to make war on Spain if other means would obtain the same result. Three days after his annual message, he sent a secret message to Congress proposing that he be empowered to use Treasury balances to negotiate with France on the Spanish question. There was reason to suppose that Talleyrand and Napoleon would exert the necessary pressure on Spain if the price were right. Jefferson had calculated the cost of war as against the cost of this sort of international bribery, and concluded that to buy would be cheaper than to shoot. Thus he favored an active military policy to keep the Spanish out of American territory, with an accompanying effort to buy the Floridas, either by bribing the French or by outright purchase from Spain. This policy, pursued for many years not only by Jefferson but by his successors Madison and Monroe, succeeded in gradually eliminating Spanish influence along the southern borders of the United States. But Congress, with John Randolph opposing the President, would not allow the funds for purchase, and, in any event, the Spanish were by no means prepared to sell.

The presence of Spain along the borders of the United States as well as the restless condition of affairs in Mexico provided Aaron Burr with reasons, persuasive to many honest men of the West, for the curious adventure upon which he presently embarked, to his own final undoing and the unleashed fury of Thomas Jefferson.

In April, 1806, Burr called on Jefferson in Washington, apparently hoping he could still rehabilitate himself in the Republican party and regain the favor of the executive. If, however, he seriously thought there was any chance that Jefferson would give him an appointment in the government, his manner toward the President was certainly poorly calculated. He reminded his former leader that he had worked hard for the party, helped in the election of 1800, and always, so he said, supported the administration. He recalled Jefferson's letter of December, 1800, suggesting that a cabinet post might have been offered to Burr if he had not become Vice-president. He then, fatally, ended his address by observing that he had it in his power to do the President great harm, but that he wished him well. To Jefferson it looked much like an attempt at blackmail. He let Burr down as easily as he could, but with sufficient firmness. He pointed out that while Burr had talents that might have served the nation well, he had lost the confidence of the people and was therefore simply not suited for a federal appointment. Without touching upon the duel with Hamilton, Jefferson discreetly referred Burr's loss of favor to his elimination in the 1804 vice-presidential race. As for the harm that Burr could do him, Jefferson records what he said on that score in some detail:

> I knew no cause why he should desire it, but, at the same time, I feared no injury which any man could do me; that I never had done a single act, or been concerned in any transaction, which I feared to have fully laid open, or which could do me any hurt, if truly stated; that I had never done a single thing with a view to my personal interest, or that of any friend, or with any other view than that of the greatest public good; that, therefore, no threat or fear on that head would ever be a motive of action with me.

One could wish that Jefferson had not spoken quite so

sanctimoniously. He was certainly one of the least corruptible men ever to hold high office in the United States. But he was not a saint. The Walker affair he conveniently forgot, unless perhaps he no longer feared its revelation. And in one case, probably only one, he had in fact gone well beyond the bounds of propriety to help an old friend. The friend was John Page, one of the two or three closest friends of his life. Page had served his country and Virginia well and had only recently served a term as governor. But his finances were in desperate condition, and Jefferson, to provide him with some income, had appointed him Commissioner of Loans in Richmond. However, Page had become so debilitated that he could no longer perform the work. At the very moment he was boasting to Burr, Jefferson was doing everything he could to keep the federal salary for his friend. He tried to appoint young Benjamin Harrison to the post, the latter having agreed in advance to make over the salary to Page. When the Senate properly refused confirmation, Jefferson proposed to appoint Page's son, with the understanding that the money would go to the father. Fortunately the Senate was not faced with the necessity of turning down this barefaced piece of nepotism, since the younger Page declined the proposition.

Jefferson's bravado was thus not only poorly suited to his own best sensibilities, but even worse, it was ineffective. Burr could not, it was true, hurt Jefferson's personal reputation, but he could and did bring upon him political tribulations such as no other embittered statesman has ever brought upon a President of the United States. The Burr conspiracy is a thorny and obscure chapter in American history which has never been wholly or satisfactorily explained. Nathan Schachner, biographer of Jefferson, Hamilton, and Burr, shows considerable sympathy for Burr and little for Jefferson. Henry Adams, on the other hand, found Burr a first-class scoundrel and Jefferson a dupe, if a somewhat vindictive one. Other historians have little good to say of Burr but divide on the propriety and effectiveness of Jefferson's role as prosecutor. Here we shall have to be content with a summary sketch to serve only the purpose of showing how Burr disrupted Jefferson's second term and how the President dealt with him.

Burr's plans had evidently been formulated well before he made his last effort to get a federal appointment from Jefferson. At any rate he put them into execution soon after leaving Washington. His scheme appears to have been twofold: (1) to raise a private army of discomfited Westerners who would march with him against the Spanish on the borders of Louisiana, then proceed into Mexico for the purpose of revolutionizing that immense Spanish colony, detaching it from Spain and establishing Burr as the head of an independent government; (2) to detach the Western states from the United States and attach them instead to the Louisiana-Mexico conquest, thus creating a vast new empire.

Burr had at least two coconspirators, who were fully informed of his plan: one Herman Blennerhasset, of Blennerhasset's Island in the Ohio River near Marietta, a wealthy Irish immigrant; and General James Wilkinson of the United States Army in Louisiana. Blennerhasset, undoubtedly influenced by his wife, seems to have been simply a well-meaning dupe of Burr's engaging personality and expansive imagination. But Wilkinson was, on any showing, a thoroughgoing scoundrel. In addition, Burr attracted to his scheme of moving against Spain—but not of detaching the Western states— several hundred men, many of whom wished to settle in Texas to make a new start at farming. And many leading figures of the Western states and territories, while not signing on, gave some degree of approval to Burr's expedition, partly because Burr let it be thought that he had the tacit approval of the Administration for a military undertaking that could be accomplished by a private army without bringing the United States into war. The intensity of anti-Spanish feeling in the West can be judged from the names of men who were in one way or another associated with Burr. Included were Andrew Jackson, Senator John Breckenridge, Henry Clay, Senator John Adair, and Governor William Henry Harrison of the Indiana territory.

Blennerhasset's Island was Burr's headquarters, and to that command post came couriers and interested citizens. From there the expedition set forth in flat boats down the river to seek their own and Burr's fortune. But nothing ever came of it. After the posting of a presidential proclamation against the enterprise, the thousand or more men Burr had told Wilkinson to expect dwindled to not more than fifty.* Wilkinson became frightened and began arresting Burr's followers wherever he could lay his hands on them, and Burr himself became a fugitive from justice until captured and brought to Richmond for trial. Wilkinson had good reason to wish he had never involved himself with Burr. He had, while enjoying the confidence of Washington, Adams, and Jefferson successively, been for many years a paid agent of the Spanish government. He was at first attracted to Burr's plan apparently because it promised riches and power far beyond what he was getting by serving at once the United States and the Spanish king. But when he saw that the wrath of the President and of the government was aroused by Burr's illegal and treasonous behavior, he quickly concluded that Burr would fail and that if he himself did not turn his coat quickly and obviously he would lose not only his various retainers but perhaps also his skin. He therefore informed on Burr and acted the part of an outraged American patriot.

Jefferson had first been warned of Burr's activities by Joseph Daviess, the United States Attorney for Kentucky. But though Daviess gave specific information and was a reliable officer, Jefferson dismissed the whole business as rumor, since Daviess appeared to be accusing all the Republican leaders of the West, including Jefferson's intimate friend Breckinridge, of plotting to split the Union. Jefferson was, of course, correct to suppose that there was no truth in such a story, but there was abundant truth in the story of Burr's intentions. When later information corroborated much of Daviess' report, the President issued his sharply worded proclamation against the expedition and ordered Burr and all his cohorts arrested. Some were apprehended at Blennerhasset's Island, others at various points along the river, and Burr himself finally was brought in after taking flight into the woods.

Jefferson never seems to have doubted that Burr was guilty,

---

* Accounts vary as to exactly how many stayed with Burr to the end. Jefferson, however, seems to have belittled Burr a bit too much by his estimate of thirty or less. See his letter to Samuel Du Pont, page 144.

not only of the illegal raising of a private army for an illegal move against Spain, but of overt treason. The two men had never liked each other, and could not have been expected to do so. Jefferson was a philosopher-statesman for whom the art of politics, and the infighting of politics, were means to the end of building a great and good society. To Burr politics was the means to personal advancement in prestige and power. His attachment to Jefferson in the 1790's may have involved some element of principle, but chiefly he had taken the short odds that the people would in the end prefer the author of the Declaration of Independence to the signer of the Sedition Act. The unreliability of his devotion was revealed clearly enough in his equivocal attitude toward the unexpected electoral tie between himself and Jefferson in 1800. Thereafter he had more than once made political medicine with Federalists. He broke with them only when he found them bent on an effort at secession by the North which he knew was impractical.

As for Jefferson, questions about Burr's character had been placed in his mind by the Clintons as early as 1791. The news he regularly received from New York was typically slanted against Burr. But Burr himself never behaved in a way to offset the prejudices planted against him in Jefferson's mind. On the contrary, as events moved, Jefferson's confidence in Burr vanished entirely. By 1806 he considered the ex-Vice-president no better than a public enemy. Convinced by Wilkinson's story and by the reports of his own investigators that Burr was a traitor, he resolved to secure his conviction and removal from the public stage. Jefferson's whole attitude toward the Burr episode is well set forth in a letter he wrote at the time of the trial to his friend Samuel Du Pont, French philosopher become American:

Burr's conspiracy has been one of the most flagitious of which history will ever furnish an example. He had combined the objects of separating the western states from us, of adding Mexico to them, and of placing himself at their head. But he who could expect to effect such objects by the aid of American citizens, must be perfectly ripe for Bedlam. Yet although there is not a man in the United States who is not satisfied of the depth of his guilt, such are the jealous provisions of our laws in favor of the accused, and against the accuser, that I question if he can be convicted. . . . This affair has been a great confirmation in my mind of the innate strength of the form of our government. He had probably induced near a thousand men to engage with him, by making them believe the government connived at it. A proclamation alone, by undeceiving them, so completely disarmed him, that he had not above thirty men left, ready to go all lengths with him . . . made up of fugitives from justice, or from their debts . . . and of adventurers and speculators of all descriptions.

Jefferson's prediction was well founded. The court proceedings at Richmond were from the beginning disheartening to the Administration. Chief Justice John Marshall, whose decision in *Marbury* v. *Madison* a few years before had dismayed Jefferson by its claim for the Supreme Court of the power of judicial review, assigned himself the duty of presiding. It was evident from the first moment that his court would give the accused every possible advantage. Marshall's honor could not fairly be questioned, but his hope that Burr would be vindicated and the standing of the Administration thereby diminished was an open secret. The grand jury, despite a parade of government witnesses, at first would not indict Burr for treason, and a new case had to be developed. Eventually there were indictments both for treason and for misdemeanors. Burr was defended by stern anti-Jeffersonian Luther Martin and by Jefferson's old friend and colleague Edmund Randolph, one of the greatest lawyers in Virginia history. Against this team U.S. Attorney George Hay, with the assistance of Attorney General Caesar Rodney, could not make a really effective case. Wilkinson, the star witness, succeeded only in alienating the court and directing suspicion toward himself. His testimony and exhibits, including a cipher letter from Burr, probably if presented by a different witness would probably have convicted Burr; but as presented by Wilkinson they probably saved him.

Jefferson, his personal feelings strongly mixed in with his sense of duty, watched from a distance with great anxiety. At one point the defense asked Justice Marshall to subpoena Jefferson himself as well as all his papers on the case. The President, shocked and angered that even Marshall would issue such a subpoena, resolved not to honor it, on the ground that the coequal status of the three branches of government forbade any one of them to require actions of another except as prescribed in the Constitution. He was sensible, of course, of the political implications of a subpoena coming from the bench of John Marshall. After consultation with his cabinet, he decided to send the relevant papers to Richmond but to ignore the summons for his own appearance. Since the summons, fortunately, had not yet been served, the court wisely decided, once the papers were delivered, not to press for Jefferson's personal appearance. Thus was a constitutional crisis averted and the unwritten but still unquestioned immunity of the President of the United States from response to court orders established.

At the conclusion of the trial Marshall instructed the jury that for conviction of treason under the Constitution there must be two witnesses to the same overt act, and that no overt act had been established in the proceedings. This, of course, amounted to a directed verdict of acquittal, and the jury acted quickly to free Burr. Jefferson was convinced that there had been a miscarriage of justice and that Marshall and other assisting judges had acted deliberately to humiliate the Administration for political reasons. He demanded that the prosecution save the face of the Administration by at least obtaining a conviction on the misdemeanor charge. At the same time he proposed a constitutional amendment to make the judges of the federal courts directly subject to the will of the electorate. He was frustrated again on both counts. Further prosecution appeared now so futile that Burr never did come to trial again, and Jefferson's amendment, though it was introduced into Congress, never generated significant support. Perhaps Jefferson's only accomplishment after nearly a year of almost frantic preoccupation with the Burr conspiracy was the final elimination of Burr himself from public life. That ill-starred adventurer of early United States political drama fled to Europe, where for a time his wild schemes excited some interest; but after the Napoleonic Wars he returned to New York to end his days in obscurity.

If Jefferson's efforts to punish Burr and his fellow conspirators ended in failure, at least his policy of forbearance with Spain was more successful. An on-the-spot agreement between military commanders to the mutual withdrawal of troops relieved the tension along the borders, and the Spanish government prudently decided to relax its irritating pressures upon American settlers. The unsettled boundary dispute was thus removed from the immediate agenda, to the relief of both sides.

But the increasing pressure from Great Britain was of another order of seriousness. Impressment of American seamen, to serve under duress on British vessels, and seizure of American ships as prizes, when suspected of being in trade with France or even in trade which might be helpful to France, were practices intolerable to a sovereign power. And both were being extended rather than limited. In April, 1806, at Jefferson's urging, Congress enacted a nonimportation act, giving the President power to stop the flow of commerce from Britain to the United States. Jefferson hoped that by economic pressure of this sort he could persuade the British to moderate their policy. With the act in suspension, but available as a gambit in negotiation, he sent Monroe to London to try for a full-scale settlement. Jefferson's hopes were high for the moment, since Charles James Fox and the Whigs, who had just come to power in England, were known to have maintained over the years the spirit of friendly acceptance of American independence they had shown before the Revolution.

But Monroe's mission ended in another failure. Fox died soon after coming to power, and his successors were differently disposed. Monroe and William Pinkney, who was sent to join him in the mission, signed a treaty with British Minister Canning which they both knew was quite unsatisfactory to the United States. It neither committed the British to stop their spoliations nor mentioned impressment. The latter was touched upon in an initialed paper not included in the treaty and not binding the British government. Monroe sent the treaty to Madison and Jefferson with regret but with insistence that it was the best that could be obtained. Monroe himself was restive in England. He had resented the arrival of Pinkney and felt himself ill used by his old friends in the Administration. And he was being flattered by John Randolph with the idea that the "true Republicans" wished Monroe, not Madison, to succeed Jefferson in the election of 1808. When the President and Secretary of State rejected Monroe's treaty, as they quite properly did, Monroe in anger and bitter disappointment left immediately for home.

The split between Madison and Monroe, which plagued the last two or three years of Jefferson's Administration, was precipitated by John Randolph. In retrospect it is difficult to see how Randolph ever wielded as much influence as he did. He was a brilliant speaker and a rather imposing personality, but at no time in his public career did he show balanced judgment or offer the kind of deference to colleagues which is characteristic of successful legislators. Yet almost upon his arrival in the House in 1798, he took a high place among the Republican leadership. In 1801 Jefferson trusted him and looked upon him as a main source of Congressional support. The House made him chairman of the Ways and Means Committee. At first he did act as Administration spokesman, but before long he was intriguing against Madison and adopting an equivocal attitude toward the President. He directed the House impeachment of Justice Chase in 1805, but by 1806 he was in open opposition. He announced that he was neither a Republican nor a Federalist but a "third something," and as "tertium quids" he and his small band of followers were afterward known. Randolph's stinging attacks on Jefferson, whom he dubbed "St. Thomas of Cantlingbury," were odious enough to the President. But to his son-in-law Thomas Mann Randolph they were so intolerable as almost to precipitate a duel. Jefferson had to plead with T. M. Randolph, himself never quite stable, to remember his family and his responsibilities instead of risking his life in a useless contest with the violent Randolph of Roanoke.

Monroe, the lifelong intimate friend of the President, but now become querulous and impatient from his diplomatic frustrations in Madrid and London, was an ideal target for John Randolph's poisoned darts—darts, that is, carrying anti-Madison venom. Monroe proved to be both honorable and gullible, as well as hurt by the treatment he was receiving from his two great colleagues. He never declared his candidacy against Madison, but he did not discourage Randolph and others who sought to use him to prevent Madison's succession. Jefferson was caught in a political and personal dilemma by this maneuver. He had settled in his mind upon Madison as the best man to succeed him, and he was satisfied that the country agreed. But Monroe had been his protégé since the Revolution, had stood by him stoutly through all the political tribulations of the 1790's, and deserved well of the Republican party, which he had played no small part in building. Referring to the two men as the "twin pillars of my happiness," Jefferson adopted a neutral public posture. Monroe seems to have been satisfied with this attitude. But he must have known that behind the scenes Jefferson could and did easily influence the Republican congressional caucus in Madison's favor.

John Randolph's apostasy in 1806 has often been regretted by historians sympathetic to Jefferson. Henry Adams, for example, lamented that "the true Virginian school of politics was forever ruined; Macon was soon driven from the speakership, and Nicholson forced onto the bench; Gallatin was paralyzed; Mr. Jefferson, Mr. Madison, and ultimately Mr. Monroe were thrown into the hands of the northern democrats, whose loose political morality henceforward found no check." But from another perspective the defection of the "tertium quids" was certainly good for the country. Randolph, Macon, John Taylor of Caroline, and their compatriots might call themselves true Jeffersonians. But unlike the founding spirit of Jeffersonian democracy, they were doctrinaire. To them the Republican system worked out by Jefferson, Madison, and Gallatin in their opposition roles of the 1790's was a "true belief" not to be altered in the face of circumstance. Jefferson was also a Jeffersonian, but his guiding adherence was always to those principles of liberty he had set forth in the 1770's as the universal rights of man. A political system he considered as means, not end, and like the skillful politician he was, he never hesitated to adapt when adaptation was best calculated to secure the liberties to which his public career was dedicated. Thus the split with the "tertium quids" had the long-term effect of putting the Democratic-Republican party on a new footing with the nation as a loose federation of the various interest groups of which the nation is composed, a footing it has sought to maintain ever since. As for the short run, before the end of 1807 Jefferson had won the allegiance of John Quincy Adams. In swapping Randolph for Adams, the President had all the better of the "deal,"—and so certainly had the nation.

What brought Adams, and many others of his former opponents, to Jefferson's side was the manner in which he handled the provocation of the "Chesapeake" affair in the spring of 1807. In March some men from the British warship "Halifax" had taken flight from their ship at Norfolk and sought asylum. They, as well as some other sailors from British ships, enlisted for service on the American frigate "Chesapeake," then preparing to join the Mediterranean squadron. British representations to Secretary of the Navy Smith resulted in an investigation which satisfied Smith that at least some of the men were in fact Americans who had previously been impressed by the British. He refused to send them back. British retaliation came on June 22, when the "Chesapeake" sailed out of Hampton Roads. A British fleet was lying out to sea waiting for a French squadron anchored at Annapolis. The commander of the British force, seeing the "Chesapeake" coming out under full sail, ordered the "Leopard" to intercept her. Before the "Chesapeake" could maneuver into fighting position, she was the victim of a surprise attack and her superstructure was blown apart. Captain Barron was forced to surrender. The British boarded the "Chesapeake" and took off the sailors who were the subject of the dispute. The American ship was then left to crawl into port as best she could.

From the President to the man in the street, Americans were instantly brought to a fighting mood. Jefferson ordered American ports closed to British warships and instructed harbor defense forces to seize any such ships if they came into American waters. A call went out for 100,000 militia to defend the coast, and the navy's platform gunboats, Jefferson's favored means of national defense, were made ready for action in all the harbors. Monroe and Pinkney in London were instructed to demand apology and reparations for the unprovoked attack on the American warship. And the President finally invoked the Nonimportation Act of 1806.

But Jefferson's anger was better disciplined than that of many other Americans. He wished to avoid the bloodshed and the expense of war, and especially he wished to avoid a precipitate declaration of war, which would find as many as 20,000 American merchant sailors at sea and helpless against the British navy. It would take weeks before he could even fully alert the American squadron in the Mediterranean. Meanwhile he felt that the time had now come when his consistent policy—in the twentieth century it would be called economic sanctions—would be effective. While public opinion boiled and while the British equivocated in London for months, Jefferson, firmly insisting upon restraint, restricted his retaliatory measures to nonimportation and to denial of port facilities and supplies to British ships of war. When the British commissioner, Rose, arriving to adjust the "Chesapeake" affair, told Madison that there would be no reparation unless Jefferson's proclamation against British warships was rescinded, the President resisted the pressure to declare war. In England, meanwhile, the government had on November 11 issued Orders in Council, so-called, which would require any American ship intending to call at any European port to call first at an English port. This was England's answer to the Berlin and Milan decrees of Napoleon. Jefferson's response to all these decrees and orders was to ask Congress for a full-scale embargo.

Over the violent but ineffectual opposition of the Federalists, Congress authorized the embargo on December 21, 1807. It was on this issue that restive Senator John Quincy

Adams crossed the aisle to join the Republicans in support of Jefferson. He was to be punished, soon after, by the loss of his Senate seat at the hands of Federalists in the Boston State-house. But old John Adams, from his retreat at Braintree, approved his son's action. Neither probably then suspected that the younger man's courageous decision had put him on the road to the presidency.

Under the terms of the embargo Jefferson could, and did, prohibit all commerce with foreign countries. Coastwise shipping was permitted, under special license. But by early spring, when Rose was trying to negotiate with Madison, all other legal shipping had stopped. The great ports of Boston, New York, Philadelphia, and Baltimore were tied up. Ships were dismantled, cargoes stored, and seamen and longshoremen laid off. Merchants, needless to say, were the first to suffer economic depression. In New England, where Federalist sympathies were still remarkably strong, there was talk of secession and there was systematic defiance of the law. Under pretense of a coastwise mission, many a New England vessel in fact left its prescribed course and headed for the West Indies or for Europe. Merchants preferred the risk of capture and seizure of their cargoes by British or French warships to the complete cessation of business. In economic terms they were right, since their carrying trade was so immense and so profitable that they could afford the loss of as many as half their ships. Torn between patriotism, in the form of obedience to the government of the hated Jefferson, and economic advantage, obtainable by defiance of that government, many New England merchants, it must unhappily be admitted, chose economic advantage. They were encouraged by some of the more extreme Federalist politicians, like Senator Timothy Pickering, the former Secretary of State. Pickering, in fact, almost as though he were the agent of a sovereign power, opened communication with British Commissioner Rose. There is reason to believe that Rose was influenced by Pickering to believe that the country was not behind Jefferson and for this reason maintained a less conciliatory attitude than his instructions required.

Given the disaffection of so many influential New Englanders, the embargo was almost unenforceable. It is always difficult to persuade a free people that self-discipline, especially costly self-discipline, is an advantageous public policy. In the case of the embargo it was doubly difficult, since the effects of the cessation of commerce were immediately felt at home and immediately discernible even by those who were not particularly affected, while the effects abroad could not be observed and would not even be heard of for weeks and months. It was under these nearly impossible circumstances that Jefferson's great experiment of peaceful economic sanctions as an antidote to aggression was tried and found wanting. All through his last months in office he had to contend not only with disobedience and with vicious political attacks in the newspapers, but with the gradual defection of his supporters. In the end almost no one was for continuing the embargo, not even Madison and Gallatin. In vain Jefferson encouraged the domestic manufactures which sprang up to provide goods to replace the interdicted imports. Manufactures flourished, and ironically enough it was the policy of Jefferson, directed to restoring the freedom of the seas, which determined that the United States should be an industrial power, not the industrial philosophy of his old enemy Hamilton. But the success of manufactures did not alter the views of the antiembargo people.

Jefferson, as always, knew when political necessity dictated a change in tactics. Acting once again through the agency of William Giles, he arranged for a measure, which Congress enacted on February 21, 1809, to repeal the embargo against all except British and French shipping. Thus he appeared to be making a major concession without seriously affecting his policy of sanctions against the aggressors. At the same time he agreed to an act to repeal the embargo entirely by June 1, 1809. Thus he extricated himself from his untenable political position by stages, and left Madison, the newly elected President, with a clear opportunity to develop a better policy if he could, or else to go to war.

Jefferson's presidency suffered not only at the hands of his antiembargo opponents at the time but for more than a hundred years thereafter was severely criticized on the same grounds by historians, including such thoughtful scholars as Henry Adams. It has only been in the period of intensive historical research following World War I that documents demonstrating the effectiveness of his policy have been extracted from archives and published. The record now available goes far toward vindicating Jefferson's judgment and his measures. There is no doubt that the British economy, as well as the French, was very severely strained by the pressure of the embargo on its North American artery and by secondary effects on its West Indies trade. The pinch was so stringent that there is good reason to believe that another year or less would have been sufficient to bring the British government to serious and conciliatory negotiations.* The Orders in Council would no doubt have been repealed or significantly modified and an agreement on impressments would probably have been reached. The War of 1812 could almost certainly have been avoided entirely. In the unlikely event that war had been the British response in 1809 or 1810, it would certainly have been under conditions much more favorable to the American side than was the case in 1812.

But such speculations will not allow us to rewrite the history of Jefferson's unhappy second term. In the events as they actually transpired, he could take satisfaction from the continued devotion of the great majority of the people, who quickly forgave him for their momentary annoyance over the embargo. Even at the height of the attacks on his policy, the nomination of Madison against Monroe had been literally "no contest," and Madison was elected by a solid majority. Jefferson could feel pride and vindication when his closest political ally was inaugurated to succeed him on March 4, 1809.

And the blessed retirement to Monticello he had so long yearned for could now no longer be denied him. Two years earlier he had written in a private letter to Dickinson of his deep distaste for office: ". . . to myself, personally, it brings nothing but unceasing drudgery and daily loss of friends." Now, two days before he left the White House for good, Jef-

---

* Commercial accounts as well as the testimony of interested commercial men and public officials are cited by Louis M. Sears in his *Jefferson and the Embargo* (1927).

ferson wrote a moving letter to Samuel Du Pont, then in France:

> Within a few days I retire to my family, my books and farms; and having gained the harbor myself, I shall look on my friends still buffeting the storm with anxiety indeed, but not with envy. Never did a prisoner, released from his chains, feel such relief as I shall on shaking off the shackles of power. Nature intended me for the tranquil pursuits of science, by rendering them my supreme delight. But the enormities of the times in which I have lived, have forced me to take a part in resisting them, and to commit myself on the boisterous ocean of political passions. I thank God for the opportunity of retiring from them without censure, and carrying with me the most consoling proofs of public approbation. I leave everything in the hands of men so able to take care of them, that if we are destined to meet misfortunes, it will be because no human wisdom could avert them. Should you return to the United States, perhaps your curiosity may lead you to visit the hermit of Monticello. . . .
>
> P.S. If you return to us, bring a couple of pair of true-bred shepherd's dogs. You will add a valuable possession to a country now beginning to pay great attention to the raising of sheep.

Perhaps the postscript is the most characteristic note in a characteristic letter. At any rate Jefferson had not by any means ignored either science—he was still President of the American Philosophical Society—or his farms, where he had spent each year one short and one long vacation. Entries in his *Garden Book* were scattered during the years of his presidency, but records and notations in the *Farm Book* and detailed records in his account books show that he never permitted public affairs to dominate his life as completely as would have been expected of most men. In fact, one of his most cherished projects, a large grain mill on the Rivanna, was finally begun in 1803, completed in 1806, and leased for its first operation in 1807. And his private correspondence, both with planter friends at home and with his numerous scientific friends abroad, was maintained throughout his whole Administration almost as zestfully as ever.

He was approaching sixty-six when the moment of retirement finally came, and he was fortunate to have better than average health. During most of 1807 and 1808 he had been plagued with headaches. He had all his life been occasionally troubled by what was then called migraine, and there is no doubt that the frequency and intensity of these attacks increased during the stresses of the Burr trials and the bitter political fight over nonimportation and the embargo. But Jefferson bore his affliction well and with little serious debility. His constitution was robust, his habits of exercise healthful, and his diet, though rich, sufficiently balanced to keep him normally in good condition to ward off the usual attacks of minor diseases. He had never had a major illness, and when he left the White House he was to enjoy more than seventeen years of active retirement, during most of which his health was good.

His letter to Du Pont was overly optimistic on the score of Madison's wisdom, as events shortly demonstrated. But Jefferson was probably correct in his estimate that the nation was in the best available hands. At any rate, he was himself no longer responsible for public policy, wise or unwise. He left the presidency with the nation in good financial condition, domestic manufactures burgeoning, agriculture reviving quickly with the end of embargo, the size of the country more than doubled, civil liberties secure, and the great majority of the citizens content. Citizens and historians would ever afterward debate, often sharply, the efficacy of his measures as President and the wisdom of his conception of the presidential office; but his place as one of the few really great Presidents of the United States was established beyond dispute.

Chapter 9.

THE "HERMIT" OF MONTICELLO

Ex-President Thomas Jefferson remained in Washington only a week after seeing his friend and successor, James Madison, inaugurated. His personal belongings, which filled an inordinate number of packing cases with the accumulation of eight years, he sent mainly by flatboat down the Potomac. To his lasting sorrow, a thief, searching the boat for valuables, threw one carton into the river, apparently in disgust when he found it contained only papers. Those papers were Jefferson's laboriously collected records of the vocabularies of North American Indian tongues, a unique work of scholarship which he had planned, in his retirement, to study and interpret. Only a few stray sheets were rescued from the mud along the shore.

Jefferson himself left Washington on the 11th and reached Monticello on March 15, 1809, to begin the final installment of his long and richly varied life. It was to be the longest installment, if not the most rewarding or yet as happy as he had so long dreamed it would be. Like all old men he had to suffer the loss of well-loved friends who died before him. His finances, never sound, eventually became chaotic and desperate. And his son-in-law, Thomas Mann Randolph, always a brilliant but moody man, finally lapsed into melancholia soon after serving a term as governor of Virginia. But these and lesser causes of unhappiness were perhaps evenly balanced by remarkable good health until almost the end of his life at the age of eighty-three, by the devotion of his proliferating family, by the continuing friendship of men like Madison and Monroe, who outlived him, by the deference paid to him by people from all over the world by letter or visit, and, not least, by the renewal in a matchless correspondence of his friendship with John Adams.

On April 3, 1809, Jefferson received a throng of neighbors and friends at Monticello. They had come to pay their respects and to welcome him home. For the occasion he wrote out a short talk which is full of the felicities that always marked his style. His theme was a restatement of the constant theme of his adult life:

> Long absent on duties which the history of a wonderful era made incumbent on those called to them, the pomp, the turmoil, the bustle and splendor of office, have drawn but deeper sighs for the tranquil and irresponsible occupations of private life, for the enjoyment of an affectionate intercourse with you, my neighbors and friends, and the endearments of family love, which nature has given us all, as the sweetener of every hour. For these I gladly lay down the distressing burden of power, and seek, with my fellow citizens, repose and safety under the watchful cares, the labors and perplexities of younger and abler minds.

He touched again upon his sense of the approval of the country for his Administration, but perhaps he was moved by fresh recollections of the bitter attacks he had suffered when he concluded with something like a plea for a credit reference from those who knew him best:

> Of you, then, my neighbors, I may ask, in the face of the world, "whose ox have I taken, or whom have I defrauded? Whom have I oppressed, or of whose hand have I received a bribe to blind mine eyes therewith?" On your verdict I rest with conscious security.

For many years Jefferson's attitude toward retirement, on the one hand, and politics, on the other, remained as ambivalent as ever. He boasted, as he had done after leaving Washington's cabinet fifteen years before, that he never read newspapers or had anything to do with public affairs. But he maintained a highly political correspondence with Madison, fairly often suggested people for appointment to federal office, and stated his opinion to the President on most of the major questions facing the government. At first, predictably enough, Madison appealed to Jefferson for advice. But Jefferson continued to give Madison the benefit of his opinions even when the new President had gained greater confidence and formed his own circle of advisers. Madison was always polite, but there is little evidence that Jefferson played a behind-the-scenes role of any consequence. When Monroe succeeded Madison in 1817, Jefferson's influence had dwindled to almost nothing, except, as we shall see, in the formulation of the Monroe Doctrine.

A famous letter to General Kosciusko, the Polish patriot who had fought in the American Revolution, is often cited to show the quality of Jefferson's life in retirement. What is less often noticed is that the passage about his personal life at Monticello occurs at the end of a long discussion of his Administration. This was in 1810. Two years later he was deeply concerned about the war with Britain. The failure of his own policy of peace with economic sanctions left him in a mood much like that of the "war hawks" who had pressed Madison to go to war. He thought the United States should make one more effort to buy Florida, failing which it should be taken by force of arms. And Cuba also should be annexed, presumably by a military expedition, as a permanent southern boundary of the United States. In the war with England he was confident Canada would be taken, and thus "we should have such an empire for liberty as she has never surveyed since the creation."

But as the war went badly, Jefferson's views changed slowly from unrestrained anger with men like General Hull, who had lost at Detroit and whom he thought should be "shot for treachery," to a more sober calculation of the need for permanent friendly relations with England. In 1815, before he knew the results of the peace conference at Ghent, he wrote to his boyhood friend James Maury, who had lived all his adult life in England, urging pacification and close cooperation between their two countries:

I hope an arrangement is already made on this subject. Have you no statesmen who can look forward two or three score years? It is but forty years since the battle of Lexington. One third of those now living saw that day, when we were about two millions of people, and have lived to see this, when we are ten millions. One-third of those now living, who see us at ten millions, will live another forty years, and see us forty millions; and looking forward only through such a portion of time as has passed since you and I were scanning Virgil together (which I believe is near three score years), we shall be seen to have a population of eighty millions, and of not more than double the average density of the present. What may not such a people be worth to England as customers and friends? and what might she not apprehend from such a nation as enemies? Now, what is the price we ask for our friendship? Justice, and the comity usually observed between nation and nation. . . .

One of the disasters of the least successful of America's wars was the British burning of Washington in 1814. But that moment of national humiliation brought Jefferson an opportunity to do yet another unique service to his country. The Library of Congress, which he had fostered, was wholly destroyed, and of all the vandalisms of the war Jefferson thought this the worst. No sooner had the British retreated and the government begun to take up its functions in Washington again than he wrote to his friend Samuel Smith, editor of *The National Intelligencer,* authorizing him to offer the Congress a chance to purchase the library of Monticello as a replacement. "I learn from the newspapers," he wrote, "that the vandalism of our enemy has triumphed at Washington over science as well as the arts, by the destruction of the public library with the noble edifice in which it was deposited." Jefferson had some ten thousand books and pamphlets, carefully catalogued, which he had collected over a period of fifty years. There is no doubt that it was the finest private library in the new world and a good deal richer source for legislative information and wisdom than the infant library lost in the

Washington fire. Congress accepted the offer and bought Jefferson's library, minus a few hundred volumes he wished to retain for himself, for $23,950. The Jefferson collection forms the nucleus from which has grown, in the century and half since, the greatest library in the world. Though it is not marked with his name, the Library of Congress is perhaps a more fitting Jefferson memorial than the Greek temple on the banks of the Potomac.

The War of 1812 once again aroused sentiments of secession in New England. Like the embargo, war cut down the carrying trade to a minimum, but, unlike the embargo, it left no safe room for piracy. The merchants were sorely hit and economic depression was felt along the wharves of the coastal towns. Paradoxically, the trend toward domestic manufactures, so long the demand of the Federalists and now begun in earnest, now seemed to the New England men of commerce and finance not the way to a strong and independent nation but to bankruptcy. Secession and separate peace were the better alternative, so at least thought such Federalists as Timothy Pickering. The Hartford Convention of 1814 brought their movement to the point of fateful decision, from which the leaders withdrew in confusion. Jefferson, who had himself been prepared to go almost to the point of secession in 1798 on the issue of civil liberties, had no fear that a movement to secede for economic reasons would carry the people with it. To his long-time friend Elbridge Gerry, a strongly antisecessionist Massachusetts Republican who was soon to become Vice-president, he expressed his views in pungent language:

> When the questions of separatism and rebellion shall be nakedly proposed to them [the people of New England], the Gores and the Pickerings will find their levees crowded with silk-stocking gentry, but no yeomanry, an army of officers, without soldiers.

Later he wrote to Lafayette that the American "yeomanry" could not be compared to the *canaille* of Paris in an earlier day:

[161]

The cement of this Union is in the heart-blood of every American. I do not believe there is on earth a government established on so immovable a basis. Let them, in any State, even in Massachusetts itself, raise the standard of separation, and its citizens will rise in mass, and do justice themselves on their own incendiaries.

Before his presidency had entirely faded from the realm of action, the ex-President found himself called upon to answer a lawsuit brought by an old friend, former New York Republican Edward Livingston. The suit was for damages in the amount of $100,000 for having ordered Livingston and his workmen off a tract of land known as the Batture along the river front at New Orleans. Jefferson was alarmed at the prospect of the suit since his financial condition was already almost unmanageable and because the case was to be tried before his old enemy John Marshall. Though Livingston had purchased the land quite legally, both Congress in a resolution and the President in an executive order had declared the Batture to be in the federal public domain. A New Orleans court had upheld Livingston, but Jefferson had nevertheless ordered Livingston to vacate, believing that the land was essential for the national defense. Livingston complied with the order, but now that Jefferson had retired he brought suit against him as a private citizen. The two men exchanged lengthy pamphlets which debated the issue in detail and set the stage for a spectacular trial. However, Jefferson's counsel, William Wirt and George Hay, argued that the suit should be dismissed for lack of jurisdiction since it should have been brought in New Orleans, where the disputed land was situated. The court agreed. Livingston thereafter gave up his efforts, Jefferson having no assets in New Orleans to sue for. Ex-President John Adams regretted, like Jefferson, that the case was settled on a technicality, thus leaving unresolved the crucial question whether a President could be sued as a private citizen for acts performed in his public capacity. "Good God!" wrote Adams to Jefferson, "is a President of the United

States to be subject to a private action of every individual?"*

The renewal of his long-interrupted friendship with Adams was certainly one of the happiest events of Jefferson's declining years. After the abortive correspondence between himself and Abigail Adams at the time of Maria's death in 1804, there had been no communication whatever between the two aging patriots. Jefferson knew in a general way that Adams approved his foreign policy, since John Quincy Adams had come over to the Republicans on that issue with his father's blessing; and he knew, of course, that the elder Adams could have no use for the high Federalists and their secessionism. But whether Adams had surmounted emotionally the hurt of his defeat in 1800, Jefferson did not know. He himself bore no grudges, and when Dr. Rush broached to him the subject of a reconciliation he was quite prepared to do his part. He sent copies of his 1804 correspondence with the Adamses to Rush so that the doctor could see how far apart his mutual friends had been at the last moment of communication. This was in 1810. Apparently Rush was discouraged, for he let his project drop for the moment. Earlier he had approached Adams, pretending to have had a dream in which Adams and Jefferson were reconciled, corresponded happily for many years, and died at about the same moment. Adams replied to Rush that such a dream was not history, though it might be "prophecy."

But at the end of 1811 the fortunate moment did arrive. Edward Coles, a neighbor of Jefferson and then secretary to President Madison, and his brother John had made a trip into New England during the summer. They called upon John Adams with a letter of introduction from the President, had been cordially received, and had stayed several days at Quincy, talking with the old man about earlier American history. At length the conversation turned to the events of 1800 and 1801. The Coleses, hearing Adams' side of the story, found it very different, in human terms, from what they had heard at Monticello. They told Adams the Jefferson side of the story. Adams was startled and then delighted to learn

---

* The whole correspondence between Adams and Jefferson has been conveniently collected by Dr. Cappon. See bibliographical note, p. 237.

that Jefferson had spoken of him privately at the time in terms of respect and deference and had attempted to direct his own movements, between his election and inauguration, in such a way as to be least embarrassing to the defeated President. Adams told the Coles brothers that he had always deplored the scurrilous attacks on Jefferson. He had differed from him on measures of administration but, he said, "I always loved Jefferson, and still love him."

Upon his return to Albemarle, Edward Coles promptly reported this momentous conversation to Jefferson. Jefferson presently reported it to Rush, expressing deep satisfaction. "I only needed this knowledge," he wrote to Rush, "to revive towards him all the affections of the most cordial moments of our lives . . . I knew him to be always an honest man, often a great one, but sometimes incorrect and precipitate in his judgments; and it is known to those who have ever heard me speak of Mr. Adams, that I have ever done him justice myself, and defended him when assailed by others, with the single exception as to political opinions." Rush, seeing his opportunity, sent Jefferson's letter on to Adams. The latter replied to Rush that he perceived that the good doctor was teasing both his friends into writing to each other. He did not give Rush the satisfaction of knowing that his ploy had worked. But on New Year's Day, 1812, the seventy-six-year-old revolutionary of Massachusetts sat down at his writing table and penned a greeting to the sixty-nine-year-old revolutionary of Virginia. When Jefferson opened Adams' letter at Monticello some days later, he missed the joke with which it opened and so did not, perhaps, quite sense the effort Adams had made to overcome his pride, being as he thought the injured one, and compose the overture:

DEAR SIR

As you are a Friend to American Manufactures under proper restrictions, especially Manufactures of the domestic kind, I take the Liberty of sending you by the Post a Packett containing two Pieces of Homespun lately produced in this quarter by One who was honoured in his youth with some of your Attention and much of your kindness.

All of my Family whom you formerly knew are well. My daughter Smith is here and has successfully gone through a perilous and painful Operation, which detains her here this Winter, from her Husband and her Family at Chenango where one of the most gallant and skilful Officers of our Revolution is probably destined to spend the rest of his days, not in the Field of Glory, but in the hard Labours of Husbandry.

I wish you Sir many happy New Years and that you may enter the next and many succeeding Years with as animating Prospects for the Public as those at present before us. I am Sir with a long and sincere Esteem your Friend and Servant

JOHN ADAMS

Though the pieces of "homespun" had not arrived, Jefferson answered immediately and zestfully with a dissertation on homespun in Virginia. He then turned to recollections of the great events he and Adams had witnessed and, finally, to something about himself:

You and I have been wonderfully spared, and myself with remarkable health, and a considerable activity of body and mind. I am on horseback 3 or 4 hours of every day; visit 3 or 4 times a year a possession I have 90 miles distant, performing the winter journey on horseback. I walk little however, a single mile being too much for me; and I live in the midst of my grandchildren, one of whom has lately promoted me to be a great-grandfather. I have heard with pleasure that you also retain good health, and a greater power of exercise in walking than I do. But I would rather have heard this from yourself, and that, writing a letter, like mine, full of egotisms, and of details of your health, your habits, occupations and enjoyments, I should have the pleasure of knowing that, in the race of life, you do not keep, in its physical decline, the same distance ahead of me which you have done in political honors and achievements. No circumstances have lessened the interest I feel in these particulars respecting yourself; none have suspended for one moment my sincere esteem for you; and I now salute you with unchanged affections and respect.

In another day or two the pieces of homespun arrived, the two volumes of John Quincy Adams' lectures on rhetoric. Jefferson hastened to acknowledge both the present and his own lack of "sagacity of conjecture."

But before this second letter could arrive at Quincy, Adams had received and replied to the first:

Sitting at My Fireside with my Daughter Smith, on the first of February My Servant brought me a Bundle of Letters and Newspapers from the Post Office in this Town: one of the first Letters that struck my Eye had the Post Mark of Milton 23 Jany. 1812. Milton is the next Town to Quincy and the Post Office in it is but three Miles from my House. How could the Letter be so long in coming three miles? Reading the Superscription, I instantly handed the Letter to Mrs. Smith. Is that not Mr. Jeffersons hand? Looking attentively at it, she answered it is very like it. How is it possible a Letter from Mr. Jefferson, could get into the Milton Post Office? Opening the Letter I found it, indeed from Monticello in the hand and with the Signature of Mr. Jefferson: but this did not much diminish my Surprize. How is it possible a Letter can come from Mr. Jefferson to me in seven or Eight days? I had no Expectation of an Answer, thinking the Distance so great and the Roads so embarrassed under two or three Months. This History would not be worth recording but for the Discovery it made of a Fact, very pleasing to me, vizt. that the Communication between us is much easier, surer, and may be more frequent than I had ever believed or suspected to be possible.

[166]

Though the posts were not often so prompt as Adams was led to expect, more than 160 letters were exchanged, including a few between Jefferson and Abigail Adams, in the fourteen years remaining before their deaths. The range of subjects they covered was immense—politics, history, political economy, agriculture, anthropology, linguistics, literature, the classics, philosophy, religion, science—and neither man seemed ever to write without verve and relish.

Rather more letters were written by Adams than by Jefferson, no doubt because there was somewhat less pressure on the former's time than on Jefferson's. Adams had been, indeed, one of the great patriots of the United States and was surely deserving of the deference habitually paid him by Jefferson. But it was Jefferson, not Adams, who had already become one of the legendary figures of modern history. Every day of his later years brought Jefferson new evidences of the esteem, often amounting to reverence, in which he was held by liberally minded men everywhere in the world. With adulation came also solicitation for anything from advice on agriculture to recollections of the French Revolution, from pleas to give money to demands for historical verifications, from mere curiosity to earnest requests for philosophical enlightenment. From the time of his retirement until his death, Jefferson received well over a thousand letters a year. His grandson and literary executor, Thomas Jefferson Randolph, found some 26,000 letters his grandfather had received and some 16,000 replies.

The management of such a bulk of correspondence, with no secretarial assistance save multicopy pens (some of his own invention), often seemed to Jefferson an insurmountable task, especially when his callers bulked proportionately numerous. At times as many as seventy people—many not invited—were housed overnight at Monticello. The curious would even make their way into the house to stand in the rotunda and watch the great man pass from his study to dinner. It is small wonder that Jefferson wrote fewer letters than Adams, or that he needed a retreat.

As he hinted to Adams in the first letter, he did have a delightful retreat in the "possession" he owned ninety miles from

Monticello. This, of course, was Poplar Forest in Bedford County. He had been fond of this place evei since it came into his possession in 1774, but it was many years before he was able to do much to improve it. In 1806, however, he began to build there a small but very fine house, in the same Greek style as Monticello. Work continued for the next several years. Though it was unfinished when he retired from the presidency in 1809, Jefferson was nevertheless able to use it for himself and a few servants. Later he usually took one or more of his granddaughters with him on the lengthy visits he made three or four times a year. One of them left a description of life at Poplar Forest which is worth citing in full:

The house at Poplar Forest was very pretty and pleasant. It was of brick, one story in front, and, owing to the falling of the ground, two in the rear. It was an exact octagon, with a centre hall twenty feet square, lighted from above. This was a beautiful room, and served as a dining room. Round it were grouped a bright drawing-room, looking south, my grandfather's own chamber, three other bedrooms, and a pantry. A terrace extended from one side of the house; there was a portico in front connected by a vestibule with the center room, and in the rear a verandah, on which the drawing-room opened, with its windows to the floor . . . Mr. Jefferson, from the time of his return home in 1809, was in the habit of visiting this Bedford plantation, but it was some years before the house was ready for the reception of his family. It was furnished in the simplest manner, but had a very tasteful air; there was nothing common or second rate about any part of the establishment, although there was no appearance of expense. As soon as the house was habitable, my grandfather began to take the ladies of his family, generally two at a time, with him whenever he went. His first visit of a fortnight or three weeks was in the spring—the second, of about six weeks, in the early or late autumn. We have staid as much as two months at a time. My Mother [Martha Randolph] went occasionally—not very often—for she had too much to do at home. I generally accompanied him with one of my younger sisters. Mr. Jefferson greatly enjoyed these visits. The crowd at Monticello of friends and strangers, of stationary or ever-varying guests, the coming and going, the incessant calls upon his own time and attention, the want of leisure that such a state of things entailed as a necessary consequence, the bustle and hurry of an almost perpetual round of company, wearied and harassed him in the end, whatever pleasure he may have taken, and it was sometimes great, in the society and conversation of his guests. At Poplar Forest he found a pleasant home, rest, leisure, power to carry on his favorite pursuits—to think, to study, to read—whilst the presence of part of his family took away all character of solitude from his retreat.*

Thus, the "hermit" of Monticello was not even a hermit at Poplar Forest. Nor was his "retirement" passed without further public service. In his own estimate, at least, his achievements in the field of education were of greater consequence than his presidency. It was an essential ingredient in his republican and democratic philosophy that free political and social institutions depend for their efficacy on the knowledge and wisdom of the citizens. All free adult males, who constitute the electorate, should, he thought, have an education in the fundamentals of literacy, in history to help them understand public affairs, and in calculation and husbandry so that they could manage their private affairs. Those who could benefit by more advanced training should have it, either at their own expense or, if they could not afford it, at the expense of the community. And there should be university education in "all the useful sciences" for the still smaller group who would be the leaders in public life and fill up the learned professions. As early as the 1770's he had drafted bills to bring about such a program and had been steadily urging its adoption for more than forty years. The principal stumbling block always seemed to be the reluctance of the legislature to lay sufficient taxes. Now that he had the time to devote to

---

* Quoted in the *Garden Book*. See bibliographical note, p. 237.

it, Jefferson poured his energies into building up education in Virginia.

While agitating among his friends in the legislature for the passage of public-education laws, he took the lead in founding a private college at Charlottesville, first known as Charlottesville Academy and then as Central College. He enlisted both Madison and Monroe on the board, as well as Joseph C. Cabell, a friend and member of the legislature who was to be his closest collaborator and loyal agent in following years. In Central College, whose campus he laid out and whose buildings he designed, Jefferson hoped to build the nucleus of a future great state university, and so it turned out.

In 1815 the state's fund for education was augmented by the application to it of the debt owed to Virginia by the national government, thus producing an endowment of more than a million dollars. The legislature now appointed a commission, with Jefferson as a member, to advise on the expenditure of the fund. Several years of plan, counterplan, and discussion, but little or no action, ensued. Finally, early in 1818, the legislature, under Cabell's prodding, accepted a plan, which granted the larger part of the income from the fund to scholarships for the poor at existing local schools, and appropriated $15,000 a year for a university. Jefferson next found himself engaged in a political tug of war between advocates of expanding his own alma mater, William and Mary, and those who, like himself, wished to build a new university. Among the latter, opinion was divided concerning the location of such an institution. But in August, 1818, after a stormy session, the commission finally decided that the university should be built at Charlottesville. In January, 1819, the legislature endorsed the plan and authorized the university. Jefferson was presently named Rector.

For the remainder of his life the University of Virginia was Jefferson's engrossing occupation. The board of Visitors, which included Madison, Monroe, and Cabell, did little more than support the decisions of the Rector. He led an annual struggle to persuade the legislature to vote funds, did all the designing necessary to convert Central College into a university, hired the contractors, supervised the construction personally, imported marble-carvers from Italy to do the decorative work, searched the United States and Europe for professors, prescribed the curriculum, made the rules for student life, conducted the administration, and even took a hand at admitting students.

The University of Virginia afforded Jefferson his last great opportunity to work for the principles of liberty and republican democracy. His behavior still displayed a characteristic element of paradox. In the name of liberty he had been willing to disobey the law of 1798 when the Congress was enacting laws curtailing the freedom of speech and press, and in 1803 he had unconstitutionally extended the empire of liberty by purchasing Louisiana. So now he did not hesitate to ignore academic freedom in order to make sure that the new university would spread the doctrines of freedom. He was not much concerned about the political opinions of the professors of languages or the sciences, or even of moral philosophy, but he wanted to make sure that the professor of law was an unswerving Republican who could be counted on to train up a generation of "Whig" lawyers to man the legislature. In a remarkable letter to Madison he unashamedly set forth his views:

In the selection of our Law Professor, we must be rigorously attentive to his political principles. You will recollect that before the Revolution, Coke Littleton was the universal elementary book of law students, and a sounder Whig never wrote, nor of profounder learning in the orthodox doctrines of the British Constitution, or in what were called English liberties. You remember also that our lawyers were then all Whigs. But when his black-letter text, and uncouth but cunning learning got out of fashion, and the honeyed Mansfieldism of Blackstone became the students' hornbook, from that moment, that profession (the nursery of our Congress) began to slide into toryism, and nearly all the young brood of lawyers now are of that hue. They suppose themselves, indeed, to be Whigs, because they no longer know what Whigism or republicanism means. It is in our seminary that that vestal flame is to be kept alive; it is thence it is to spread anew over our own and the sister states. If we are true and vigilant in our trust, within a dozen or twenty years a majority of our own legislature will be from one school, and many disciples will have carried its doctrines home with them to their several States, and will have leavened thus the whole mass.

This conception of a university dedicated to the training of youth in Republicanism, with a specific mission to infiltrate the various state legislatures, is the more revealing of Jefferson's character and lifelong convictions when one remembers that he was already eighty-two years old and could not hope to see the results of his scheming. He might write to John Adams in lofty terms about the necessity for both Whig and Tory in all civilized societies, but with his other hand (he could write with either) the author of the Declaration of Independence was still doing what he could to carry on a revolution that he had long ago conceived to be for the elimination of Tories, English or American.

Jefferson's prodigious labors to build the university were carried on under numerous frustrations. Though his health remained fundamentally good, rheumatism made walking and riding more difficult so that his almost daily trips into Charlottesville became more and more painful and burdensome. Money was always short, partly because the legislature was tightfisted, but partly also because Jefferson's ambition for the university was not to be satisfied with less than the best in buildings, equipment, or faculty. Though some of the buildings rose rapidly and the design of the campus was soon well enough along toward completion to catch the admiring eyes of visitors, work was often held up for lack of materials or funds, and faculty recruitment was very slow. In all it took six years from the enactment of the university statute in the legislature to the opening of the doors at Charlottesville. But when, on March 5, 1825, the moment of commencement at last came, the eighty-two-year-old Rector was well satisfied with the results of his labors. And so, too, were the citizens of Virginia and the 125 students of the university. The citizens congratulated the Rector and supported his budget. The students were amused at the almost motherly attitude he took toward their health and morals, but revered him and were quick to accept his frequent invitations to dine at Monticello. If the University of Virginia, for all its superb architecture and its distinguished history, is yet not quite a sufficient memorial to the founder, at least it is a great one.

While the university absorbed nearly all the hours of activity Jefferson in his old age could afford, he never wholly cut himself off as a witness to the stream of history. In 1816 he had the satisfaction of seeing his party triumph again at the polls under the leadership of James Monroe, who had been the first in the long line of distinguished men whose education he had supervised. In 1820 he was gratified when Monroe was re-elected without opposition. The Federalists, whom he had fought so long and who had so viciously maligned him in so many campaigns, had been at last wholly routed.

But in 1820 another event filled him with fear for the future of his country. The application of Missouri for admission to the Union as a slave state was the first jarring note in that cacophony of misery which was to end only in civil war. In the compromise whereby the admission of Missouri was balanced by the admission of Maine as a free state, while it was agreed that the area north of Missouri should not be open to slavery, Jefferson saw only a momentary lull before other storms would break. He set forth his views in an incisive letter to John Holmes of Massachusetts, an ex-Federalist who had gone over to the Republicans on the issue of secession at the Hartford Convention and had been thereafter a leading unionist in New England. After his usual disclaimer of reading the papers, Jefferson continued:

> . . . this momentous question, like a fire-bell in the night, awakened and filled me with terror. I considered it at once as the knell of the Union. It is hushed, indeed, for the moment. But this is a reprieve only, not a final sentence.

The division of the nation into two zones, it seemed to him, augured only permanent antagonism. Once established, he said, "and held up to the angry passions of men, [it] will never be obliterated; and every new irritation will mark it deeper and deeper." Neither slavery nor antislavery was, in Jefferson's view, worth such portentous measures. He himself was as strongly opposed to slavery as he had ever been:

> The cession of that kind of property, for so it is mis-named, is a bagatelle which would not cost me a second thought, if, in that way, a general emancipation and *expatriation* could be effected; and gradually, and with due sacrifices, I think it might be.

He thought that under the prevailing circumstances the diffusion of slavery would tend more toward emancipation than would confinement of it within geographical boundaries. The difficulty, as he had come to see it, was that too many men of the South had become so entirely dependent on slave labor that "justice is in one scale, and self-preservation in the other." His own best hope was in compensated emancipation with expatriation of the freed slaves to Africa. His support and subscription had been readily forthcoming when the colonization societies were formed. In this he had been joined by both Madison and Monroe. But he knew that it was a forlorn hope. Meanwhile he thought best to let matters take their course, recognizing the right of each state to regulate its internal affairs, including the maintenance or the abolition of slavery. As he suggested to Holmes, it was no more logical for Congress to interfere in the South than it would be in the North. "Could Congress, for example, say, that the freemen of Connecticut shall be non-freemen, or that they shall not emigrate into any other state?"

The issue compromised in 1820 had been, of course, embryonic since the first slave ship reached American shores in 1619. For more than 150 years slavery had grown only slowly. In Jefferson's youth it was the fashion among Southern gentlemen to deplore slavery, and many, like Jefferson himself, Madison, and Monroe, were deeply opposed to its extension and to the slave trade, and sought means to abolish the in-

stitution altogether. But the longer it continued in existence
the harder it was to get rid of it. Jefferson hoped it would die
out of its own accord over a period of years; meanwhile he
would encourage it to dissolve by a system of compensated
emancipation. But the invention of the cotton gin had made
slavery more advantageous economically than ever before,
and Southern planters ceased talking of emancipation and
even began finding virtues in the system. In the North, abolition sentiment grew about in proportion as slavery increased.
Now, in 1820, Jefferson could see only a future in which there
was no escape from disaster:

> I regret that I am now to die in the belief, that the use-
> less sacrifice of themselves by the generation of 1776,
> to acquire self-government and happiness to their coun-
> try, is to be thrown away by the unwise and unworthy
> passions of their sons, and that my only consolation is to
> be, that I live not to weep over it. If they [both sides]
> would but dispassionately weigh the blessings they will
> throw away, against an abstract principle more likely to
> be effected by union than by scission, they would pause
> before they would perpetrate this act of suicide on them-
> selves, and of treason against the hopes of the world.

In the fall of 1823, President Monroe, who had behind the
scenes supported the Missouri Compromise as better than
rupture of the Union, turned to his eighty-year-old mentor for
advice on a quite different and far more hopeful matter. The
British government, fearing that the alliance of Europe,
formed in the wake of the Napoleonic Wars, had plans for
further colonization in the new world, was anxious to maintain
the *status quo* there as an anchor of permanent policy, and
had approached the American President to seek an understanding. For Monroe there was a kind of belated vindication
of his efforts many years before to mend American relations
with England, and an opportunity to lay down a major line
of future policy. He applied to Jefferson for his advice on the
question of making an agreement with Britain that would
secure the American position by the unbeatable combination

[175]

of American ground forces and the British navy, in exchange
for similar guarantees of the security of British possessions in
the Western hemisphere. Jefferson was excited at the prospect. In the vision of permanent security for his beloved empire of liberty he easily sloughed off his lifelong antagonism
to England:

> The question presented by the letters you have sent
> me, is the most momentous which has ever been offered
> to my contemplation since that of Independence. That
> made us a nation, this sets our compass and points the
> course which we are to steer through the ocean of time
> opening on us.

His advice was to accept the British proposal:

> Our first and fundamental maxim should be, never to
> entangle ourselves in the broils of Europe. Our second,
> never to suffer Europe to intermeddle with cis-Atlantic
> affairs. America, North and South, has a set of interests
> distinct from those of Europe . . . While the last is labor-
> ing to become the domicile of despotism, our endeavors
> should surely be, to make our hemisphere that of free-
> dom. One nation, most of all, could disturb us in this
> pursuit; she now offers to lead, aid, and accompany us in
> it. By acceding to her proposition, we detach her from
> the bands, bring her mighty weight into the scale of free
> government, and emancipate a continent at one stroke . . .

Jefferson took the occasion to repeat his belief that the
United States ought somehow to acquire Cuba. But recognizing that it could not be taken short of war, and that its independence, "especially its independence of England," was a
better possibility, he was willing to give up the objective. At
any rate Monroe had finally succeeded in acquiring both
Floridas, so that the southern borders of the United States
were extended to the sea all the way to Mexico. The President did not react to Jefferson's discussion of Cuba, but otherwise he followed the course Jefferson had advocated, as had

Madison and Secretary of State John Quincy Adams. On December 2, 1823, he set before Congress the controlling American policy which became known as the Monroe Doctrine.

In November, 1824, occurred one of the most dramatic and moving human events in American history when the aging Lafayette, making a triumphal return to the United States, called upon Jefferson at Monticello. In the presence of a great crowd of well-wishers, the two old revolutionists met and embraced on Jefferson's lawn. Later, at the university, Jefferson gave a dinner at which President Monroe and ex-President Madison were the other honored guests. In the speech he drafted for the occasion, Jefferson praised Lafayette with characteristic generosity, but he could not and did not speak so definitively as Lafayette spoke of him. "The history of the human race," said Lafayette, "tells us of no one who has ever had a broader mind, a loftier soul, a stronger republicanism."

The last months of Jefferson's life were saddened by the lapse of his son-in-law into permanent melancholia and by the desperate condition of his own finances. The fatal blow to his always shaky financial position was dealt him when his friend of many years, Wilson Cary Nicholas, went bankrupt, leaving Jefferson as endorser on notes of over $20,000. Added to his own pile of debts this was more than could any longer be endured. Early in 1826 he decided to sell off most of his property by lottery, in the belief that the proceeds would secure Monticello and some surrounding acres for his last days and for his family after he was gone. It was only with difficulty that his friends were able to get a bill through the legislature authorizing the lottery. But it was never held. The news of Jefferson's troubles spread about the country and led to the taking of public subscriptions of money to rescue him from disaster. It would be pleasant to record, as some of his biographers have in fact done, that Jefferson's debts were paid and his last days made secure by the generosity of his fellow citizens anxious to repay in some measure their measureless debt to the author of the Declaration of Independence. But such was not the case. The deluge was staved off only until Thomas Jefferson Randolph had to settle up after his grandfather's death. Jefferson's debts amounted to over $100,000.

In the late spring of 1826, Jefferson's health at last began to fail. He made his will, in which he gave freedom to several of his most devoted slaves, set down instructions for his burial, and wrote a number of farewell letters to his surviving friends. Of these a great letter to Madison is an appropriate swan song:

> The friendship which has subsisted between us, now half a century, and the harmony of our political principles and pursuits, have been sources of constant happiness to me through that long period. And if I remove beyond the reach of attentions to the University, or beyond the bourne of life itself, as I soon must, it is a comfort to leave that institution under your care, and an assurance that it will not be wanting. It has also been a great solace to me, to believe that you are engaged in vindicating to posterity the course we have pursued for preserving to them, in all their purity, the blessings of self-government, which we had assisted too in acquiring for them. If ever the earth has beheld a system of administration conducted with a single and steadfast eye to the general interest and happiness of those committed to it, one which, protected by truth, can never know reproach, it is that to which our lives have been devoted. To myself you have been a pillar of support through life. Take care of me when dead, and be assured that I shall leave with you my last affections.

Jefferson was invited to be guest of honor at the celebration in Washington of the fiftieth anniversary of the signing of the Declaration of Independence, but he was forced to decline because of feeble health. As it happened, death came to him precisely on that anniversary day, July 4, 1826. Up in Quincy death came also on the same day to his hard-bitten old friend. John Adams is said to have muttered with his last breath, "Thomas Jefferson still lives." And so he does. And so he will, so long as love of liberty can stir the human heart.

Part 2

THE MIND OF THOMAS JEFFERSON

It has long been the fashion among students of the history of American thought to prepare systematic accounts of the ideas of major American "thinkers"—writers, politicians, propagandists, naturalists, educators, artists—in short, anyone who made some impact on the public notice by reason of his intellectual achievement. Such studies are often helpful short cuts to understanding how an important person grappled with his experience; taken together, they constitute one useful mode of composing the intellectual history of the United States. But from time to time there occurs a madness in the method. Systematic accounts are so much easier to write when the subject being accounted for is also systematic that there is great temptation to find system where no system was. Thomas Jefferson had an orderly mind, kept notes of his reading, catalogued his library with care, organized his opinions for his correspondents with an eye to logical progress and even, perhaps, to posterity. He applied well-known philosophical and religious labels to himself, like "materialist" or "unitarian." Hence it is not difficult to organize his thinking for him into a sort of systematic philosophy. This is sometimes done, but not without unfortunate distortions. For Jefferson was neither systematic nor was he a philosopher, at least in the more common acceptation of these terms. He was, of course, a philosopher in the Enlightenment sense that he was a man of the mind, a lover of learning. But he built no system, either of metaphysics or of moral philosophy, or even of government; he set forth no science of society; he had little taste for theological studies; he was less interested in cosmology than in other sciences. His mind was restless and curious, active rather than reflective, given to the search for practical applications rather than to grand speculations. His bequest to his countrymen might take the form of rice culture, not philosophical doctrine; of an educational institution, not an educational theory; of a political party, not a myth of political unity; of the uses of liberty, not a political system. As Matthew Arnold told his American listeners that Ralph Waldo Emerson was neither a great poet, a great writer, nor a great philosopher, but only "the greatest man of letters of the nineteenth century . . . a friend and aider of those who would live in the spirit," so we can say of Jefferson that he was neither a great philosopher nor a great scientist, but only the most effective intellectual man of his time, and a friend and aider of those who would live in liberty.

It was in keeping with Jefferson's intellectual bent that among all the men of the founding generation whom he knew (and he knew them all, most of them well), his affinity was for Franklin among the older men and Madison among the younger. Franklin he revered as his senior in the world of science and letters. He fully appreciated Franklin's immense contribution to the achievement of American liberty, but it was Franklin the enlightened philosopher who most stirred his affection and admiration. The feeling was strongly reciprocal. When the three great Americans, Franklin, Jefferson, and Adams, were together in their joint diplomatic mission to Europe (surely the most remarkable delegation one nation ever sent to wait upon another), Franklin quickly chose Jefferson as his companion for the private hours. John Adams he could admire for his integrity and learning. But Adams was something of an egotist; he was not anxious to learn, either from Franklin or from Europe. He was suspicious of the intellectuals in Paris and unwilling to suspend his prejudices for the moment, even to enrich his own perspective on human affairs. He would not relax. Franklin could not be much attracted by such a man.

Jefferson, on the other hand, went to Paris prepared to drink deep of the Pierian springs he knew were running there. Like Adams, he suspected that their waters might be adulterated, but he trusted the antibodies in his own constitution to ward off attacks of virus should any strike. He turned immediately to Franklin as a guide to the intellectual geography of Paris and as a patron to introduce him into its society. Jefferson was better impressed by Adams' quick wit and rugged patriotism than Franklin was, but he much preferred his private hours with Franklin in the French world of art and letters.

When Franklin retired, Jefferson moved easily into his place, not, of course, in the affections of the French, which no one could do, but in their esteem and in their company. In all the years thereafter he never lost touch with men like Condorcet, Du Pont de Nemours, Rochefoucauld, Marbois, Lafayette, or Volney except through the curtains of time. Adams read the books of the French writers and penciled caustic—sometimes brilliant—comments in the margins; Jefferson, like Franklin, made the authors his friends without losing his own intellectual identity.

Jefferson's already well-established friendship with Madison ripened into unrestricted intimacy after he returned from France. Beginning in 1790 the two men collaborated in political matters for twenty years and on intellectual matters for thirty-five. In their correspondence political subjects usually received first attention, but the continuing themes of agriculture, science, education, political economy, and practical invention show why their friendship was more than an alliance.

Madison suffered so long at the hands of Henry Adams, and of the historians who followed his lead without studying the record for themselves, that it has been a great relief to have him rescued by scholars of the mid-twentieth century. Like most movements of historical rehabilitation, however, the enthusiasm of the therapists tends to encumber their judgment. It is not, for example, really possible to make the War of 1812 into an American triumph, even if it is entirely possible to show that Madison was a more effective President than Henry Adams supposed. Nor is it credible to make Madison responsible for all of the achievements of the Jefferson Administration, even if it is entirely possible to show that as Secretary of State Madison was a close collaborator of the President. And it is stretching both evidence and credibility too far to assign Madison prime credit for those political ideas and dedications of Jefferson, which became the national heritage—freedom of conscience, civil liberties, and republican government.

Madison, as he himself was never ashamed to confess, generally took the lead from his older friend. But his role as critic and conscience to Jefferson's always fertile but occasionally headstrong improvisation was nevertheless crucial. It was Madison, to cite the classic example, who by quiet persuasion saved Jefferson from going further than was wise, or necessary, in the crisis over the Sedition Act. It was Madison, too, who earlier reassured Jefferson when the legislature would not entertain his bill for religious freedom and who eventually saw and seized the moment which was politically propitious for it. Madison assisted Jefferson also in matters of science. Though never a scientist of the stature of Franklin or Jefferson, he nevertheless, at Jefferson's suggestion and for Jefferson's use, took measurements of animals, made records of rainfall and temperatures, and collected all sorts of specimens of flora and fauna. Jefferson, drawn by the younger man's fine intellectual quality, his humane sensibility, his consummate skill in the arts of legislation and in the refinements of political theory, and influenced by their immense areas of political and intellectual agreement, may have overrated Madison's qualifications for leadership, but he did not and could not overrate his qualifications for friendship.

Among Jefferson's other American friends, many were noted for their intellectual pretensions and attainments rather than for their leadership in public affairs. A few, like Benjamin Rush, were active patriots as well as men of science, but others were scientists and philosophers like David Rittenhouse, the mathematician; Benjamin Waterhouse, physician and biological researcher; Joseph Priestley, the radical British preacher who came to America; and Benjamin Smith Barton, physician and natural historian. With them Jefferson exchanged ideas, observations, instruments, specimens, books, and papers. It was the same with his many friendly correspondents overseas. English philosophers like Price, French social theorists like Cabanis, Destutt de Tracy, Say, and Volney, and German scientists like Von Humboldt he thought of as colleagues in the pursuit of knowledge, an objective he always preferred to that of power.

The recognition accorded him by the men of learning in Europe, like his membership in the Agricultural Society of Paris, meant more to Jefferson than the holding of public office. His twenty-year presidency of the American Philosophical Society attested not only to the fact that his contemporaries thought him, after Franklin, the first scientist of the United States, but to his devotion to the discovery and diffusion of knowledge by others. He encouraged Whitney in the perfection of his cotton gin, and issued him his patent; he encouraged Fulton to launch his steamboat; he was delighted with Paine's single-span bridge. His own contributions ranged from a much improved plow to the breeding of sheep to produce a better quality of wool; he was so highly regarded as a naturalist that a new plant was named for him; he brought his mathematics to bear on the problems of weights, measures, and coinage and developed the American decimal system; and he founded a university.

If Jefferson's philosophical and scientific leanings are well displayed by his network of friends both at home and abroad, his two implacable animosities tell us almost as much about the quality of his mind. John Marshall he considered a subtly calculating enemy of the people. Jefferson was himself a lawyer, well trained by George Wythe and well read in the literature of the law. But, as he put it to Madison when they were seeking a suitable man to teach law at the university, it was to Coke Littleton and the ancient and forthright British tradition that he looked for principles of legal justice and propriety. He did not trust either Blackstone or those who were brought up on his text. Marshall was a skillful follower of Blackstone and Mansfield. He could and did change the force of the law by interpretation. Marshall thought Jefferson a "speculative theorist," a kind of Republican he considered but one cut above the "absolute terrorists." But Jefferson, who prided himself on being forthright on matters of good and evil, right and wrong, justice and injustice, turned the argument about. In Marshall's hands, he said, "the law is nothing more than an ambiguous text, to be explained by his sophistry into any meaning which may subserve his personal malice." Marshall, distantly related to Jefferson on the Randolph side and the son-in-law of Jefferson's boyhood "Belinda," was, for all his legal hairsplitting, precisely the kind of insensitive, uncurious, intellectually self-satisfied, gregarious, and hearty drinking companion that Jefferson was not.

So too was Alexander Hamilton. Between him and Jefferson the differences in temperament and sensibility were greater even than the political. Hamilton was a brilliant and incisive but quite uncultivated man. He was guided by ambition and a yearning for power, not by the love of knowledge. When the United States was forming under General Washington's anxious auspices, one can discern already the inner contradiction and ambivalence which have ever since characterized American development and growth and the quality of American life. In Hamilton the nation was served by a man who put property at the top of his scale of values, doubted the wisdom of the common man, and thought that the reins of power should be tightly held by men of wealth and substance, who distrusted intellectuals and considered force the only significant counter in the games of human and international relations. In Jefferson the young country had an example of what Emerson was to call "man thinking," who placed civil liberties above property in his scheme of values, even, if necessary, above government itself, who trusted the common man and doubted the wisdom or the disinterestedness of the men of wealth and substance, who welcomed intellectual inquiry as the best hope for human betterment, and who thought of his own education as a process to continue at least until his mind and perceptions should be dulled by age. It was Hamilton who was hopelessly puzzled, in 1790, when Jefferson expressed the opinion that Bacon, Newton and Locke were the greatest men who had ever lived, and who asserted that, on the contrary, Julius Caesar was undoubtedly the greatest of men. Between a Caesar and a Bacon, a Newton, or a Locke is an almost unbridgeable chasm. But the affinities among the latter three are not hard to find, nor is it difficult to see why they served Jefferson as symbols of the intellectual things he valued most: the uses of reason, the philosophy of nature, and the philosophy of society.

Chapter 1.

BACON, OR THE USES OF REASON

Francis Bacon is, above all, the sign and symbol of the modern movement toward science, technology, and the improvement of material life. When a profound scholar like Irving Babbitt sought for the wellsprings of modern thought, he found them in Rousseau and Bacon. To Rousseau, Babbitt assigned responsibility for inspiring the modern tendency to substitute humanitarian sympathy for individual discipline and collective progress for personal character. To Bacon he attributed the origination of the revolution in modern thought which made humanitarianism possible, but absolved him from responsibility for the consequences. Rousseau, according to Babbitt at least, was the model for the emotional excesses of romanticism; Bacon gave the impulse, for good or ill, to modern thought. Babbitt was a conservative who preferred Burke to all other modern political thinkers, John Adams to all other American founders, and Aristotle to both. He was no admirer of Jefferson, but he was less well-informed about Jefferson's views than he should have been, or than Adams was. Had he studied the Americans with the care and thoroughness he devoted to Rousseau, he would have found that Jefferson's liberal temper was disciplined by a bold and skeptical mind not unlike his own. It was no oversight that led Jefferson to ignore Rousseau almost completely while installing Bacon in his modern pantheon.

Thomas Jefferson, it should be quickly added, was no prophet of the nineteenth-century cult which lavished upon Bacon praise more extravagant than perhaps any other modern man has received. His tough mind would not have been attracted by the notion that Bacon was really Shakespeare or Edmund Spenser or the designer of the flintlock gun. Jeffer-

[188]

son was fooled by "Ossian," the literary hoax of the eighteenth century, but this was a matter of taste, not a rewriting of history. What Jefferson saw in Bacon was a breaking out of the confinements of formal logic, wrought by the *Novum Organum* and *The Advancement of Learning.*

Bacon thought and wrote at the moment when the medieval mind, which had slipped almost unnoticed through the Renaissance, was mortally wounded by the upthrust of science. He saw that knowledge was not expanded by the applications of Aristotelian logic at the hands of schoolmen, but only refined. If the eternal and absolute principles of life and nature and religion were known by means of revelation, the realms of knowledge must be limited by the range of those principles and would be distorted to the extent that the principles might turn out to be neither eternal nor absolute. Bacon had no quarrel with Aristotle. In the *Organon* he found a spirit of inquiry which had broadened the scope of knowledge beyond measure. In setting forth with mathematical precision the rules by which deduction must proceed, Aristotle had made no claim for the exclusive use of deduction. If one were to go, as Bacon did, to Aristotle's scientific writings, he would find that his descriptions of animals, of plants, even of the celestial bodies, rested on the best observations he could make. Even his lectures on poetry and ethics and government were based upon careful analysis and classification of the types of poetry then being recited, the modes of behavior then taught, the forms of government then known to history and to contemporary practice. It was not, clearly, Aristotle's formal treatise on the rules of thought, nor yet his intellectual bequest to posterity, that led to the smug medieval synthesis which Bacon found sterile and unpersuasive. It was, on the contrary, the insistence of the schoolmen that all the important premises are known, which had rendered Aristotle's deductive system formal only and incapable of expanding the human intellectual horizon. What needed study, Bacon saw, was the premises. It was this insight which led him to write a new organization of the methods of learning and thought, which added the essential dimension of induction.

Bacon was not himself a scientist and gave no important

demonstrations of the virtues of his method. But its clarity and simple credibility guaranteed its influence in the intellectual turmoil of the seventeenth century. Scientific method would henceforth require a beginning in direct observation. Data would have to be collected, instruments designed, measurements taken. The results would be classified, again according as observation showed likeness or unlikeness. The classifications would lead, in turn, to the cautious formulation of general statements, hypotheses which might, with further evidence, become theories or even, if never unaccountably contradicted, laws. Thus would reliable major premises be formed and made available, and then only would the older methods of deduction be applied, in order to predict specific instances or occurrences. Like his colleague Babbitt, but for different purposes and with far deeper understanding, Alfred North Whitehead also derived the modern movement in thought from Francis Bacon. It was Baconian science, more than anything else, he said, which made the modern world.

Thomas Jefferson was a faithful disciple of Bacon. As a boy at Shadwell he developed a knack for observation of nature, both wild and cultivated, as a necessary skill for living and farming in the still raw country on the slopes of the Alleghenies. As a young student he read both Bacon and the works of later writers who extended the lines Bacon had opened. At William and Mary he was impressed by George Wythe's attention to cases as the best mode of studying law. William Small and Governor Fauquier, men of cultivation and a speculative cast of mind, encouraged him to explore the realms of science and displayed to him in their conversations the advantages of speaking from observation.

His reading in the classics was prodigious, however, both in youth and in later life. He mastered both Latin and Greek at an early age and always preferred the original texts to translations. But the most admired of the ancients, Plato, he never read with pleasure and confessed, late in life, that though he had read the whole of *The Republic* he was never able to get through any of the other dialogues. Platonizing and Baconizing, it is fair to say, simply do not go together. Jefferson seems never to have been moved by the vision of Plato or of any other seer. And the woods of Socrates' hardhanded grasp of reality he seems not to have seen for the trees of Plato's mythmaking. He valued for himself, and commended to his nephew Peter Carr, especially the Greek and Roman historians, because in their descriptions of life in the ancient world could be found firsthand evidence of its relevance to his own day. He was no antiquarian. The classics were to be valued only because they remained wonderfully useful.

But the bulk of Jefferson's reading was of the modern era. One of his favorite authors was the Scottish empiricist Dugald Stewart, whom he knew in Paris. Stewart acknowledged a direct obligation to Bacon:

> To ascertain those established conjunctions of successive events which constitute the order of the universe;—to record the phenomena which it exhibits to our observation, and to refer them to their general laws, is the great business of philosophy. Lord Bacon was the first person who was fully aware of the importance of this fundamental truth. The ancients considered philosophy as the science of *causes;* and hence were led to many speculations, to which the human faculties are altogether incompetent.

This was Jefferson's view precisely. He conceived reason as capable of endlessly applying knowledge to use, but not of discovering the first and last things of the universe. Like his friend the French philosopher Tracy, he thought metaphysics an idle pastime. "We rank metaphysics," wrote Tracy, "among the arts of the imagination, intended to satisfy us and not to instruct us." Jefferson's admiration of Tracy was extravagant. The latter's studies of Montesquieu and other political writers he thought the wisest political writing of the day, and his psychological essays on ideology he considered correct interpretations of the workings of the human mind. Tracy has been forgotten, except as Jefferson's advocacy of his writings keeps him alive. But his ideas well fitted the pattern of Jefferson's thought. Tracy, like Stewart, considered Bacon the founder of his school. He rested his formulations on observation, or at least upon the principle that observation should underlie generalization, and he rejected the claims of evidence not derived from the senses. In fact Tracy was so thorough a materialist that he cast his whole system of thought in biological terms. In this Jefferson did not follow him, but was content to accept the sensationalism of Locke's *Essay on the Human Understanding*. Indeed, Jefferson's agreement with Locke's central proposition, that there are no innate ideas, was a prime reason for his confidence in the efficacy of education, both for the development of the mind and character and for the benefit of democratic societies.

If Bacon was not himself an observer and collector of specimens so much as an advocate of empirical methods, Jefferson was both. He began, as a very young man, with careful notations of the behavior of plants and animals on his own lands, and kept up his notebooks all his long life. The *Garden Book*, for example, was begun in 1766 and continued through 1824. There were, of course, many interruptions in his life at Monticello, so that the book is full of long gaps. But even as an old man Jefferson kept in it tables of his plantings, showing when and where his seeds were sown, and when their fruits first "came to table." Scattered over the years are many entries detailing the nature of his experiments with vegetables and flowers and the results he obtained. The *Farm Book* is less revealing, since it contains chiefly matters concerned with the farms as a business enterprise. But Jefferson's letters, from early to late years, show how closely he observed the growth of farm crops, methods of farming used both in the American states and in Europe, and how carefully he followed the current history of agriculture. Some of the entries in his household books dealing with other matters, such as building and engineering, show his attention to exact measurement and calculation. For example, here is a notation he made in 1769 about the digging of the main well at Monticello:

> . . . in digging my well, at the depth of 14 f. I observe one digger, one filler, one drawer at the windlace with a basket at each end of his rope very accurately gave

one another full employment, but note it was yellow rotten stone with a great many hard stones as large as a man's head and some larger, or else the digger would have had time to spare. They dug and drew out 8. cubical yds in a day.

Or again, when he was setting up his kilns: "A bed of mortar which makes 2000. bricks takes 6. hhds. of water."

A curious entry in the *Garden Book* for 1795 shows Jefferson in the act of improvising a way of getting something done with the least inconvenience, in this case measuring, without getting off his horse, distances along a roadbed being laid out by his men:

. . . for clearing the road along Belfield and Slatefield, where there was no digging, but every thing was grubbed up which could be grubbed, and the larger trees were cut down to a width of 1.pole, 4 men did 220. yds a day which was 10. square poles each. I tried on that line the step of my horse, as a rough way of estimating distances without getting down to stride them off. When pushed into a brisk walk he stepped the 220. yds at 112 steps descending and 116. steps ascending. 110 steps would have been 2. yds a step. 114 (the medium) is 5 f 9½ I. the step.

Jefferson's letters, papers, and notebooks contain an immense store of interesting observations and measurements in almost every category of human concern. But these were recorded only for his own use or for the edification of his friends. His public reputation as a scientific observer rested in his own time quite safely on his *Notes on Virginia*. Jefferson's devotion to the inductive methods of Bacon is demonstrated in every section of this prodigious book. Random examples serve as well as any. In discussing the geology of Virginia in Query VI, he points out that "near the eastern foot of the North Mountain are immense bodies of *Schist,* containing impressions of shells in a variety of forms." Like Anaximander in ancient times, the enlightened philosopher cannot be content to attribute the fossils he observes to the whimsical acts of a supernatural being. Instead he digresses from his main business to entertain and examine three different hypotheses: that there had been at some ancient time a deluge bringing the sea to the mountain tops; that there had been in the remote prehistoric ages an upheaval from within the earth; that, borrowing from Voltaire, there had been some kind of metamorphosis in the earth itself making shell growth possible by chemical change. Adducing whatever evidence he has available, he examines each possibility carefully and rejects each one as unproved. In true scientific spirit he leaves the matter unresolved and his own judgment in suspense pending the accumulation of conclusive evidence.

The best-known instance of Jefferson's proclivity for measuring almost anything measurable occurs in the same query, when he takes issue with Buffon on the size of animals. Buffon had asserted that the animals of America were smaller than those of Europe of the same species. Measuring animals was the only sensible way to test such a proposition. Jefferson did so, and persuaded such friends as Madison to assist him in the enterprise. Drawing also upon available records from other American and European sources, Jefferson constructed a set of tables which easily won him his celebrated victory over the French naturalist. In this matter Jefferson's pride as an American, as well as scientific accuracy, was no doubt involved. He may be forgiven, perhaps, if he hinted that Buffon's errors arose less from faulty observation than from prejudice resting on no observation at all.

It was not Jefferson's pride as an American but as a human being which led him to resent and to refute Buffon's contention that his hypothesis regarding the inferiority of American creatures applied as well to Indians as to animals. Calling upon his own observations of Indians and gathering together the abundant experiences of other Americans, he asserted categorically:

> . . . in contradiction to this representation [Indian inferiority], that he is neither more defective in ardor, nor more impotent with his female, than the white reduced

to the same diet and exercise; that he is brave, when an enterprise depends on bravery; education with him making the point of honor consist in the destruction of an enemy by stratagem, and in the preservation of his own person free from injury; or, perhaps, this is nature, while it is education which teaches us to honor more than finesse . . .

Jefferson continued the last irony by suggesting that the North American Indian would at least compare favorably with the barbarians of northern Europe as they were at first discovered by the Romans.

A quite different sort of observation and calculation Jefferson provided in answer to the query about population. He was always much interested in demography and later, of course, actively supported the decision of Congress to have a decennial census taken. As for Virginia in 1781, he took issue with the notion that it would be best to increase the population by immigration. In the *Notes* he printed a table showing the results of a projection he had made. According to his calculations, starting with the most recent census of the state, population would reach a given desired figure by "proceeding on our present stock" within twenty-seven and a quarter years of the time the same figure would be reached by "proceeding on a double stock." That would be soon enough, Jefferson thought.

The *Notes on Virginia* contained mistakes and errors of calculation. Sometimes Jefferson's passion for mathematical precision led him to hypothesize too rigorously to be realistic. His population projections may be an example of the latter. An instance of the former is his willingness, on the basis of unauthenticated Indian reports, to believe that the mammoth still existed. His belief that nature never permits any species to become extinct rested on very flimsy evidence. To his credit it should be said that he later rejected this proposition. As an old man he remarked to Adams that "certain races of animals are become extinct." But for all its imperfections, Jefferson's record as geologist, naturalist, agriculturalist, demographer will compare favorably with any of his contemporaries or predecessors. His small treatise on obtaining fresh water from salt water, for example, is a good introduction to that still vexing subject.

The point is not so much whether Jefferson's observations and hypotheses were correct as that he thought it necessary to make observations in order to reach meaningful propositions. He was unwilling to suppose that knowledge could be increased or wisdom attained by logical deductions from one's personal prejudices or from inherited superstitions. The bent of his mind was toward the new, not the old, toward intellectual adventure, not conformity to the long-accepted. In such adventurings there were certain to be cul-de-sacs and wrong turnings, as well as miscalculations and misapprehensions. Jefferson knew this well enough, but the risks were slight compared to the prospects for the betterment of mankind and the delight of extending his own knowledge.

In one respect Jefferson did follow Bacon literally. In cataloguing his library he borrowed Bacon's classification of the human mind into "Reason," "Memory," and "Imagination." Under these headings he grouped his books in the categories of "Philosophy," "History," and "Fine Arts" to correspond with the functions of the mind. While Jefferson might here be charged with precisely the sort of uncritical acceptance of past opinions he disparaged (Bacon's classification of mental activity was out of date even in Jefferson's time), he might persuasively answer that if a more useful classification for a library catalogue were to come along he would adopt it. At any rate his own system was an honorable forerunner of the Dewey system, and at least as manageable for the searcher-out of titles.

The uses of reason were not, in any case, to be lost in psychological subtleties. The point, as not only Jefferson's beliefs but his consistent actions gave abundant testimony, was to make new applications of reason to ancient problems, and to redefine those problems where older formulations had proved sterile. Reason was the gift of nature which distinguished the human species from others. Not to use it was to deny oneself the best opportunities of life for growth and happiness, and for wisdom. Peoples and institutions, which were content to ignore the prospects suggested by the use of reason would stagnate and eventually die, either of inanition or at the hands of other peoples and institutions not so hesitant. The uses of reason, in short, were for Jefferson what they had been for Bacon, the appropriate and promising exercise of the human faculties throughout the cycle of birth and death.

Chapter 2.

NEWTON, OR THE PHILOSOPHY OF NATURE

In Paris in 1789, when he expected to return soon to the United States, Jefferson commissioned John Trumbull to paint a picture showing the busts of Bacon, Newton, and Locke. It was this picture which he afterward showed to Hamilton in New York. He told Trumbull, as he was to tell Hamilton, that he regarded these three as the "greatest men that have ever lived, without any exception, and as having laid the foundation of those superstructures which have been raised in the physical and moral sciences." At the time he was perhaps more under the spell of the Enlightenment than he had been earlier or would be again. Epicurus, indeed, was always his favorite philosopher, and in his later years he would no doubt have given a high place to the historical Jesus. At least his efforts to disentangle what might be credited as the actual teachings of Jesus from the webs of dogma built up in eighteen hundred years suggest that he himself saw no magic in a trinity and would welcome such others onto his Olympus as seemed worthy.

But he assuredly had no doubts of Bacon or Newton or Locke. It is noteworthy that he identified all three with both physical and moral science. The continuity of knowledge was a characteristic proposition of the positivists of the Enlightenment, and Jefferson was no exception. Each man had, however, contributed his compelling formulations with emphases sufficiently different to stand as signposts on various intellectual routes. Sir Isaac Newton's was the highway, as John Adams put it, to the "heaven of the Heavens." He soared with mind's eye and practical instrument to the very heights, leaving what was below permanently altered. Jefferson inherited the world of man, nature, and God as redefined by

Newton in his *Principia*, and it seems never to have troubled him, as it troubled so many thinkers of the eighteenth century, that the whole corpus of Western thought had now either to be revaluated or discarded.

Newton, who was a humble man and a devoted Christian, dedicated his book to the greater glory of God, which he believed he had demonstrated. But the God of the Christian churches was soon lost in the argument for the laws of motion and the mechanistic hypothesis. God was needed, perhaps, to account for those laws being in operation, but there was no evidence that he interfered with them. Rational religion would henceforth have to be natural religion. If laws of physics could be mathematically formulated and demonstrated to be applicable to phenomena, then reason was efficacious in explaining and describing the physical universe, as Bacon had foretold. Thus revelation would give way to instruments, if not as the source of moral exhortation then at least as the source of knowledge.

From Bishop Butler to Bishop Warburton, from Clarke to Atterbury, and from Boyle to Priestley, British students of religion in the eighteenth century wrestled with the problem of reconciling Newton and orthodox interpretations of the New Testament. Priestley concluded, finally, that it was an impossible task, and declared himself a unitarian. Jefferson thus found his work largely done for him. Though he was exposed to it as a boy at Shadwell, he never displayed any affinity for the trinitarian theology of the Church of England. The awful possibility that Jesus of Nazareth had indeed been God the Son never affected his imagination. A devout theologian like Joseph Butler could be tormented by an inner need to reconcile the apparent revelations of reason, as set forth by Newton, with the ancient revelations of the Scriptures; or a Samuel Johnson could satisfy himself that Newtonian science was untrustworthy because it was misused by superficial men like Soame Jenyns to explain away the fact of evil; but Jefferson's pragmatic cast of mind enabled him to escape both the dilemma and its emotional consequences. There is no shred of evidence that he was ever concerned with formal religion in any but the most objective and intellectual terms.

But religion was nevertheless a lifelong interest, as it must be in the life of any cultivated man. As a student Jefferson made extensive notes of cases in which British judges had professed to find the common law supporting the teachings of the Church. It may be that this early reading helped to fix his mind with prejudice against both judges and priests. But he did not allow his repugnance to stand in the way of acquiring as much learning about the Christian religion as he could. By the time of the Revolution, he felt sufficient confidence in his knowledge to prepare notes for speeches to the Virginia Assembly arguing for the disestablishment of the Episcopal Church. These notes show a remarkable degree of learning in the Christian fathers and in later Christian writings. Jefferson's purpose was to show that no one community of Christians, Protestant or Catholic, could be said to have possession of truths denied to others, and that no one sect ought to be preferred by the state above others. His views, of course, went far beyond this point to a firm insistence that the state and churches ought to be wholly separated. But in 1776 he had in mind audiences of Protestants only, and he wished to address them in terms that might effectively persuade them, as lay legislators, that neither the Episcopal nor any other group had a sound claim to preferment. Thus he cites the reliance of the churches upon St. Paul's epistles, observing that they were addressed to people who were already Christians. "A person might be a Christian then before they were written." This and similar lines of argument he employed to maintain that "the fundamentals of Christianity were to be found in the preaching of our Saviour, which is related in the Gospels." But he cites the Fathers, too. "Origen, being yet a layman, expounded the scriptures publickly and was therein defended by Alexander of Jerusalem." St. Peter himself had given "the title of *clergy* to all God's people till Pope Higinus and the succeeding prelates took it from them and appropriated it to priests only." He cites Ignatius as writing to the Philadelphians " 'that it belongs to them as to the church of god to chuse a bishop.' "

Jefferson, apparently with some relish, also displayed an extensive knowledge of the various heresies. He noted that "a heretic is an impugner of fundamentals," but observed that there is no reliable evidence as to what the fundamentals in fact are. He cites Irenaeus as asking Christians only to believe in the Father and the Son. The Holy Ghost, Jefferson points out, is never mentioned in the extant papers as part of a trinity until the Council of Nicaea (325). He sets down the beliefs of the Socinians, Arians, Apollinarians, and Macedonians as examples of heresies, but without adverse comment.

Whether this freight of learning in both church history and Christian disputation would have enlightened his colleagues in the legislature, or annoyed them, or merely confused them, we do not know, since, as was so often his practice, Jefferson left the actual speechmaking to others. But we can be certain, at any rate, that he approached the post-Newton English writers on religion, especially Priestley, with more than adequate equipment to understand and to judge what they were talking about. His own studies of the doctrines of Jesus and his extracts of the "true" sayings of Jesus were prepared by a mind that had not only cleared away centuries of theological encrustations, but knew what he was clearing away:

> It is too late in the day for men of sincerity to pretend they believe in the Platonic mysticisms that three are one, and one is three; and yet the one is not three, and the three are not one: to divide mankind by a single letter into *homoousians* and *homoiousians*. But this constitutes the craft, the power and profit of the priests. Sweep away their gossamer fabrics of factitious religion, and they would catch no more flies.

But Jefferson had no difficulty in accepting the existence of *one* God. The notion of a single pre-existent and creative agent not only fitted in with his apprehension of experience, but seemed to him a necessary explanation of the perfection of nature. Here he follows directly in the path of the natural religionists, starting with Newton's new definitions of the laws of nature. He touched upon the subject many times over the years in letters to friends and even to unknown inquirers. But the most satisfactory account of his views is to be found in a long letter to Adams, written on April 11, 1823, two days before his eightieth birthday. The cogent, if familiar, argument attests not only to Jefferson's grasp of the relation between cosmology and theology but to the vigor of his octogenarian mind (which Adams, in reply, saluted):

They say [Spinoza, Diderot, d'Holbach] that it is more simple to believe at once in the eternal pre-existence of the world, as it is now going on, and may forever go on by the principle of reproduction which we see and witness, than to believe in the pre-existence of an ulterior cause, or Creator of the world, a being whom we see not, and know not, of whose form substance and mode or place of existence, or of action no sense informs us, no power of the mind enables us to delineate or comprehend. On the contrary I hold (without appeal to revelation) that when we take a view of the Universe, in its parts general or particular, it is impossible for the human mind not to perceive and feel a conviction of design, consummate skill, and indefinite power in every atom of its composition.

The key to this passage is the parenthetical serving of notice that Jefferson does not appeal to revelation. Design is to be found in nature and can only be accounted for by the existence of a designer. The argument, of course, is ancient. Newton had no intention of disturbing it. What was essentially Newtonian was the conviction that the argument was better demonstrated after his formulation of the laws of nature than had been possible before:

The movements of the heavenly bodies, so exactly held in their course by the balance of centrifugal and centripetal forces, the structure of our earth itself, with its distribution of lands, waters and atmosphere, animal and vegetable bodies, examined in all their minutest particles, insects mere atoms of life, yet as perfectly organized as man or mammoth, the mineral substances, their generation and uses, it is impossible, I say, for the human mind not to believe that there is, in all this, design, cause and effect, up to an ultimate cause, a fabricator of all things from matter and motion, their preserver and regulator while permitted to exist in their present forms, and their regenerator into new and other forms.

This was a Jeffersonian version of the "great chain of being." As A. O. Lovejoy so brilliantly showed* some years ago, this complex of ideas derives from early Greek speculations and has seldom been allowed to fade very far out of the reach of the scientist and philosopher. But its era of widest acceptation among men of thought was certainly the eighteenth century, in the wake of Newton. Excepting only such skeptics as Hume and Kant, scarcely a single philosopher of the Enlightened Era would have disputed Jefferson's observation that there is a "necessity of a superintending power to maintain the Universe in its course and order." Newton had explained *how* it was done, but assumed, as did his followers, that it was God who *did* it.

It was Newtonian natural religion, as well as his own temperamental bent, that made Jefferson a sensationalistic materialist and a unitarian. The laws of motion and the ideas of force had now made immaterial beings and existences unnecessary to the explanation of reality, so Jefferson thought; they had never been attractive to reason. "I feel, therefore I exist," he said, not "I think, therefore I am." To Adams, again, he outlined his materialism:

I feel bodies which are not myself: there are other existences then. I call them *matter*. I feel them changing place. This gives me *motion*. Where there is an absence of matter, I call it *void*, or *nothing*, or *immaterial space*. On the basis of sensation, of matter and motion, we may

* Arthur O. Lovejoy, *The Great Chain of Being*, (1936).

erect the fabric of all the certainties we can have or need. I can conceive *thought* to be an action of a particular organization of matter, formed for that purpose by its creator, as well as that *attraction* is an action of matter, or *magnetism* of loadstone.

Thus he sharpened the primitive materialism of Democritus and Epicurus upon the mechanistic hypothesis of Newton. The consequences were devastating, at least in Jeffersonian logic, for the theists of the churches:

To talk of *immaterial* existences is to talk of *nothings.* To say that the human soul, angels, god, are immaterial, is to say they are nothings, or that there is no god, no angels, no soul.

He appealed to the moderns, Locke, Tracy, Dugald Stewart, for support. "I cannot reason otherwise," he said. As for immaterialism, he asserts that it is a heresy imported into Christianity at some unspecified time, certainly after Jesus himself and after such Fathers as Origen, Tertullian, Justin Martyr, Macarius, all of whom he cites as maintaining that no contradiction exists between the assertion of Jesus that God is a spirit and the materiality of such a spirit.

Jefferson concluded this incisive letter to Adams with a paragraph celebrating materialism in language that suggests the moving cadences of George Santayana, the classic materialist of the twentieth century:

Rejecting all organs of information therefore but my senses, I rid myself of the Pyrrhonisms with which an indulgence in speculations hyperphysical and antiphysical so uselessly occupy and disquiet the mind. A single sense may indeed be sometimes deceived, but rarely: and never all our senses together, with their faculty of reasoning. They evidence realities; and there are enough of these for all the purposes of life, without plunging into the fathomless abyss of dreams and phantasms. I am satisfied, and sufficiently occupied with the things which are, without tormenting or troubling myself about those which may indeed be, but of which I have no evidence.

The best statement of the unitarianism Jefferson erected upon his studies of ancient religious history, the history of science, the Newtonian hypothesis, and sensationalist psychology he made in 1822 in answer to a letter of inquiry about his religion from a religious writer named James Smith. He began by saluting Smith for his efforts to revive "primitive Christianity." Primitive, of course, meant true:

> No historical fact is better established, than that the doctrine of one God, pure and uncompounded, was that of the early ages of Christianity; and was among the efficacious doctrines which gave it triumph over the polytheism of the ancients, sickened with the absurdities of their own theology.

Jefferson considered it equally undeniable that the Platonizing of Christianity was achieved not by persuasion but by force:

> Nor was the unity of the Supreme Being ousted from the Christian creed by the force of reason, but by the sword of civil government, wielded at the will of the fanatic Athanasius. The hocus-pocus phantasm of a God like another Cerberus, with one body and three heads, had its birth and growth in the blood of thousands of martyrs.

Since this "hocus-pocus" and its underlying immaterialism were, in Jefferson's view, the real heresies in Christian history, it followed that Arianism was the primitive teaching of Jesus himself and of his church. It was a teaching that rested on reason and observation. It would require freedom of religious inquiry in order to flourish. Jefferson, consequently, thought that the separation of church and state would inevitably foster unitarian Christianity:

> And a strong proof of the solidity of the primitive faith,

is its restoration, as soon as a nation arises which vindicates to itself the freedom of religious opinion, and its external divorce from the civil authority.

He assured Smith that "the pure and simple unity of the Creator of the universe, is now all but ascendant in the Eastern States; it is dawning in the West, and advancing towards the South; and I confidently expect that the present generation will see Unitarianism become the general religion of the United States." It is fortunate, perhaps, for his reputation that Jefferson did not often undertake the role of historical prophet. Indeed, it is hard not to conclude that his information about the "Eastern States" was hearsay rather than knowledge obtained empirically by reading the sermons of the Congregational, Presbyterian or even Unitarian clergymen of New England. Less than ten years later another American Unitarian, devoted like Jefferson to "primitive Christianity," was to leave his pulpit in the Second Church of Boston precisely because he could not square the "hocus-pocus" still prevailing there with the life of reason. Emerson would have found in the scholar of Monticello not only the "American Scholar" he celebrated but an enthusiastic and empathetic admirer of his Divinity School Address.

Jefferson not only adopted Newtonian natural religion but made some small contribution to its advancement. It is difficult to imagine that a President of the United States could at any time have afforded the leisure to devote to serious literary, philosophical, scientific, or religious studies. Yet President Jefferson read, meditated and wrote in all these fields while carrying on the business of state in the White House. But he never found time or quiet to accomplish one task that he wanted greatly to do. This was to extract the teachings of Jesus and compare them with the teachings of pre-Christian wise men like Socrates, Cicero, and Epictetus. He was hopeful that a compendium of acceptable moral truth would be the result, as well as a new demonstration of the efficacy of "primitive Christianity." And so when Priestley sent him a copy of his *Socrates and Jesus Compared* he encouraged his English friend to undertake the larger work. Priestley did so in 1804, the last year of his life, and published the work under the title *The Doctrines of Heathen Philosophy Compared with Those of Revelation.* Jefferson, whose prompting Priestley had acknowledged in correspondence, was delighted with the book and recommended it to many friends. Ten years later he was extolling its merits to Adams. Soon after his urging of Priestley, he had himself prepared a syllabus of the subject, an extensive outline which shows that Jefferson would have been fully capable of writing such a book, had the time been available to him.

This "Syllabus of an Estimate of the Merit of the Doctrines of Jesus, compared with those of others," he sent to Rush in 1803 and to Adams in 1813. Both men respected his confidence and returned the paper without showing it to others. He was not so fortunate in the case of his letter to Priestley. After the latter's death it was widely circulated, apparently in the belief of some enemies of the Administration that it would reveal Jefferson as the atheist they always accused him of being. His popularity, of course, was well able to withstand this revelation of his private views. Perhaps, indeed, it struck more responsive than unfriendly minds. If Unitarianism was not to sweep so convincingly over the land as Jefferson expected, at least adherents of "primitive Christianity" and its Arian heresy were not likely, after the age of Newton, to be burned at the stake—or even turned out of office by a free electorate.

Chapter 3.

LOCKE, OR THE PHILOSOPHY OF SOCIETY

In starting with the political principles of the "Great Mr. Locke," Jefferson was not different from other cultivated men of the American Revolution. But whereas conservatives like Hamilton, or even Adams, retreated from some of the more advanced grounds Locke had staked out, and others promptly forgot all about Locke's *social* contract once the war was over and *business* contracts occupied their minds sufficiently, Jefferson assimilated the whole Lockean philosophy both of human nature and of society. He not only occupied the entire area Locke had claimed for social philosophy but extended it considerably. It is a salubrious experience to read Locke's *Essay on the Human Understanding, Treatises of Civil Government* and *Letter Concerning Toleration,* and then to read the papers and letters of Thomas Jefferson. At the least, such an exercise will disabuse the reader of the notion that Jefferson was a visionary follower of Rousseau, for which the romantic historians, and others who should have known better, miserably mistook him. At the most it will provide a reliable insight into both the flexed muscles and the originality of Jefferson's social thinking.

To start with Locke meant that Jefferson started with the Lockean notion of the laws of nature. The idea of natural law is, of course, an ancient one. Political theorists, and students of that often sterile discipline, dispute endlessly about both the origins and the validity of natural law, natural rights, and other corollaries of a social philosophy based upon the premise of design or order in nature. But neither Jefferson nor Locke had the slightest interest in the genesis of these ideas among the ancients or their history among the schoolmen. Nature, after Newton, was a new and radically different concept from anything known to earlier social thought. Nature now meant the total field of energy and mass as explained by the instruments of science and the laws of motion. Newton had not merely asserted that there was order in nature, he had demonstrated it and accounted for it with a grand and persuasive hypothesis. Locke, and Jefferson after him, adopted the Newtonian concept of nature and set to work to see what it meant for the human species contained within it.

Arguing from his opinion about the nature of man, Thomas Hobbes, in his *Leviathan*, had asserted that man's life in a state of nature, that is, without government, is an endless war, "nasty, brutish, and short." To have peace, people contracted with a strong individual to protect them and maintain public order. Thus the transition from "nature" to civil society was a transition from anarchy to despotism. Locke rejected this view, for reasons both scientific and political. The latter did honor to human dignity but did not enrich the argument. The former have often been called specious by sticklers for anthropological accuracy, but have not been improved upon by their critics. If nature, as Newton had shown, was governed by "natural" laws discoverable to reason, so must men, as contained within nature, be governed by laws rooted in nature and similarly discoverable by reason. Locke sought to find these natural laws in human behavior. Observation disclosed that some men are aggressive and appetitive, others meek and subservient, and still others without pronounced leanings either way. In his psychological investigations Locke concluded that there are no innate "ideas" in the human mind. Men develop their leanings of character according to their experience of life and, of course, their natural endowment and capacity. Thus, unlike Hobbes, Locke thought it would be scientifically accurate to argue that without government the typical traits of behavior would keep men neither in a state of war nor a state of harmony but in a state of uncertainty. They would contract together in order to do away, as much as possible, with uncertainty.

Characteristic of the uncertain state of man in nature was the precarious condition of his rights. According to Locke men have certain natural rights, that is, rights, which belong to them simply because they are men. Natural rights belong to human beings by their nature, not by the gift of society. As Locke detailed them, these are rights to hold on to one's life, to individual liberty, and to hold property improved and used by one's labor. But in the state of nature the rights of the weak would be infringed by the stronger and more appetitive, while the rights of the many who were neither strong nor weak would be constantly at hazard. The application of reason, man's natural gift, would suggest that everyone would be more secure in his rights if institutions of mutual protection were established. People would proceed to do so by agreement to accept limits upon their liberties in order to protect what was within the limits. They would set up instruments of government to secure the liberties agreed to, protect the whole group from attack by outsiders, and make rules for the ownership and use of property. They would, in short, form a "body politic, wherein the majority would have a right to act and conclude the rest." It would be the responsibility of the majority to protect the minority so long as the minority peaceably accepted the will of the majority. It would be the duty of the minority peaceably to accept the will of the majority so long as the means were available to persuade members of the majority to change their minds. The whole agreement was a kind of social contract which should remain in force so long as the authorized agents of government lived up to its terms. If the government should violate those terms, the people had an indubitable right to declare the contract void and to overthrow the government. Locke, writing in 1689, had argued that this was precisely what Parliament had done in ousting James II. Jefferson, writing in 1776, argued that this was precisely what the Americans were doing in ousting George III.

Like most of the American Revolutionaries, Jefferson was satisfied that the Lockean theory had never been truly put into practice in England. He granted that the English were better off than the French in matters of liberty and rights. But the colonial Americans were still better off. In his *Summary View of the Rights of British America* he argued as early as 1774 that the Americans should be understood by the British as people who had exercised their natural right to move their residence out of one jurisdiction into another they had set up by social contract for themselves. Their recognition of the English king as their sovereign was a voluntary act. By granting the colonial charters, the kings of England had acquiesced. For Parliament to enact statutes contrary to the interests of the Americans, as defined by themselves, or for the king to deny the Americans his protection was to violate the social contract and leave the Americans free to rebel. The English king, said Jefferson, "is no more than the chief officer of the people, appointed by the laws, and circumscribed with definite powers, to assist in working the great machine of government, erected for their use, and, consequently, subject to their superintendence."

When the petitions of the colonials fell only upon deaf or hostile ears and the king "withdrew his protection" by ordering his troops to fire upon Americans, the contract was torn up. This is the meaning of the Declaration of Independence. The truths Jefferson proclaimed, he asserted to be self-evident; that is, they flowed from the Newtonian concept of nature and the Lockean concept of man's place in nature. The equality of men was determined not by their individual characteristics but by their common humanity. Their rights were theirs by nature. The sole function of government was "to secure these rights." Government derived its "just powers" from the consent of the governed only. Justice was the law of nature. Injustice was real enough; governments did indeed exercise unjust powers. But when injustice prevailed, the law of nature was violated. The task of reason was to bring government into line with nature, so that harmonious social institutions, protecting the natural rights of men, would correspond to the harmonies in physical nature described by Newton's laws.

Thus far Jefferson makes no significant additions or modifications to the Lockean system as he inherited it from Locke's own writings, from later English writers, and from his own seniors in Virginia like Richard Bland and George Mason. But his concept of liberty was rather more fully developed than Locke's, or at least it developed with experience beyond any definition Locke had offered. In a letter to Isaac Tiffany in 1816, Jefferson offered his own definition of liberty in terms which, unaccountably, have not often been attributed to him but for which many years later John Stuart Mill's essay *On Liberty* became famous:

> Of liberty then I would say, that, in the whole plenitude of its extent, it is unobstructed action according to our will, but rightful liberty is unobstructed action according to our will within limits drawn around us by the equal rights of others. I do not add 'within the limits of the law', because law is often the tyrant's will, and is always so when it violates the right of an individual.

Jefferson here draws the classic lines between anarchy and order, on the one side, and between order and tyranny, on the other. It is these careful distinctions which range him, more than any of his specific programs, among the liberals of the modern era.

Jefferson's language in the Declaration of Independence also expressed at least one idea not found in Locke or anywhere in the British tradition. This, of course, is the natural right to "the pursuit of happiness." The importance of this phrase was in part rhetorical. It would persuade more people of the justice of the revolutionary cause than would the Lockean assertion of the rights to property. No doubt the expression, borrowed in some measure from Mason's language in the Virginia Declaration of Rights, was intended to include property and safety. But its larger significance in Jefferson's mind, if not to his fellow members of Congress, was its elevation of human over mere property rights. Locke nowhere speaks of individual happiness as an objective of government or as a natural right. Jefferson thus extends the dominion of the social contract by suggesting what life and liberty—and property—may be good for.

But the most radical of Jefferson's departures from Lockean doctrines flows not from his interpretation of the social contract so much as from his acceptance of Locke's psychology. It was, at bottom, Locke's own psychological insight which led Jefferson to reject the Lockean notion of toleration and the Lockean concern for some form of external religious discipline upon the citizens. What Jefferson sensed was a discontinuity between the conception of the human mind as in infancy a *tabula rasa* capable of education and, with growth, of self-direction and gifted with a moral sense, and the insistence of Locke, and even of a skeptic like David Hume, that an established church was a necessary cohesive force in society. This was not, it should be quickly said, a matter of the interpretation of Christianity. Jefferson admired Locke's *The Reasonableness of Christianity*, which was one of his guidelines in the field of natural religion. It was, rather, a question of political theory.

If equality was the natural condition of the human race and equal liberty a natural right, it would contradict the laws of nature to enforce upon anyone the religious opinions of another. So far Locke was prepared to go, as a theoretical matter. But in practice he thought that atheists and Roman Catholics ought not to have the privileges of the British Constitution: the former because their doctrines tended to undermine the public morals, the latter because they owed allegiance to a foreign prince. For the rest, dissenters should be allowed to worship freely. They should be *tolerated*. Toleration, evidently, assumes a power to do the tolerating, and this was the Church of England. The assumption was that the Church of England was in possession of the Truth and could, in confidence, put up with such errors as led neither to moral nor political corruption.

Toleration was an advanced doctrine in 1690, when most of the civilized nations of the world gave religious matters into the sole and authoritative custody of one denomination. But it was this doctrine which Jefferson utterly rejected. There was, in his view, neither liberty nor equality in a system which assumed any body of men to possess a monopoly on truth with an attendant right to be supported by public money, no matter how tolerant they might be. The idea of toleration was, in fact, arrogant and unscientific. It contradicted Locke's own notion of the structure and growth of the human mind; it had no proper place in a Newtonian world.

On the contrary, "Almighty God hath created the mind free."

The Virginia Statute of Religious Freedom, though it is less celebrated than the Declaration of Independence, is the more revolutionary of the two documents. It was so recognized in its own time and place; for the same men, in the Virginia Assembly, who were willing to disestablish the Church of England and who had voted for Mason's Declaration of Rights, were not by any means prepared to underwrite the absolute freedom of conscience. Jefferson's bill could not pass in 1779. Madison got it through in 1786 only because the intense jealousy of competing denominations made it politically feasible. The Virginia revolutionaries feared Jefferson's proposal because it attacked the premises of toleration and left the individual to decide for himself in matters of religion. In his *Notes on Virginia* Jefferson indicated the practical ground on which he would separate church and state:

> The legitimate powers of government extend to such acts only as are injurious to others. But it does me no injury for my neighbor to say there are twenty gods, or no God. It neither picks my pocket nor breaks my leg.

On the contrary, it was the state which was picking his pocket by requiring citizens to pay taxes for the support of a church. What is less often noticed is that this famous passage is preceded by a statement of precisely those theoretical propositions which form the preamble to the statute of religious freedom:

> The error seems not sufficiently eradicated, that the operations of the mind, as well as the acts of the body, are subject to the coercion of the laws. But our rulers can have no authority over such natural rights, only as we have submitted to them. The rights of conscience we never submitted, we could not submit. We are answerable for them to our God.

Thus a state church, even a tolerant one, is not covered by the social contract, and cannot be numbered among the "just powers" of government. And it violates the contract because it rests upon the prior assumption that some men know the truth while others do not. The identity of church and state is tyranny; toleration is offensive to reason; only full freedom of conscience is compatible with free government.

In his astonishing bill for Virginia, Jefferson spelled out his whole theory in what is surely his most masterful piece of sustained thought. Its texture is so rich that it cannot be cut to pieces without damage to the fabric:

Well aware that Almighty God hath created the mind free; that all attempts to influence it by temporal punishments or burdens, or by civil incapacitations, tend only to beget habits of hypocrisy and meanness, and are a departure from the plan of the Holy Author of our religion, who being Lord both of body and mind, yet chose not to propagate it by coercions on either, as was in his Almighty power to do; that the impious presumption of legislators and rulers, civil as well as ecclesiastical, who, being themselves but fallible and uninspired men have assumed dominion over the faith of others, setting up their own opinions and modes of thinking as the only true and infallible, and as such endeavoring to impose them on others, hath established and maintained false religions over the greatest part of the world, and through all time; that to compel a man to furnish contributions of money for the propagation of opinions he disbelieves, is sinful and tyrannical; that even the forcing him to support this or that teacher of his own religious persuasion, is depriving him of the comfortable liberty of giving his contributions to the particular pastor whose morals he would make his pattern, and whose powers he feels most persuasive to righteousness, and is withdrawing from the ministry those temporal rewards, which proceeding from an approbation of their personal conduct, are an additional incitement of earnest and unremitting labors for the instruction of mankind; that our civil rights have no dependence on our religious opinions, more than our opinions in physics or geometry; that, therefore, the proscribing any citizen as unworthy the public confidence by laying upon him an incapacity of being called to the offices of trust and emolument, unless he profess or renounce this or that religious opinion, is depriving him injuriously of those privileges and advantages to which in common with his fellow citizens he has a natural right; that it tends also to corrupt the principles of that very religion it is meant to encourage, by bribing, with a monopoly of worldly honors and emoluments, those who will externally profess and conform to it; that though indeed these are criminal who do not withstand such temptation, yet neither are those innocent who lay the bait in their way; that to suffer the civil magistrate to intrude his powers into the field of opinion and to restrain the profession or propagation of principles, on the supposition of their ill tendency, is a dangerous fallacy, which at once destroys all religious liberty, because he being of course judge of that tendency, will make his opinions the rule of judgment, and approve or condemn the sentiments of others only as they shall square with or differ from his own; that it is time enough for the rightful purposes of civil government, for its officers to interfere when principles break out into overt acts against peace and good order; and finally, that truth is great and will prevail if left to herself, that she is the proper and sufficient antagonist to error, and has nothing to fear from the conflict, unless by human interposition disarmed of her natural weapons, free argument and debate, errors ceasing to be dangerous when it is permitted freely to contradict them.

If such unqualified freedom of conscience is to prevail, the only legitimate course for government must be to stay out of the realm of opinion entirely, except to guarantee that it shall be unmolested. And so the operative portion of the statute is also stated in absolute terms:

Be it therefore enacted by the General Assembly, That no man shall be compelled to frequent or support any re-

ligious worship, place or ministry whatsoever, nor shall
be enforced, restrained, molested, or burthened in his
body or goods, nor shall otherwise suffer on account of
his religious opinions or belief; but that all men shall be
free to profess, and by argument to maintain, their
opinions in matters of religion, and that the same shall in
no wise diminish, enlarge, or affect their civil capacities.

In time, of course, the whole country followed Virginia in
thus placing between religion and the state a "wall of separation." And the Constitution of 1787, together with its first
amendment, restrained the national government in the same
way. There has never been a time when Jefferson's view was
accepted by everybody, nor is such a condition of affairs
likely in a free society. Jefferson would himself no doubt have
been astounded if unanimity had grown up around his doctrine of the free conscience. But happily for that conscience,
there seem always to be enough citizens—and judges—to
give it the protection it needs to carry out its mysterious functions freely.

Jefferson placed this total separation of church and state at
the top of his scale of requisites for a free society. What T. V.
Smith has called the "property of privacy" he considered more
valuable than acres or even books. Jefferson told Rush, in a famous letter, that he was "averse to the communication of his
religious tenets to the public; because it would countenance
the presumption of those who have endeavored to draw them
before that tribunal, and to seduce public opinion to erect
itself into that inquisition over the rights of conscience, which
the laws have so justly proscribed." The principle, Jefferson
insisted, was reciprocal or it was nothing:

It behooves every man who values liberty of conscience
for himself, to resist invasions of it in the case of others;
or their case may, by change of circumstances, become
his own. It behooves him, too, in his own case, to give
no example of concession, betraying the common right
of independent opinion, by answering questions of faith,
which the laws have left between God and himself.

Beyond Locke, Jefferson thus went a long way. Beyond Jefferson it would be difficult for anyone to go.

But there was still another clause in Jefferson's Statute of Religious Freedom not dealing with religion directly but with those laws of nature from which the doctrine of the free conscience was derived. The purpose of the clause was simple enough; that is, to declare that the law should not be tampered with. But such a declaration, as Jefferson well knew, came very close to contradicting another law of nature which he thought he had discerned and to which he attached high value. Here is the concluding clause of the statute:

> And though we well know this Assembly, elected by the people for the ordinary purposes of legislation only, have no power to restrain the acts of succeeding assemblies, constituted with powers equal to our own, and that therefore to declare this act irrevocable, would be of no effect in law, yet we are free to declare, and do declare, that the rights hereby asserted are of the natural rights of mankind, and that if any act shall be hereafter passed to repeal the present or to narrow its operation, such act will be an infringement of natural right.

The problem, of which Jefferson must have been nervously sensible, was the inevitable and irreconcilable tension that would arise if and when two natural rights, each deriving from the laws of nature, should come into conflict with each other. The legislature here wished to proclaim an inviolable natural right which would bind all succeeding generations. If freedom of conscience was indeed a natural right, it would, in any case, be thus binding. But, Jefferson believed, it was also a law of nature that "the earth belongs always to the living generation." On this premise "no society can make a perpetual constitution, or even a perpetual law." The contradiction was avoided in the language of the statute on religious freedom by casting the perpetuity of the law in declaratory form only. In the Jeffersonian vision, reasonable men would perpetually avoid a conflict between the absolute rights of one generation to legislate for itself and the absolute rights of conscience for all generations by never failing to observe that the exercise of the one right against the other would be in itself an irrational act, hence contrary to the law of nature.

Jefferson's speculation about the rights of generations of men was a part of the larger discussion of the principles of free government in which he was engaged with his French friends in Paris in the late 1780's. His views are contained, among many other places, in a well-known letter to Madison. Beginning with the question of the rights of property inheritance by one individual from another of a prior generation, he argues that while a man may deed his property to his child, his legatee, or his creditor, "the child, the legatee or creditor, takes it, not by natural right, but by a law of the society of which he is a member, and to which he is subject." No one questions the authority of a legislature to make rules controlling inheritance; at Jefferson's insistence Virginia, for example, had abolished both primogeniture and entail. But if "by nature" one man's property reverted to society and could not be encumbered except by the will of society, what of a generation? "The question," Jefferson observed, "whether one generation of men has a right to bind another, seems never to have been started either on this or our side of the water."

Jefferson "started" the question, and with Madison's help finished it, at least to his own satisfaction. Laying down the principle that "what is true of every member of the society, individually, is true of them all collectively; since the rights of the whole can be no more than the sum of the rights of individuals," he examined in detail hypothetical cases in which a whole generation was born on the same day and died on the same day. Such cases, so he thought, demonstrated that generations, like individuals, could not justly bind their successors. And there would be no legitimate means of making civil determinations:

> But a material difference must be noted, between the succession of an individual and that of a whole generation. Individuals are parts only of a society, subject to the laws of a whole. These laws may appropriate the

[219]

portion of land occupied by a decedent, to his creditor, rather than to any other, or to his child, on condition he satisfied the creditor. But when a whole generation, that is, the whole society, dies, as in the case we have supposed, and another generation of society succeeds, this forms a whole, and there is no superior who can give their territory to a third society, who may have lent money to their predecessors, beyond their faculties of paying.

The logic of the position, as Madison politely suggested, left something to be desired. To assert that the whole is no more than the sum of its parts is an ancient fallacy of which Jefferson himself was at other times aware, though he seems not to have noticed that he was guilty of it here. He had maintained, for example, in defending the Articles of Confederation only two years earlier, that Congress had power to compel contributions of money from the states "by the law of nature," even though such power was not delegated under the document. This proposition could not stand unless Congress were more than the sum of its parts, unless the rights of government were more than the sum of the rights of the citizens. Another difficulty, of course, was that Jefferson's model of a generation bore no relation to reality, in fact was not intended to. But this was to make reality conform to preconceived ideas in order to demonstrate a principle, an exercise both unscientific and Platonic and thus, one might have expected, abhorrent to Jefferson.

But despite the flimsy logic of the argument, Jefferson clung tenaciously to its conclusions throughout his life. He might have done better to rest the case on moral grounds, where he would certainly have been more persuasive. For the notion that the "earth belongs to the living" is not only appealing to the living but an effective measure of the justice of legislation. Jefferson, indeed, was on much firmer ground when applying his principle, as he often did, than when he was defending it. The Republican attack on Hamilton's funding policy as well as the Republican policy of debt liquidation both rested on Jefferson's "law of nature." But such cases will

not justify the appeal to Jefferson's name by latter-day wor-
riers about the immorality of saddling future generations with
supposedly intolerable burdens of debt. On Jefferson's own
principle that governments may, by the law of nature, act to
preserve themselves, debts contracted for the national defense
do not bind the future so much as guarantee that there will
be one. Jefferson would not perhaps condone the contraction
of debt for social-welfare spending, but this is not to justify
citing him as opposed to spending. He was, in fact, the first
to advocate public expenditures for welfare purposes, for
public works, and for education; he simply insisted that the
people tax themselves to raise the money. His plan of spending the federal surplus on public works is suggestive of Keynes-
ian methods of balancing investment, and would result in
the improvement of the earth for the "usufruct" of the next
generation.

When he was eighty, Jefferson was still vigorously expressing this favorite law of nature which, argument or no argument, he considered self-evident. To an inquirer after his
political principles he gave this answer:

> That our Creator made the earth for the use of the
> living and not for the dead; that those who exist not can
> have no use nor right in it, no authority or power over
> it; that one generation of men cannot foreclose or burthen
> its use to another, which comes to it in its own right and
> by the same divine beneficence; that a preceding genera-
> tion cannot bind a succeeding one by its laws or con-
> tracts; those deriving their obligation from the will of
> the existing majority, and that majority being removed
> by death, another comes in its place with a will equally
> free to make its own laws and contracts; these are
> axioms so self-evident that no explanation can make them
> plainer.

It was this conviction that the earth belongs to the living
to live in as they see fit which led Jefferson to his various remarks about the necessity for rebellion and the right of
revolution. These ravelings from a whole political philosophy

have so often been represented as the whole by the thoughtless or the mischievous that it is important to see where they really belonged in the Jeffersonian pattern. The right of revolution Jefferson and his contemporaries thought of as a natural right. They understood well enough that no civil government can be expected to tolerate subversion. When a people rises up against established institutions, it must be because conditions have become unbearable. This was the point of the Declaration of Independence. Tyranny is sufficient cause for rebellion; tyranny abrogates automatically the social contract. It does not matter, at least in theory, whether the tyranny rebelled against is living or dead. The dead hand of the past, in the form of unwanted laws or customs, may be thrown off by the law of nature.

Most of Jefferson's oft-quoted pronouncements about rebellion belong to the period of his residence in France and refer either to the coming French Revolution or to the rebellion of Shays in Massachusetts, which took place in 1786. Writing to Colonel Smith, John Adams' son-in-law, Jefferson said, for example, that the Shays rebels had acted "honorably" and that their motives "were founded in ignorance, not wickedness." He was prepared to condone what they had done. "God forbid," he said, "we should ever be twenty years without such a rebellion." He calculated that one rebellion among eleven states in thirteen years would project to "one rebellion in a century and a half, for each state." This seemed to him a not unreasonable record. Contrasted with earlier American experience or with the tyrannies of Europe it was indeed a remarkable record. It must be remembered that a revolutionist was speaking, not an executive bent with the responsibilities of discovering and acting upon the wishes of a free people. "The tree of liberty," said Jefferson, "must be refreshed from time to time, with the blood of patriots and tyrants." Again, writing to Madison about Shays' Rebellion, he laid it down that "a little rebellion, now and then, is a good thing, and as necessary in the political world as storms in the physical. It is a medicine necessary for the sound health of government."

But to justify Shays under the conditions prevailing in

Massachusetts in the 1780's or to justify the French in their rebellion against the King was not to say that rebellion must always be violent. Nor is the blood of patriots necessary to nourish the tree of liberty where there are no tyrants. Jefferson was satisfied that the amending process allowed Americans plenty of room to make such drastic or radical alterations in their ways and forms of government as they might, from generation to generation, think fit. At least twice during his own Administration he invoked it as a means of giving legal sanction to acts he considered unauthorized by the social contract. On the other hand, when the Congress, in his judgment, violated the First Amendment to the Constitution, he was prepared to rebel, if necessary, to bring about a repeal. Thus the revolutionary of the eighteenth century became the constitutionalist of the nineteenth, but without changing his basic view that individual liberty is a natural right not to be infringed by any tyrant, living or dead.

If, as Jefferson's statute of religious freedom declared, there were no religious opinions so certainly correct that people who held them should also hold privileged positions in society, neither were there any other reasons for such privileges, excepting only merit. It was the same fundamental principle of equal freedom that led Jefferson to develop his theory of natural aristocracy, and to build up his plan of education. And again his starting point was John Locke.

Among all the topics discussed in their wise and voluminous correspondence, Adams and Jefferson were at their best when they talked about the vexed question of who should be the rulers of society. Neither was deceived by their apparent agreement on the general proposition that power ought to reside with the aristocrats—nor even by their agreement that there is a "natural aristocracy" among men. What Adams meant by natural aristocracy has provided conservatives with the best American formulation of their views; what Jefferson meant by the same phrase has become classic liberal doctrine.

Adams began the discussion by raising a rhetorical question: "who are the *aristoi?*" He answered it himself in these famous words:

Philosophy may answer "The Wise and Good." But the World, Mankind, have by their practice always answered, "the rich the beautiful and well born." And Philosophers themselves in marrying their children prefer the rich and handsome and well descended to the wise and good.

"What chance," asked Adams, "have Talents and Virtues in competition, with Wealth and Birth? and Beauty?" He thought it was no contest. He then laid down a general proposition: "The five Pillars of Aristocracy, are Beauty, Wealth, Birth, Genius and Virtues. Any one of the three first, can at any time over bear any one or both of the two last."

Jefferson received this letter on October 12, 1813. He must have known that it was partly playful, as were so many of Adams' sallies. No doubt it was intended to bait the great democrat. But Jefferson took his time before replying. When he did so, on October 28, it was with one of his most brilliant essays. "I agree with you," he wrote, "that there is a natural aristocracy among men." But from this innocent point it was Jefferson who, in effect, teased Adams by putting an opposite view in compelling terms:

The grounds of this are virtue and talents. Formerly bodily powers gave place among the aristoi. But since the invention of gunpowder has armed the weak as well as the strong with missile death, bodily strength, like beauty, good humor, politeness and other accomplishments, has become an auxiliary ground of distinction.

He was now ready to administer the *coup de grâce* to Adams' pretentions for inherited aristocracy: "There is also an artificial aristocracy founded on wealth and birth, without either virtue or talents; for with these it would belong to the first class." The true *aristoi*, in effect, rested on the law of nature, for, Jefferson observed, "it would have been inconsistent in creation to have formed man for the social state, and not to have provided virtue and wisdom enough to manage the concerns of society." Since virtue and talents do in fact exist in adequate supply, it follows that the best government will be that "which provides the most effectually for a pure selection of these natural *aristoi* into the offices of government."

Turning to the long-standing differences between Adams and himself on the structure of government, Jefferson argued that to give the pseudo-aristocracy a share of power, as Adams or the British constitution would do, even though the intent was to "hinder" them from doing mischief, was to give the undeserving what cannot be in the best interests of society. On the contrary, he was content with the republican system:

> I think the best remedy is exactly that provided by all our constitutions, to leave to the citizens the free election and separation of the aristoi from the pseudo-aristoi, of the wheat from the chaff. In general they will elect the real good and wise. In some instances, wealth may corrupt, and birth blind them; but not in sufficient degree to endanger the society.

Jefferson's recognition here of the normality of social evil and corruption even under the freest sort of republican government is answer enough to those in his own day, and later, who sought to misrepresent him as a believer in the natural goodness and perfectibility of man. He was, he told Adams, a "meliorist," not an optimist. From the unpredestined beginnings of the human life cycle, as understood by Locke and Jefferson, would come both good and evil, wisdom and folly. The point was to secure as much good and as much wisdom as possible by means of the best possible institutions. Thus the best system was that which gave each man the fullest opportunity to display his virtues and talents, educating all men to their maximum capacity, so that they could make precisely the "election and separation" which would put the natural aristocracy where it naturally belonged, in the seats of power and influence. Operative equality would be equality of opportunity.

To serve this purpose, Jefferson devised his plan of education and placed it in the center of his social philosophy. His original Bill for the More General Diffusion of Knowledge

[225]

was drawn at the same time, 1779, as his statute on freedom of conscience, and has much of the same quality of close reasoning and penetration into the roots of freedom. Again it is the preamble which most deserves attention. Asserting that even under the best forms of government "those entrusted with power have, in time, and by slow operations, perverted it into tyranny," Jefferson proposed that the legislature should now declare that

> . . . the most effectual means of preventing this would be, to illuminate, as far as practicable, the minds of the people at large, and more especially to give them knowledge of those facts, which history exhibiteth, that, possessed thereby of the experience of other ages and countries, they may be able to know ambition under all its shapes, and prompt to exert their natural powers to defeat its purposes . . .

Jefferson's belief that the mass of men could be thus educated, and that, if educated, they could be trusted to forestall tyrants, rests upon Lockean psychology, not upon uncritical faith in the natural altruism of man such as characterized Rousseau's *Émile* and *Contrat Social*. Universal primary education, in Jefferson's view, will not guarantee civic virtue but will "enable" the people to "know ambition." Elsewhere Jefferson frequently points out that public ignorance has always been the secret weapon of tyrants and of priests. Their great fear is the fear of being found out, of being recognized as no more than "fallible men." Universal education will provide society with enough understanding to minimize the dangers that government will fall into the hands of tyrannical laymen, just as the free conscience will minimize the danger that religious life will be dominated by tyrannical churchmen.

But equally important for free society will be the availability of men whose skills and character are worthy to govern. Forty years before his epistolary essays to John Adams, Jefferson used almost identical language to identify the kind of leadership appropriate to free government:

And whereas it is generally true that that people will be happiest whose laws are best, and are best administered, and that laws will be wisely formed, and honestly administered, in proportion as those who form and administer them are wise and honest . . . it becomes expedient for promoting the public happiness that those persons, whom nature hath endowed with genius and virtue, should be rendered by liberal education worthy to receive, and able to guard the sacred deposit of the rights and liberties of their fellow citizens, and that they should be called to that charge without regard to wealth, birth or other accidental condition or circumstance.

These natural aristocrats, since they are to be so designated by the people and not by themselves, their families, or their privileges, must be drawn by the purest possible equality of opportunity from the mass of men. There is an almost Platonic tone to the passage in which Jefferson underlines this crucial point:

. . . but the indigence of the greater number disabling them from so educating, at their own expence, those of their children whom nature hath fitly formed and disposed to become useful instruments for the public, it is better that such should be sought for and educated at the common expence of all, than that the happiness of all should be confined to the weak or wicked.

But it is only the tone that is Platonic. In Jefferson's plan the wise and virtuous men will be chosen by the people, or by the representatives of the people, not by philosopher-kings. And once in power they will not, of course, be kings either, but public servants subject to recall at elections. Jefferson's educational plan did no violence to the sovereignty of the people. Nor did it eliminate any risks that the people will be mistaken, but, frankly recognizing that such risks are the price of freedom, undertook to minimize them as far as is compatible with freedom. No doubt, as he wrote to William H. Crawford many years later, ". . . a government regulating itself by what is wise and just for the many, uninfluenced by the local and selfish views of the few who direct their affairs has not been seen . . . on earth." But it would not be for lack of trying the experiment in Virginia.

To implement these principles of education for freedom, Jefferson's bill proposed to lay off the state into "hundreds," each of which would have a common school. All the children would attend these schools for three years at public expense, or longer if their parents wished to pay the cost. Reading, writing, and arithmetic would be the subjects taught. But Jefferson would take care that "the books which shall be used therein for instructing the children to read shall be such as will at the same time make them acquainted with Graecian, Roman, English, and American history."

Beyond the common school would be established a system of grammar schools at central locations throughout the state. To these would be sent each year, at public expense, the best scholar from each district from among those whose parents could not afford to educate them further. Other boys would be admitted to the grammar schools, if qualified, to continue their education at their parents' expense. In these schools would be taught "the Latin and Greek languages, English Grammar, and the higher part of numerical arithmetick, to wit, vulgar and decimal fractions, and the extrication of the square and cube roots." Thus Jefferson, even as a younger politician, ventured to prescribe the curriculum.

Finally, from among the seniors in each grammar school each year one would be chosen, again from among those who could not afford further education, to be sent at public expense to William and Mary. At the time he offered his bill, Jefferson seems to have taken it for granted that William and Mary would continue as the capstone of the arch of education in Virginia. But renewed residence in Williamsburg when he was governor gave him a chance to observe what was going on there, and he soon concluded that so unimaginative a private college would neither satisfy the needs of his ideal republic nor train up leaders who might, in the next generation, guide the state of Virginia toward the continuing improvement of its republican institutions which, as a practical man, he was prepared to accept. While he was still in his thirties he began to conjure in his mind's eye a university of Virginia.

Jefferson's ambitious plan for the educational system of Virginia was politely complimented by his legislative colleagues, but neither they nor their successors ever fully enacted it into law. And so it was Horace Mann in Massachusetts who came to stand as the American symbol of faith in the efficacy of education for freedom. But Jefferson never ceased to urge the adoption of his or a similar plan and, of course, he lived to see his hopes for a university realized.

Meanwhile, over all the years, Jefferson took the most active interest in the education of the young men of his own family and of others who applied to him for help. He spent countless hours outlining courses of reading for his nephew, Peter Carr, and his grandson, Thomas Jefferson Randolph. He prescribed the classics above all, not because of their antiquarian interest but because of their relevance to the recurring problems of life. But it was history rather than speculative philosophy, Thucydides rather than Plato, that he chose from the ancients. Of modern languages he was partial to Spanish because he saw in Latin America a permanent and vital interest of the United States and apparently also foresaw a more abundant growth of Latin-American culture than has thus far developed. French he considered indispensable but advised Carr not to study Italian, since people who spoke Spanish, French, and Italian often mixed them up. He thought every educated man should absorb as much mathematical and physical science as he could. He was never satisfied with his own immense scientific learning and often complained that immersion in public affairs had prevented him from filling in gaps in his scientific education.

In addition to formal study, Jefferson urged his young friends to follow a steady plan of exercise. Like the Greeks who balanced learning with gymnastics, he thought a certain portion of each day should be set aside for walking. He told Peter Carr that competitive games were not well suited to the fullest development of coordination between mind and body. Instead he suggested walking and shooting. From the Greeks he also borrowed the idea of universal military training. The national defense, he always believed, should be in the hands of the citizens in a republic, not those of a professional army. "Where there is no oppression," he said, "there will be no pauper hirelings." If a militia was to be effective, the citizens should have sound instruction. In a letter to Monroe in 1813, he proposed that military training should be a requirement in "collegiate education."

In Jefferson's mind the whole course of education had as its objective the development of civic virtue. "When your mind shall be well improved with science," he wrote Peter Carr, "nothing will be necessary to place you in the highest points of view, but to pursue the interests of your country . . ." Thus the high contracting parties to the social contract might be worthy of their freedom to make it.

Chapter 4.

EPICURUS, OR THE PURSUIT OF HAPPINESS

Thomas Jefferson did not include Epicurus among the immortals, perhaps because he knew that the ancient Greek moralist was no believer in immortality. But his spiritual kinship with Epicurus was nevertheless at least as close as with Bacon, Newton, and Locke. To the last three Jefferson owed his intellectual origins and tutelage, but to the former he owed his own private way of pursuing happiness.

In the late years of his life Jefferson was moved by a letter from his old secretary and friend William Short, then still living in Paris, to celebrate the teachings of Epicurus in one of his own finest epistolary essays. It seems not often to have been noticed that he enclosed to Short a "syllabus" of what he believed to be the true teachings of Epicurus, just as he had done with the teachings of Jesus, and, at about the same time. "Epictetus and Epicurus," he said "give laws for governing ourselves, Jesus a supplement of the duties and charities we owe to others." He had sometimes thought, he said, of translating the sayings of Epictetus and of adding "the genuine doctrines of Epicurus from the Syntagma of Gassendi." Thus his source for Epicureanism was apparently not Lucretius, a poet whom one might have expected him to take to his heart. However, Jefferson was highly conscious of the distortions to which Epicurus has always been subject, and the sublime poet himself would certainly have approved Jefferson's syllabus.

The point, of course, was the similarity between self-indulgence for its own sake, on the one hand, and discipline for its own sake, on the other. "Nothing," as Irving Babbitt once observed, "resembles a hollow so much as a swelling." Jefferson deplored either extreme, as had his "master," Epicurus. The Cyrenaics with their doctrine that "virtue is not excellent" and the Stoics with their austerity were both not only mistaken but irrational. Jefferson regretted that Cicero, who, he thought, should have known better, was among those who "misrepresented" Epicurus. He put it down to Platonizing, a sin in the Jeffersonian canon for which there was little hope of remission. Plato, he thought, had corrupted pure morality by his "mysticisms," and his doctrines had been used to mythologize Christianity. This view, at least on the findings of so eminent a Christian scholar as Paul Elmer More, proves Jefferson doubly heretical. That he was an Arian was bad enough, but that he was an Epicurean made him also a "Platonic heretic," for Epicurus, content with the Democritean vision of atoms and the void, had eliminated the ideal element in the Platonic dualism.

Jefferson himself began his Epicurean syllabus with the atomic theory:

> The Universe eternal. Its parts, great and small, interchangeable. Matter and void alone. Motion inherent in matter which is weighty and declining. Eternal circulation of the elements of bodies.

Here is the classic, if condensed, formulation of the materialism Jefferson found most congenial to his own experience and meditation. Upon it a Newtonian world could be constructed; within it a Baconian logic could bring endless increase in knowledge, and a Lockean society could and should be established.

But most efficacious of all was the personal moral philosophy which flowed from such thoroughgoing materialism. To Jefferson, as to Epicurus, happiness was the "aim of life." But experience showed that "virtue is the foundation of happiness." Undisciplined indulgence produced pain; but the "summum bonum is to be not pained in body, nor troubled in mind." The true felicity, therefore is "in-do-lence," the absence of pain. Action may be agreeable but it is the state produced by action which is desirable. "Thus the absence of hunger is an article of felicity; eating the means to obtain it." Even more important is "tranquillity of mind." This condition is to be achieved only by "avoiding desire and fear, the two principal diseases of the mind." Man has the power to avoid desire, or to satisfy it moderately, and to control fear, since "man is a free agent."

Finally Jefferson noted the Epicurean canon of virtues and their opposites:

Virtue consists in
1. Prudence. 2. Temperance. 3. Fortitude. 4. Justice.

To which are opposed,
1. Folly.   2. Desire.   3. Fear.   4. Deceit.

Following Jefferson's outline to this conclusion suggests again the great twentieth-century Epicurean, George Santayana. Jefferson would have felt a sure moment of empathy on reading this epitome of their master's teaching: "Eat, drink, and be merry for tomorrow we die, but moderately and with much art, lest we die miserably and die today."

There is no way of knowing when Jefferson first felt himself at home with the teachings of Epicurus, or when he began to read them. But the tone and temper of his moral precepts were always profoundly Epicurean. For example, in 1785, when he was prescribing reading lists and a code of conduct for Peter Carr, he combined a Kantian imperative with the classic motives of his habitual Epicureanism:

Whenever you are to do a thing, though it can never be known but to yourself, ask yourself how you would act were all the world looking at you, and act accordingly. Encourage all your virtuous dispositions, and exercise them whenever an opportunity arises; being assured that they will gain strength by exercise, as a limb of the body does, and that exercise will make them habitual. From the practice of the purest virtue, you may be assured you will derive the most sublime comforts in every moment of life, and in the moment of death.

[233]

Again, two years later, he advised Carr to conduct a rigorous inquiry, without fear, into matters of religion. "Don't be frightened from this inquiry," he said, "by any fear of its consequences. If it ends in a belief that there is no God, you will find incitements to virtue in the comfort and pleasantness you feel in its exercise, and the love of others it will procure you."

Jefferson's own inquiry had satisfied him that God exists. But his "Creator" and "Author of our religion" was thoroughly de-Platonized to conform with a creation Newton could describe in physical and mathematical terms and where the moral sense planted in man was to be induced from experience, not justified by scripture. "The Creator would indeed have been a bungling artist," he wrote Thomas Law in 1814, "had he intended man for a social animal, without planting in him social dispositions." But even this mild dogmatism is immediately qualified to harmonize with naturalism and materialism:

> It is true they are not planted in every man, because there is no rule without exceptions; but it is false reasoning which converts exceptions into the general rule. Some men are born without the organs of sight, or of hearing, or without hands. Yet it would be wrong to say that man is born without these faculties, and sight, hearing, and hands may with truth enter into the general definition of man.

What mattered in the moral sphere was what one did with his moral sense. He could cultivate it and exercise it, as a man could and should exercise his limbs and senses, or he could allow it to atrophy from disuse. Short, though a much younger man, had retired to "repose." Jefferson's response to this news welled up from his deepest moral convictions:

> Your love of repose will lead, in its progress, to a suspension of healthy exercise, a relaxation of mind, an indifference to everything around you, and finally to a debility of body, and hebetude of mind, the farthest of all things from the happiness which the well-regulated

indulgences of Epicurus ensure; fortitude, you know, is one of his four cardinal virtues. That teaches us to meet and surmount difficulties; not to fly from them, like cowards; and to fly, too, in vain, for they will meet and arrest us at every turn of our road. Weigh this matter well; brace yourself up. . . .

As for Jefferson, only once in his long life had he needed to "brace himself up," and that had been in the depths of his grief over Martha's death almost forty years before. Now, in 1819, at the age of seventy-six, he was pursuing the happiness both of the future for his country and of the moment for himself by building the University of Virginia. "I like the dreams of the future better than the history of the past," he said on another occasion. It is pleasant to think of him, finally, as he thought of himself one evening in January, 1814, finishing an inspired letter to his ancient friends: ". . . so good night! I will dream on, always fancying that Mrs. Adams and yourself are by my side marking the progress and the obliquities of ages and countries."

BIBLIOGRAPHICAL NOTE

The sources for a book on Thomas Jefferson are more voluminous than for any other American, partly because he was
more prolific as a correspondent than most, and partly because
so much of what he wrote is both worth publishing and worth
writing about. His unparalleled public life, his engrossing
private life—to the extent that he was allowed to have one—
and his influence upon his country, deeper and wider than
any other man's, combine to excite biographers, essayists, historians, and pamphleteers to produce a never-ending flood of
Jefferson literature. The differences which, hopefully, dis-
tinguish this book from others, as suggested in the Preface,
do not include a hunt for fresh, original sources. Fortunately
this is not necessary in the case of Jefferson. The hunt, so to
speak, is for all practical purposes completed. The massive
edition of *The Papers of Thomas Jefferson,* edited by Julian
Boyd and others and published by the Princeton University
Press, (1949—), will ultimately extend to fifty-two volumes.
Mr. Boyd and his associates have undertaken to find and to
print every scrap of Jefferson's writings still extant, and many
thousands of the letters he received. Thus it is now possible to
follow Jefferson's relations with many different people in their
full reciprocity, adding a priceless dimension to our knowledge of Jefferson himself. For the years of Jefferson's career
not covered by the Boyd volumes already published there
are three other useful editions. The best is *The Works of
Thomas Jefferson,* ed. P. L. Ford (10 vols., 1892–99). Important letters not found in Ford may appear in *The Writings of Thomas Jefferson,* ed. A. A. Lipscomb and A. E. Bergh
(20 vols., 1903); and in *The Writings of Thomas Jefferson,*
ed. H. A. Washington (9 vols., 1854, often reprinted).

The principal manuscript collections of Jefferson papers are in the Library of Congress, the Alderman Library of the University of Virginia, the Massachusetts Historical Society, the American Philosophical Society, and the New York Public Library. Smaller collections are scattered among many libraries and historical-society archives.

Important specialized publications of Jefferson materials include *The Adams-Jefferson Letters,* ed. L. J. Cappon, 2 vols., published by the University of North Carolina Press, Chapel Hill (1959) for the Institute of Early American History and Culture at Williamsburg, Virginia. The correspondence is complete and well edited. The *Farm Book* has been edited by E. M. Betts and published by the Princeton University Press (1950) for the American Philosophical Society, and The *Garden Book,* also edited by Mr. Betts, was published by the American Philosophical Society in 1944. Jefferson's *Literary Bible,* his commonplace book of philosophers and poets, was edited by Gilbert Chinard and published by the Johns Hopkins Press (1928). I have made liberal use of all of these books, as well as all of the editions noted above

There are many one-volume collections of Jefferson's writings, but two are worth particular notice. *The Life and Selected Writings of Thomas Jefferson,* ed. A. Koch and W. Peden (1944), is readily available, rich but manageable, and fairly represents the many facets of Jefferson's career and thought. A better and fuller collection is that by Saul Padover, *The Complete Jefferson* (1943), but unfortunately it has been allowed to go out of print.

An excellent selection of Jefferson's political writings, drawn from both documents and correspondence, is *The Political Writings of Thomas Jefferson,* ed. E. Dumbauld (1955).

There is no standard life of Jefferson. Biographies, of course, abound, but none is at once scholarly, complete, and without the distortions of its author's bias. The best is that by Dumas Malone. It is both scrupulously detailed and scrupulously fair, so far as it goes. But the three volumes so far published carry the story only through 1800. These are *Jefferson the Virginian* (1948) and *Jefferson and the Rights of Man*

(1951) and *Jefferson and the Challenge to Liberty* (1962). The whole work is to be called *Jefferson and His Time*. Marie Kimball has published three volumes of a projected complete life of Jefferson, which are somewhat sentimental but done with exacting scholarship: *Jefferson, The Road to Glory* (1943), *Jefferson, War and Peace* (1947), and *Jefferson, The Scene of Europe* (1950). Saul Padover's *Thomas Jefferson* (1942) is full scale and sympathetically written but shows signs of hasty preparation.

I would recommend especially three books, all of which are marked by the bias of the author but nevertheless succeed in bringing Jefferson to life as something like what he must have been. Gilbert Chinard's *Thomas Jefferson: Apostle of Americanism* (1929) is based on its author's invaluable original research in documents both in the United States and abroad. It is finely written and goes far to correct the worm-eaten tradition, sanctified by Henry Adams, of Jefferson's incompetence and impractical idealism. But the book suffers from Chinard's preoccupation with what he sees as French origins of much of Jefferson's thought and from his too sharply defined notions of what "Americanism" is. Claude Bowers' three volumes, *Jefferson and Hamilton* (1925), *Jefferson in Power* (1936), and *The Young Jefferson* (1945), are the most refreshing and exciting books about Jefferson I know. They span his whole life, with particular and highly sophisticated attention to his political involvements and battles, and they make extensive and illuminating use of the contemporary press, as other writers do not. But Mr. Bowers' journalistic impatience and his political avocation as a distinguished Democrat mark almost every page. Despite its occasionally faulty scholarship and its undisguised partisanship, however, I rather think Jefferson would recognize himself in Bowers' books more readily than in any other. Finally, I have found Nathan Schachner's *Thomas Jefferson, A Biography* (2 vols., 1951) a very useful detailed account of its immense subject. Mr. Schachner has done a great deal of original research and made use of much manuscript material not only of Jefferson himself but of other figures of the time. Yet his claims for his book are modest; he wishes it to serve, as it is serving, in the place of a standard life until such time as Malone's work is finished or someone else does the job. But the reader should be warned that while Mr. Schachner admires Jefferson, in many ways he does not really like him, giving rather more attention to his faults and failures, which were abundant, than to his virtues and successes, which were a good deal more abundant. Mr. Schachner has written excellent biographies also of Aaron Burr and Alexander Hamilton. He seems, however, to prefer both to Jefferson; and, perhaps, prefers Burr to either of the others.

Three specialized studies of Jefferson deserve particular notice. Adrienne Koch's *The Philosophy of Thomas Jefferson* (1943, 1957) is a brilliant attempt, which appropriately won a prize in philosophy, to make Jefferson into a positivist, that is a positivist philosopher. Read alone, the book is persuasive. Jefferson certainly said all the things and maintained all of the views Miss Koch says he said and maintained. They do add up to a kind of positivistic system like Dugald Stewart's. Thus the book is valuable for students who have read a great deal of Jefferson, because it looks at him steadily from one angle. But Jefferson is so much more than he appears from that angle, and so much less angular in his full complexity, that Miss Koch's book ought not to be relied upon by a beginner. The opposite is true of another book by Miss Koch, *Jefferson and Madison, the Great Collaboration* (1950). This brilliant and highly readable book is well calculated to seduce its reader into a lifelong devotion to the mind and world of Thomas Jefferson. If it is a bit more generous to Madison than it needs to be, its claims for him are not so extravagant as Irving Brant's, and the substance of the book—the ideas the two men developed together—does certainly constitute one of the most remarkable collaborations in intellectual history. Another highly readable book is Daniel Boorstin's *The Lost World of Thomas Jefferson* (1948). This is a careful and sensitive account of the ideas and preoccupations of the intellectual circles in which Jefferson moved, with Jefferson himself as the central focus. It is invaluable for discussion of Newtonian science and other systematic thought of the Enlightenment.

Finally, a recent book by Merrill Peterson, *The Jefferson Image in The American Mind* (1960), has brought the history of Jefferson's reputation and influence in America from the time of his death in 1826 down to the present. The book, as Peterson puts it, "is not a book on the history Thomas Jefferson made but a book on what history made of Thomas Jefferson." It is based upon prodigious research and written with charm and vigor. Not the least of its merits is that its author's sophistication not only in matters Jeffersonian but in matters generally political, has enabled him to deal fairly but firmly with those unreconstructed "Jeffersonian Democrats" who have for generations done most violence to the ideas and character of the founder of the Democratic party.

INDEX

Adair, John, 142
Adams, Abigail *see* Adams, John (Mrs.)
Adams, Henry, 141, 153, 183
Adams–Jefferson Letters, The (Cappon), 237
Adams, John, 13, 14, 16, 18, 22, 39, 43, 44-46, 54, 62, 63, 90, 92, 93, 94, 96, 104, 109, 111, 114, 152, 162-65, 178, 182, 183, 188, 208, 223-25
Adams, John (Mrs.), 45, 132, 163
Adams, John Quincy, 67, 68, 114, 150, 151, 163
Adams, Samuel, 10-11, 13, 112-13
Advancement of Learning, The (Bacon), 189
Alien Act, 95, 98, 115
Ambler, Jacquelin, 6
American Philosophical Society, 185
Ames, Winthrop, 66
Aristotle, 188, 189
Arnold, Benedict, 33, 34
Arnold, Matthew, 182
Aurora (newspaper), 90

Babbitt, Irving, 188
Bacon, Francis, 188, 189-97
Barbary pirates, 118
Barbé-Marbois, Marquis de, 38, 119

Barton, Benjamin Smith, 184
Bayard, James, 107
Beckley, John, 67
Bellini, Charles, 47
Bergh, A. E., 236
Betts, E. M., 237
Biddle, Nicholas, 126
Bill for the More General Diffusion of Knowledge (1779), 225-26
Bill of Rights, 55
Bland, Richard, 5, 211
Blennerhasset, Herman, 142
Bonaparte, Napoleon, 103, 117, 118-19, 120
Boorstin, Daniel, 239
Botetourt, Lord, 9, 11, 12
Bowers, Claude, 238
Boyd, Julian, 236
Breckinridge, John, 97, 100, 142, 143
Buffon (naturalist), 39
Burke, Edmund, 12
Burnwell, Rebecca, 6
Burr, Aaron, 90, 91, 92, 102, 105, 106, 114, 139-40, 141-47
Burwell, William, 129
Butler, Joseph, 199
Byrd, William, 3

Cabell, Joseph C., 170
Cabell, Samuel, 96-97
Callender, James, 128